FROM A DARK STREAM

First published in United Kingdom 1986 by Dyllansow Truran
Trewolsta, Trewirgie, Redruth, Cornwall.
Copyright 1986 Henry Blackwell.

ISBN 1 85022 019 0

Printed in Great Britain by A. Wheaton & Co. Ltd, Exeter

FROM A DARK STREAM

Being an account of how the history and geological formation of Cornwall affected its inhabitants and led to the great impact they had on many parts of the world with special reference to the history of certain Cornish families.

Henry C. Blackwell

Fellow of the Institute of Petroleum.

Dyllansow Truran

ORIGINS

Blackwell

Leofric Blacwellan	*A.D. 1012*
Mauricius de Blacwella	*A.D. 1175*
Benedictus de Blackwelle	*A.D. 1243*
Robert Blakewell	*A.D. 1296*

Derived from Blackwell
(Derby, Durham, Worcestershire)
or from a residence near a dark well
or stream

"For inquire, I pray thee, of the former
·age, and prepare thyself to the search of
their fathers. For we are but of
yesterday, and know nothing, because
our days upon the earth, are as a
shadow. Shall not they teach thee and
tell thee?"

Job VIII v. 8-10

CONTENTS

PLATES

DOCUMENTS

MAPS

ACKNOWLEDGEMENTS

I am grateful to so many people who have given help in providing photographs, information and documents for this book.

To Mr. H. L. Douch, Curator of the County Museum in Truro and his staff, Miss Angela Broome and Mr. Roger Penhallurick, my thanks for their guidance over a period of many months when I was a daily visitor to the Royal Institution of Cornwall Courtney Library.

To Mr. P. I. Hull, County Archivist and his staff at the County Records Office, Truro, Mrs. C. R. North, Mr. J. C. Edwards and Mr. D. E. Ivall, for keeping my reading table supplied with records and volumes of information.

My thanks also to the Cornwall Local Studies Library at Redruth where Mr. T. Knight and Mrs. B. Olds have always been extremely helpful, and at Camborne Library, where Mr. Alan Thomas has always come up with answers to my questions.

Falmouth Library, too, has been most useful in helping me unearth my Falmouth connections.

I must not forget the invaluable help received from Registrars' Offices throughout Cornwall in supplying me with copies of birth, marriage and death certificates covering a period of almost one hundred and fifty years, the bulk of these from Mrs. D. M. Thomas, Superintendent Registrar and her staff at The Leats in Truro; Mr. Douglas Ward, Deputy Superintendent Registrar at Redruth; and Mrs. G. Westran, Superintendent Registrar at Falmouth.

I wish to thank the Michigan Technological University for allowing me to research in their library when I was a guest there in the summer of 1983 and the Houghton County Court House for allowing me to examine the registers of births and marriages to trace the descendants of my family who travelled to the Copper Country in the 1870's.

To the lady supervisor at the Forest Hills Cemetery in Houghton who took time from directing the digging of a grave to show me the burial places of those I had come to find, my thanks.

In particular, I wish to thank all those good Americans who, during my travels around Michigan's Copper Country, treated me with great courtesy, especially so on discovering that I was Cornish. Cornwall is not the only place where pasties and saffron buns are enjoyed! I had visited Michigan's Flint and Detroit in 1941 when H.M.S. Furious, the aircraft carrier I was serving on, was undergoing repairs at the Navy Yard in Philadelphia. The Cornish Americans at that time were perhaps more closely tied to Cornwall and many felt their absence from the "Old Country" at the time of her great peril with sadness, but how glad they all were to see me!

I especially wish to thank William Faull from Arizona who took time to show me so much of Copper Country. His forebears left Wheal Rose in Scorrier around 1852 for the mining areas of America, but he is still Cornish.

My thanks to all those private people mentioned below who have answered my questions, allowed me to empty old boxes, pore over albums and rummage through attics in the search for photographs, documents or anything that would reveal the past, help my research and add to this book.

XI

Mrs. Patricia Alcock (daughter of Captain Charles Blackwell)	*South Africa*
Mrs. Prudence Bagge (daughter of W. J. Bennetts)	*Camborne*
Mrs. Dorothy Petersen (grand-daughter of Prudence A. Mitchell)	*Houghton, U.S.A.*
Mrs. Estelle Davey	*Houghton, U.S.A.*
Mr. Glenn Richards	*Houghton, U.S.A.*
Mrs. Florence Mayne (Walter Mayne's widow)	*Illinois, U.S.A.*
Miss Leslie Fiedler (Walter Mayne's grand-daughter)	*Illinois, U.S.A.*
Mrs. Hazel Ingwersen (grand-daughter of Henry Blackwell, 1870 - 1912)	*Toronto*
Mr. Howard Dunn (grandson of Prudence Ann Mitchell)	*Florida*
Mrs. Avis Blackwell (Garry Blackwell's widow)	*Beacon, Camborne*
Mrs. Marion McGeorge (daughter of A. E. Blackwell)	*Beacon, Camborne*
Mr. David McGeorge (for research at St. Catherine's House)	*London*
Mrs. L. Salamone and Jane	*Camborne*
Mr. Stanley Mayne	*Beacon, Camborne*
Mrs. Sheila Willis	*Camborne*

Special thanks to my wife June who worked without complaint to type the manuscript.

If any acknowledgements have been unwittingly omitted, please accept sincere apologies.

The author wishes to thank the following who have kindly given permission for the use of the following copyright material:

The Royal Institution of Cornwall for the Stannary Order and List of Tinners, 1798.

The Houghton County Historical Society and John H. Forster Press of Michigan, U.S.A. for "The Long Winter Ends" by Newton G. Thomas and extracts from "The Atlantic, Copper and Community of South Portage Lake" by Sandra Hollingworth.

Professor Charles Thomas of the Institute of Cornish Studies for passages from his book "Christian Antiquities of Cornwall".

Dr. A. C. Todd for extracts from "The Search For Silver" and "The Cornish Miner in America".

The South African Newspapers: Sunday Chronicle, Sunday Times, Newcastle Advertiser, The Times, The Star, Rand Daily Mail, for accounts and photographs of the 1922 South African Revolt.

The County Records Office, Truro, for the Will of Thomas Blackwell, 1719 and Inventory of William Blackwell, 1666.

The Secretary for Education, Cornwall, for Admission Registers, Zelah Board School, 1878 and 1889.

The West Briton, various extracts from 1812 onwards.

Camborne Redruth Packet, Cameo of R. G. Blackwell, 1958 and Walter Mayne, 1960.

Royal Cornwall Gazette, various extracts nineteenth century.
Cornish Telegraph, Poem "Chosen Race", 1906.
Lyson, History of Cornwall, 1322 Crusade.
Fortescue Hitchins, History of Cornwall , 1824.
J. C. C. Probert, Primitive Methodism in Cornwall.
John Miller, "Cornubia".
Thomas Spargo, extracts from "Mines of West Cornwall", 1865.
Treve Holman, Historical Relationship of Mining Silicosis and Rock Removal, 1946.
Charles Wittlesey, "Ethnology, the Ancient Mines of Lake Superior", Cleveland, 1852.
The Encyclopaedic History of the Transvaal, 1906, edited by L. V. Praagh. Extracts covering early history, mining, railways and Harvey's of Hayle.
Smuggling. The murder of William Odgers, 1768, from notes based on extracts from Customs Books now unobtainable, compiled by J. A. D. Bridger of Penzance.
Account of the blizzard in Cornwall: extracts from "The Blizzard in the West" published by A. H. Swiss, Devonport, various newspaper reports and local family recollections.

Illustrations

The author wishes to thank the following who have kindly given permission for use of the following copyright material:

Africana Museum, City of Johannesburg, for photograph of staff and volunteers at the Johannesburg Power Station, 1922, via Mrs. P. Alcock, Pinetown, South Africa.
Mr. P. S. Butt of Truro for "General Arrangement of Tin Mine, late nineteenth early twentieth century".
James Gibson, photographer, Isles of Scilly, for R.M.S. Scillonian, 1956.
Quincy Mine Hoist Association Inc., Hancock, Michigan, for 'Labourers posed in front of Quincy rock house, 1880'.
'Quincy, Pewabic and Franklin Mines, 1873.'
Hand rock drills shaft sinking as depicted in the "Scientific American", December, 1880.
Reference and Information Library, Truro, for 'Cornish Wrestlers'.
Zennor Wayside Museum for 'Early Stamp Mill'.

For the use of the following illustrations my thanks to:

Camborne Library and Cornwall Local Studies Library, Redruth, for the following:-
Beacon - The Blizzard, 1891.
Beacon Sub Post Office, nineteenth century.
Camborne - Redruth Mining District, 1893.
Camborne Wesley Chapel, 1902.

The Ghost Train at Stray Park, 1891.

John Wesley's Tree, 1900.

The Randfontein Rugby Club, 1909.

Osborne Studios, Falmouth for:-

Bal Maidens and Old Jan, Dolcoath, 1890.

Bal Maidens, Pednandrea Mine, Redruth, nineteenth century.

Falmouth Docks, 1890.

Falmouth Docks, 1900.

Gwennap Pit, 1900.

Mr. George Holman, Weeth, Camborne, for 'Camborne Rugby Team, 1902/1903'.

Compair Maxam Ltd., Pool, for 'Climax Dust Allayer'.

Mrs. Walter Mayne, Steger, Illinois, U.S.A., for:
    'First Annual Banquet' and 'Chicago Southern's Rugby Team',
    'Memorial Service, Walter Mayne, Steger, Illinois'.

The Encyclopaedic History of the Transvaal, 1906, edited by L. V. Praagh for:
    'Central Johannesburg from Robinson Deep Mine, 1904.
    Chinese gambling between mine dumps, 1904.
    Chinese mine workers, 1904.
    General View, Jumpers Deep Mine, 1905.
    Johannesburg Offices, Messrs. Harvey & Co., 1895.
    Tailings Wheel, 1905.

Mr. Edward Williams, Camborne, for:
    'In Memoriam, the seven miners who lost their lives at Dolcoath, 1893.'

The County Court House, Houghton, Michigan, U.S.A. for:
    Return of Marriage, Richard Williams and Ellen Mitchell at Franklin Township, Houghton, Michigan, 1874.
    Return of Marriage, Alfred Moyle and Prudence Ann Mitchell at Houghton, Michigan, 1878.
    Return of Marriage, Charles Davey and Prudence Ann Moyle, widow, at Franklin Mine, Houghton, Michigan, 1882.

And especially Constance Stuart Larrabee of Kings Prevention, Chesterton, Maryland, U.S.A., for "Warriors with their Knobkerries", from her world renowned "Tribal Photographs" collection.

Many of the photographs not mentioned above are from the private collection of the author.

Preface

In the search for our ancestors, we are conscious of a desire to retreat into the past, and reluctant to look ahead to an increasingly hostile and irreligious world.

The past was turbulent and violent, but the world survived, thanks to the courage and fortitude of those who resisted and overcame all the hardship that fate could inflict upon them.

The way back is uncertain too, with a myriad of unanswered questions concerning the origins, relationships and movements, of our forebears. The urge to unravel the truth, in spite of all obstacles, persists, and it is possible to succeed, but only as far as existing knowledge and recorded facts allow.

Some searchers are fortunate in finding the path clear, others delve unceasingly, without success, and are left with feelings of great frustration.

What do we expect, or hope to find, when we embark on the quest into the past?

The overriding thing is the truth. It would be absolutely unwarranted to indulge in wishful thinking and fantasy. To have descended from lines of good, honest, God-fearing men and women, is sufficient.

To discover ancestors who could not be so described, is not always less satisfying. Many of us relish the idea of a black sheep, or perhaps a grey wolf, with an air of romantic mystery attached.

Having begun the search, it is soon evident that family history cannot be divorced from the great social upheavals and events that have dictated the paths of humanity.

The creation of the earth gave man the stage on which to act out his destiny, and its physical make-up has, to a large extent, dictated these paths.

Therefore, it is to the origins that we must turn and which we must examine, before considering the lives of individuals.

Historians, writing about figures in the public eye, usually have their task helped considerably by the amount of information available to them from various sources.

Historic events have been well documented; battles had eye witnesses, usually focussed on the Commanders and not on the individuals who made up the mass, but who, in the end, won or lost the day.

These individuals are members of ordinary families, although in truth, there is no such thing as an ordinary family; each is part of, and collectively the whole of, the population of the world, and the makers of history.

The people we are concerned with in this family history are, in the main, Cornish, and no discussion can be contemplated without reference to, and knowledge of, the land which gave them birth.

To The Memory Of Our Ancestors
To Those Buried In Distant Lands
To The Family At Home
    And In Foreign Parts
To All Those Yet To Come

SETTING THE STAGE

The great deluge which almost wiped out life on earth many thousands of years ago eventually subsided leaving sufficient human and animal life somewhere in the Middle East to begin anew the process of multiplying the species.

As their numbers increased, people formed themselves into tribes and later dispersed from the plains of Shinar to venture into new lands.

As mankind trekked, many of them passed through different regions towards the more fertile west and in doing so they left permanent settlements.

Gaul, or France as it is now called, Germany and Spain were peopled and mankind multiplied mainly because of favourable climates and fertility of the soil. With these areas peopled, the journey across the water to Britain was not long delayed.

Among the early arrivals into Cornwall, around 2500 B.C., could have been people from the settlements in the Basque mountains of Spain and Brittany. The supposed Iberian aspect of some Cornish people could be accounted for if this assumption is correct.

Tin has been mined in Spain from earliest times and this could account for the ability of the new settlers in the metal bearing areas of Cornwall to quickly establish a mining industry and to trade with merchants from the Mediterranean countries and Spain who obviously knew about the value and uses of tin, otherwise why should they have ventured so far to obtain it. It is logical to assume that the early settlers in Cornwall had preknowledge as well. After all, they came across the world on foot and had ample time to gain from their experiences during the long period of emigrations. This was also the order of the day, centuries later with the great exodus of peoples - tribes - from Europe to the Americas and other sparsely populated countries beyond the seas.

The journeys of recent history were full of hardship and sorrow but the trials and tribulations of the dispersed tribes from the plains of Shinar must have been awe inspiring. The leaders of some tribes can be likened to so many Cornishmen especially of the nineteenth century, unsettled, changing from country to country as the need arose or the prospects of fortunes to be made in green fields far away seemed good. Very often these wanderers, driven to seek a livelihood away from the bleak, desperate and miserable conditions that existed all too often in Cornwall, would be accompanied by their wives and children no doubt bewildered but, in spite of the undoubted fraility of many caused by years of privation, they were still prepared to endure everything including death that an uncompromising and sometimes hostile world could throw against them.

Desperate conditions at home were not always the reasons which persuaded some Cornish to venture abroad. Hundreds of years before the period of the great exodus of its mining community others journeyed for quite different reasons. In 1147 a body of Cornish volunteers on their way to a crusade assisted the Portuguese in expelling the Moors from Lisbon and some of them settled on the banks of the Tagus, calling their town Cornwallia. In 1322 a great host of Cornish men, women and children went on another crusade with less happy results. They set out in one of those great enthusiastic outbursts not uncommon in Cornwall to set free the Holy Land. After encountering great dangers and losing many of their numbers by famine, imprisonment, torture and other perils, the survivors returned home greatly depressed by their misfortune.

With the settlement of migratory tribes in Cornwall with its deposits of tin and copper, here then were the ingredients of history already setting in motion the later events that were to take place. These changed the face of many parts of the world, drawing Cornish people, tin, trade, religion, colonisation and politics into a great and dramatic stream of events.

The Cornish, who produced the finest hard-rock mining men the world has ever known, were one of the major elements in the changing pattern of the western world throughout the nineteenth and twentieth centuries.

Emigration was the order of the day. Beacon men resting on their travelling trunk on the way to Camborne Station and the mines of everywhere, 1900.

STAGE PROPERTIES AND REHEARSALS

Without tin and copper, Cornwall would probably have developed into a purely agricultural area, with fishing playing an important role.

Experience gained in the recovery of metals, enabling thousands of Cornishmen to travel the world and claw the depths apart for everything of value concealed in the darkness.

The art of relatively deep mining was not practised in Cornwall until the reign of Elizabeth I. Tin, nevertheless, was recovered in abundance by methods described by the historian, Fortescue Hitchins, who wrote in 1824:

"Mines of considerable value have been discovered by chance, or the vagaries of nature. Sometimes, veins of ore have been exposed by torrents of water issuing from hills and mountains, laying open such beds of the mineral. On other occasions, quarries, which have been laid open to raise stones for building, have led to valuable discovery. It is from causes such as these that we must suppose the early inhabitants of Cornwall, to have derived their first knowledge of these metals, which have rendered this county so conspicuous in the pages of history.

The advantages of stone and timber to build shelter from the weather would have been obvious, and loose stones, scattered around, would be the first to be used. Some were partly buried and the removal of these, must, naturally, lead to the discovery of others lying beneath the surface, and finally, point out the quarries in which the solid rock appeared.

To procure fragments from these would call forth their mental and muscular abilities, and it must be perceived that between quarry and the underground mine, the transition is at once obvious although far from easy. It seems plain, therefore, that the early dwellers in Cornwall were led gradually to search the bowels of the earth for metals because of the accidental discoveries.

In an area that was impregnated with tin, some was found on the low grounds where it had been deposited by the floods, or rains, that brought it from the hills.

Some was found pulverised among the sands of the sea having been originally washed either from adjacent rocks or separated from veins covered with water. Tin was also found among the sands of rivers and resting heavily in sheltered places, able to defy the efforts of the sea and tides to move it further".

Probably this was the first situation in which tin was discovered, for tin, in the language of the Chaldeans, signifies slime or dirt, and when traders from the Mediterranean came here and saw this metal in its slimy bed they called it the mud, and so has the name tin continued.

Handling the ores at once showed those who had turned their attention to it that it was heavier than any of the surrounding strata. Naturally, further search would proceed beneath the surface. On finding a continuance of the ore, until they came to it resting on the solid rock, they would proceed to trace it through those vales in which the floods had passed. It was this distribution of tin, as deposited in valleys, that constituted what became known as stream works. In these streams we may suppose that the ancient tinners discovered a large proportion of their tin.

But, besides the stream of tin ground, a stream of water was always necessary to separate the ore from the surrounding rubbish and it was probably from the streams of water assisting the tin workers in their labours, as well as from the tin distribution along the valleys, that these stream works got their name.

The manner in which the Cornish procured their tin before the time of the Romans was not by sinking perpendicular shafts to reach the lode, for this method seems to have been introduced by Crassus, a Roman. The method adopted appears to have been that of laying open the ground from the surface of the higher lands whenever they discovered a vein of ore, and thus pursuing it through this aperture to an indefinite length and depth, until stopped by their inability to penetrate hard rock or the vein becoming of little value. Of this method of mining, which appears to be the earliest ever practised in Britain, many signs were still in existence over a hundred years ago and may still exist.

Stone wheel similar to that used for crushing rock.

These excavations were given the name "koffens", or "goffens". Several were found in the Parish of St. Just in Penwith in the last century. Little is known about the tools used by the ancients, or the methods used to excavate the koffens. The tin stuff now dug out was washed in the running stream so that the earth and sand would be removed leaving the pure tin, or at least as pure as it could be, in its present condition. This was then passed through a sieve. The small fragments of rock containing the ore were then pulverised by a machine described from one that remained on the Isles of Scilly:

"About a quarter of a mile south west of the Blockhouse, upon the top of a hill, is a natural rock about nine inches above the surface of the ground, with a hole in its centre, eight inches in diameter, supposed for a vertical post to work round in; and at the distance of two feet from this, is a gutter, cut round in the rock out of solid stone, fourteen inches wide and a foot deep, wherein a round, wheel-like stone, four feet in diameter and nine inches thick, went around upon its edge. The round stone has a hole through its centre, about eight inches in diameter, and there must have been the axle, or shaft, connecting from the centre post, across to and passing through the wheel sufficiently far for it to be pulled by horse or men".

This was the first known machine to pulverise the ore before stamping mills were introduced and was described by a Mr. Troutbeck more than one hundred and fifty years ago.

The material thus pulverised would again be washed, and eventually the tinners were able to extract and to bring it to a state of purity, ready for another process to transform the ore into metal.

The manner in which the ancient Cornish passed their ores through the fire has been lost to us because of the unfortunate loss of a description of it by the Roman, Polybius. The only authority whose writings remained, concerning the preparation of the metal by fire, is the Scillian-Greek historian of the first century B.C., Diodorus Siculus. He merely stated that . . ."The tinners manufacture the tin by working the grounds which produce it, with great art. For though the land is rocky, it hath soft veins of earth running through it, in which the tinners find their treasure; extract, melt, and purify it, then, shaping it by moulds into a kind of cubical figure".

It is believed that the mineral ore was procured chiefly in the four western hundreds of Penwith, Kerrier, Pider and Powder and there smelted into white tin by charcoal fires, and, as there was nothing else to burn, the entire demolition of all the woods near the tin workings was plain to see.

From conjecture, fact and authority, we know that the natives of Cornwall and the Isles of Scilly discovered the art of bringing their ore into a state of fusion, and when brought into this state, it was not difficult for them to purify it from its natural dross, the scum, thrown off from the metal in melting.

Having first discovered the possibility of fusion, however incomplete their first efforts might have been, it was easy for them to make improvements and to carry this treatment to the level required for the constant demand and state of the market. Cornwall and the Isles of Scilly were supplying the world with tin many centuries before the birth of Jesus and the fame of its metals and its mining men has ensured its good name in the pages of history. With the decline of the production of Cornish tin during the nineteenth century, Cornwall exported another commodity to the waiting world, a commodity of untold value, in the form of its miners.

From mining developed engineering wonders, and here too the Cornish shone with brilliance, especially in exploration and adaption of the uses of steam in the mining industry and locomotion. As the mechanisation of the mines advanced with more inventions, and as crude machinery was perfected, the old methods of pumping out the water always present in Cornish mines were discarded and many men found new ways of life in manufacturing, installing and maintaining great engines and works for this purpose.

The working depths of Cornish mines had nevertheless been increasing before the power of steam had been introduced to the industry . Much thought had been given to methods of removing the ore and water from the shafts.

Before this great and exciting period of invention and increased mining activity, the industry had made little or no progress in the mechanical field or in the production of copper and tin.

An early stamp mill.

THE DOLDRUMS AND A FRESH WIND

When the Romans left Cornwall mining lost its importance, mainly because the country was being attacked by the Saxons. The warlike activities of these invaders effectively prevented any trading for tin. The Saxons also appeared to have no knowledge of the value of the metal, completely ignored the industry and latterly, when their own claim to dominion over Britain was challenged by the Danes, thay had no time to indulge in mining.

The Danes were similar in their attitude to mining. Blood letting was more to their liking and so, for a long period until the arrival of the Normans, the mines lay stagnant and the miners a forgotten breed, but, as we shall see, they had not entirely forgotten the art and were working under the management of the Jews who were brought in at about the time of King John early in the thirteenth century.

This was not to the liking of the Cornish who saw their rights being taken away, with the result that they displayed no interest in recovering the metal to line the pockets of a disliked King.

To the credit of King John he saw that the tin trade of Cornwall was being ruined but he was prompted in his change of attitude mainly because of the loss of revenues from the sale of metal.

Laws had been earlier introduced preventing the tinners from cutting down trees for the smelting of the metal but John now rescinded these and placed mining activities under the law of the realm.

There has always been a question regarding the Jews in Cornwall. It is certain that they were in evidence at the time of King John and there are some who maintain that they left their mark on the Cornish long before that period.

Traditionally, they were here; the money to be made in the tin trade would have been another reason, and it is also clear that Jewish features are evident on some Cornish faces. A Jewish rabbi, who was much travelled, once remarked that the only country in which he could not tell a Jew was in Cornwall, because he had met so many Cornishmen who, at first sight, appeared to be Jewish. A striking example is on record of a Newlyn boatman whose face was so Hebrew that he sat for an artist and portrayed St. Peter.

When it came to mining, the Cornish did not see eye to eye with the Jews, and turned away from producing tin. Edward I, (1272 - 1307) alarmed at the way the industry had declined, banished the Jews, but this alone was not enough to rekindle the old spirit of the mining fraternity, who had very little encouragement, and in addition, distrusted the King.

Some influential Cornish gentlemen, being aware of the stagnant state of mining, approached Edmund, Earl of Cornwall, strongly requesting him to confer upon them certain grants essential for the working of the mines. These requests were granted and confirmed by his personal seal. A charter was drawn up giving miners and the industry privileges that had never before been allowed.

By this charter, the miners were enabled to hold courts of judicature, to decide all pleas of action and all stannary causes. At their discretion, they were permitted to hold parliament and to receive, as their own due and property, one fifteenth part as a legal toll, of all tin that should be raised.

In return, the miners agreed to pay to the Earl of Cornwall, one halfpenny for every pound of tin brought to a marketable state. To prevent fraud it was agreed that all tin raised and manufactured should be brought to certain towns to be weighed, coined and kept, until all dues had been paid.

To the Charter a seal was affixed, depicting a pick-axe and shovel.

According to the historian Tonkin, the Charter was granted in the thirty-third year of Edward I, 1305, to several gentlemen living in the parishes of St. Austell, St. Ewe, Lanlivery, Luxulyan, Roche, St. Stephens, St. Mewan and St. Dennis. The charter was supposed to have been kept in the tower of Luxulyan church, secured in a coffer, with eight locks and eight keys, each of which was kept in the parishes mentioned. During the civil war, the Charter, together with other important papers and documents concerning the Stannaries, was taken to Lostwithiel, where the forces under the command of Essex, destroyed them in 1644.

At this time, however, and because of the Charter, rights of bounding, the setting of bounds to certain portions of land for the encouragement of those searching for tin, were first applied. Accordingly, if any man found tin in any ground that was enclosed, but not bounded by another, he could ask leave of the owner to work the area. If the land was bounded, then whether it was enclosed or not, all that was required was to obtain leave of the bounder. If the land was neither bounded or enclosed, then any person could mark out the bounds to the land and, observing the legal forms, begin his search for tin.

A great deal of time and effort went into the search for tin. Men would spend their whole lives prospecting, in the hope of striking it rich, but few luckier than two beautiful dreamers who found tin works of great value through means no less strange than extraordinary, by dreams.

In Edward VI's time, a gentlewoman, heir to one Tresculierd, and wife to Lanine, dreamed that a man of seemly personage told her how in such a tenement of her land she would find so great a store of tin as would serve to enrich both herself and her posterity. This dream she revealed to her husband and he, putting the same in trial, found a work which in four years was worth many thousand pounds.

Also a man called Taprel, lately living in the parish of St. Neot, by a like dream of his daughter, made the like essay, met with the effect, farmed the work of the unwitting lord of the soil, and grew, thereby, to a good state of wealth.

STREAM TIN - ITS DEVELOPMENT

Legal matters concerning the search for tin now being settled, the real business of production could begin. The early methods of recovery of tin have already been briefly covered; now, after the idle years, miners could let their imagination and inventive abilities run free, driving the industry from crude workings to a mammoth worldwide phenomenon.

Tin ore, scattered near the surface of the earth, was deposited in veins running through the strata of Cornwall. Large amounts of ore have been broken from these veins by some violent acts of nature and carried from the hills by water into valleys leading to the sea. Carried, probably by the great floods, it was found in particles of various sizes, sometimes incorporated with stones and mixed with other metals. When found in stones, scattered beneath the surface of slopes, it was usually 'shode'. Shode would vary from one foot to ten in depth and the bed of stone and sand resembled a stream. A stream of water was required to recover the ore.

Having discovered the shode, the tinner then obtained from the owner the right to work. This right was called a Sett, and Stannary laws being complied with, the tinner now directed a stream of water on to the surface to remove waste soil. A lower level would be dug up to the water workings to allow the sand and soil to be carried away. The ground was then opened at the extremity nearest the sea, or the discharge of water, from which place the workers made their way towards the hill. On the ground which had been opened up, a stream of water was directed in from the surface, which, running over the almost perpendicular descent, washed off the lighter parts of such ground as had previously been broken by picks, carrying them through the under level called a 'tye' and leaving behind the sands and heavy stones. In this stream the men stood wearing boots, keeping the sand and gravel at the bottom agitated. The larger deposits would be lifted out and thrown to one side, at the same time selecting any shode that showed on their shovels.

The man-made cliff, over which the water ran, was called a 'breast', the material thrown away 'stent', the sand with its tin was called 'gard', the walls on each side of the tye were called 'stiling' and the last particles washed away by the water were the 'tailings'. The streams were worked by this method until they were exhausted, a process sometimes lasting many years.

The gard, shode and pebbles of tin ore that were found would be selected from the stent and tailings. The pebbles containing pure tin would be held, waiting the preparation of the shode, which, if large, would be broken by heavy hammers until reduced to a size the mill could handle and pulverise. The gard would pass through another process before being ready for the mill. Before being pulverised it would be taken from the tye and laid on its banks, then collected together and carried to a small floor where an oblong pit was dug, about three feet deep and about eight feet long, by four feet wide. This pit was the 'gounce'. Above it was placed a sloping frame of iron bars called a 'ruddle', something similar to a gridiron. At the head of this was a stream of water into which was shovelled the gard, which, on being carried to the ruddle, would be separated, the finer parts bearing the tin passing through it into the gounce

9

Engine belt driven Cornish stamps, Jerome, Arizona, 1895. Similar to very early stamps operated by hand and water wheels and invented by Sir Francis Godolphin.

below. The floor, or bed, of the gounce, being on a slight incline, the heavier gard remained near the upper level, while the lighter and less productive parts would be carried down to its lower end. When the gounce was full the material would be removed and placed in heaps, according to the various sizes deposited. All these would then be taken to a stamping mill and crushed to powder.

Sir Francis Godolphin is credited with the invention of the stamping mill. A member of a famous family which gave its name to the Cornish village, he was the owner of several tin mines thereabouts in the sixteenth century. He was also a sailor of some repute and a few years after the Armada, the waters around Cornwall were again troubled by Spanish buccaneers; Sir Francis on one occasion sailed down to Penzance to teach a company of these a lesson and hasten their return to Spain.

Before the introduction of the mill, crushing machinery similar to that described earlier was used but was very limited in its usefulness by its design. The new mill consisted of a water wheel and up to eight large pieces of timber placed under a shed perpendicularly within a frame close by the side of a

10

revolving axle. At the bottom of these timbers, called lifters, were attached large pieces of iron weighing from 80 to 180 pounds. The axle was fitted with a number of projecting timbers, called 'tappets', which as it revolved, connected with 'tongues' of timber attached to the vertical lifters, thereby lifting them to a height which could be adjusted according to the length of the tongue. When the tappets lost contact with the tongues, the heavy lifters would fall, crushing the ore to a powder. The material for crushing would be fed into the mill through a large opening at the back called the 'pass'. This opening was higher than the mill, and steep, to allow the materials to fall easily to the crushing base. In front of the lifters was placed an iron grate about a foot square, standing vertically and perforated with small holes to which size all the ore had to be crushed. The stamps, working in the water, would force the crushed material against the grate with every blow, driving particles of the correct size through the holes. The pulverised materials, having passed through the grate, would be carried along by the stream of water which forced them through into a sump, in which the richer parts would settle near the head, while the lighter parts would be carried further on. There would be a succession of these sumps, each retaining crushed ore, according to their weight and purity.

Electric motors driving a stamp mill, Johannesburg gold mine, early twentieth century.

When the sumps were full, the contents were divided into separate piles, and the more refined parts were carried to another pit, called a 'buddle', where a man was constantly employed keeping the whole in a state of agitation, under another stream of water, dividing and smoothing with his

11

shovel the small quantities placed on the buddle head, which was elevated about three feet above the floor of the buddle where he stood. Brooms were also used to expose the ores now being refined by the action of the water. When the buddle was full the contents were again divided, the better parts being against the head. These would then be removed to a large tub, called a 'keeve', and thrown carefully in, using a shovel. The water in the keeve was constantly agitated and stirred into a circular motion, by which method the tin was drawn towards the bottom, so bringing about further separation. When the keeve was full, it would be drained and the lighter parts skimmed off to undergo a further process, with the better materials passing through a sieve immersed in a second keeve, in which the water was agitated as before, to assist in the removal of any remaining impurities. The motion of the water in the keeve was increased by men beating the sides with mallets. This was called 'packing' and was intended to promote separation.

From the top of the keeve, the upper parts would be skimmed off with a shovel to undergo further purification. The remaining parts bore the general name of black tin, and as such, was taken to the blowing houses for sale.

In all these works, it is seen that water played an indispensable part, but to purify the black tin further, another process was necessary.

In addition to the miners and streamers, there were other trades connected with the industry in early days, just as there are at the present time. The blowers, or smelters of tin, together with assayers, were prominent in these subsidiary trades, although the blowing houses no longer remain, except in naming places where they once operated.

Samples of black tin were taken to an assay furnace to be melted, and the results estimated, according to the weight of the ore, and that of the metal. Sometimes, twenty pounds of ore would produce twelve to fourteen pounds of metal, but this was rare. By various estimates, the batches of ore were purchased, and the tinners paid according to the prices established at the coinages.

The samples now having been assayed, the rest of the black tin had to be carried to a blowing house, where it was laid out with its proper flux on great moorstone hearths, and by action of charcoal, fanned to intense heat by huge bellows worked with a water wheel, and when in a molten state, would be passed into an iron gutter, leading to a very large kettle sunk into the ground.

Here it would remain for several hours, being stirred to allow the dross or impurities to rise to the surface and be skimmed off. The tin would then be removed using iron ladles, and poured into stone moulds. These moulds would contain blocks of tin weighing about three hundredweight each, and bearing the marks of the owners of the blowing house. The ingot was then carried to the coinage town for examination, and to receive the impression of the Duchy seal.

It is apparent that the amount of carrying about was very great. Apart from the problems of materials and supplies, the tin stuff had to be brought from the mine to a place where sufficient water power could be made available for operating the stamps used for crushing it; then to the blowing house, and on to one of the coinage towns, where tax was levied, and finally, to the ports for shipping to London.

All this in an area where scarcely any roads existed, necessitated some form of pulling power, and mules where used to a great extent. Looking after

To the Conſtable of the *Pariſh of Cambourne*

to wit.} **B**Y Virtue of an Order from Sir *John Morſhead*, Baronet, Lord Warden of the STANNARIES in and for the ſaid County, unto me directed, you are hereby required to make out a fair and true Liſt, in Writing, of all the Miners and Working Tinners uſually, and at this Time dwelling within your Conſtablewick, between the Ages of *Fifteen* and *Sixty* Years, diſtinguiſhing therein which of them are willing to engage themſelves to be armed, arrayed, trained and exerciſed, for the Defence of the Realm, and which of them are willing to engage, in Caſes of Emergency, either gratuitouſly, or for Hire, as Pioneers or Labourers, and ſuch of them as by Reaſon of Infirmity are incapable of active Service, according to the Form hereunto annexed: which Liſt, ſo fairly made as aforeſaid, you are hereby required to ~~to the Deputy Lieutenants and Juſtices of the Peace for the ſaid County, at their Meeting for that Purpoſe to be held, on the~~

Given under my Hand this **24** Day of

of *April* **1798**

John Hichens High Conſtable.

13

Name	Ages	Name	Ages
William Cara	30	James Pascoe	38
Thomas Webster	20	John Reynolds	55
William Rodda	18	Samuel Vial	18
Richard Harris	48	Reynold Thomas	45
Stephen Webster	30	Abraham Rowe	27
James Eddy	20	Joseph Commons	29
John Webster	38	James Oates	40
Samuel Bastard	17	Henry Hicks	30
William Clemence	20	John Hicks	30
William Hart	30	James Reynolds	20
Jacob Kneebone	47	Richard Reynolds	16
James Kneebone	20	Thomas Harvey	40
Samuel Vial	30	John Daw	31
Matthew Vivian	40	Bennett Libby	32
Thomas Williams	40	William Leaty	17
Thomas Williams Jun.	19	James Guard	22
Henry Williams	17	William Guard	24
William Pascoe	35	Henry Poll	54
William Rogers	20	John Polkinhorne	36
Richard James	24	Thomas Blackwell	21
William James	22	Richard Dunn	16
James James	17	Samuel Toms	21
Samuel Noble	45	Richard Berryman	17
James Noble	16	Thomas Ingrim	58
Thomas Sincock	30	George Eustis	59

these animals was a major occupation in itself.

Before 1838, tin might only be sold at the coinage towns like Helston on two or at most four times a year. This meant that the tinners were forced to apply to the merchant for an advance, to enable them to live from one sale to another.

Money was lent on the condition of so much tin being produced by the next coinage and as many moneylenders usually planned to get their pound of flesh, the rate of loan was high and the tinners output always overpledged.

'Poor as a tinner'! Maybe, but there were compensations. In return for taxes which he paid, he received many privileges, paying no tithes nor dues at the fairs or markets. He had a court of laws and a stannary parliament of his own. He could not be summoned for military service unless the Lord Warden issued a special command.

In 1798 an order was issued from Sir John Morshead, Lord Warden of the Stannaries, requiring a list of all miners and tinners who would be willing to defend the Realm. The list shown is for Crowan but the 'Order' is for Camborne, the Crowan Order having been lost.

The most important privilege and one which prevented him from becoming a slave as miners in other parts of Britain became, was his right to enter freely all waste and unclosed land to search for tin.

Usually the tinner was content with his lot and enjoyed his work. It was labour of a special kind requiring a special breed of men and women to carry it out.

This enjoyment of work was to a great extent lost as the mines got deeper and conditions underground became extremely harsh, but even so there were many miners who experienced a sense of satisfaction from knowing that they could handle and in their own fashion, master the situation.

V

I HAVE A WHIM IN MY HEAD

With tin streaming becoming exhausted, the tinners' attentions were drawn toward the conclusion that the only places remaining to be searched lay under the surface and therefore to release the ores greater depths had to be worked.

In deep level mining among the main problems encountered was the raising of the ore, rubbish, and water. To raise these materials a simple machine called a whim was used. This is supposed to have got its name from a man called Coster who was of more than average intelligence, being seen by his friends erecting some strange contraption of a mechanical nature. When asked what he was doing, he replied. . ."I have a whim in my head and am trying to put it into practice".

He was laughed at but when it was completed and seen to work, the machinery proved invaluable.

In its original design the whim was a perpendicular pole up to eighteen feet in height, the upper end of which was held within a transverse fixed beam the bottom resting on a solid foundation in which it turned. Connected to and turning with the vertical pole was a large hollow drum or cylinder of wood called the cage. Around this was fastened a strong rope extending outwards in a horizontal manner so that its two ends each passed over a pulley erected over the shaft down which the ends of the rope descended. At each end of the rope a bucket was fastened. These buckets were known as 'kibbals', an old Cornish name, and were used to raise and lower not only materials in the shaft but men as well. Connected under the cage and to the vertical pole, a strong beam extended horizontally and which when being harnessed to horses moving in a large circle, caused the cage to revolve in the horizontal plane thus bringing one kibbal up and at the same time lowering the other. At every cycle the horses would reverse their circular path and repeat the process.

When used to carry men, kibbals could be a dangerous method of travel. A report from Gwennap in February 1818 noted that, "on Thursday last a miner named Collins belonging to Gwennap was killed in Poldory mine. He had just exploded a charge in a hole which contained six pounds of powder and went down to see that the blast had properly taken effect. Finding the smoke which had not cleared out of the shaft too powerful he desired to be drawn up. Just as he came to the surface, but before he could be laid hold of, he fell from the kibbal in which he stood and being precipitated to the bottom was killed on the spot. The unfortunate man has left a wife and six children".

The raising of water from the depths was the most difficult problem facing the miners. Kibbals were used for this purpose but as shafts got deeper and deeper and the amount of water to be discharged increased, this method proved totally inadequate and more ingenious engines were brought into use. These were the practical outcome of the ideas of an imaginative people.

In shallow workings where only small amounts of water had to be raised an amazing contraption called a flopjack was used. It was cheap to build and to operate and was the nearest thing to perpetual motion.

A wooden beam suspended at its centre was fitted at one end with a rod hanging vertically down into the flooded shaft at the bottom of which was a tube. The rod and tube constituted the cylinder and piston of the pump. At the other end of the beam was placed a large box open at its far end. The beam, or bob as it was called, was balanced so that naturally the rod extended down into the shaft, and the cylinder or tube at the bottom. The box at the other end of the beam being a part of it would when so inclined retain water. Above this box was a container secured on a frame which was not part of the beam. The container which received a supply of water from a stream, was fitted with a free moving hatch which was opened by the action of the beam until the balance turned in its favour, causing it to descend and at the same time closing the hatch on the container.

The other end of the bob, now rising, would withdraw the rod bringing up water from the shaft. This motion of the beam would naturally allow the water in the box to flow out and the beam now becoming heavier at the rod end would balance towards the shaft. These actions of the working parts continue to cycle continuously, discharging water from the shaft.

It was the steam operated pumps that saved Cornish mines from being abandoned. Without the benefit of steam power mining would have stagnated throughout most of the nineteenth century, or at least until electrically operated machinery became available.

It was thanks to such pioneers in the field of the steam engine as Savery and Newcomen that mining was able to continue at great depths and the problem of water accumulation at lower levels overcome by the use of the steam driven pump.

The first of these pumps was installed at Wheal Vor tin mine in Breage where it operated from 1710 - 1714

> "And then they had an injin good
> That drawed the water like a flood
> And sucked right up the very mud
> Of the mine of Balleswidden".

Following the inevitable acceptance of steam power it was natural that many engineers would turn to the building of steam engines. Cornwall produced a number of famous men in this field including Woolf, Trevithick and the notable Jonathan Hornblower who had a younger brother, Josiah. He was an experienced engineer and was chosen to go to America in the middle of the eighteenth century to install the first steam pump ever to work in that country. The copper mine where the pump operated was in north Arlington. Josiah never returned to Cornwall but continued to be associated with mining in America, where in the late eighteenth century he is reputed to have installed the first ore stamping mill.

As mining developed around the world, the demand for experienced engineers and miners increased, especially in Mexico, America, Australia and South Africa. In Cornwall village blacksmiths found that in addition to fitting shoes to horses, their services were now in demand to carry out maintenance and repairs on the new generation of machinery being used in the mines. Many of these blacksmiths and their sons became greatly experienced and progressed from repairing to the installation of engines, pumps, whims and stamp mills. A few became world famous and founders of great engineering works, supplying mining machinery to all parts of the globe.

17

In the relatively short space of time of intensive deep mining in Cornwall requiring the use of a great variety of mechanical equipment, it is amazing that almost overnight hundreds of great works were installed. What manner of men were they in this remote corner of the world who could progress in ability and become capable of performing these miracles of achievement in so little time?

When one considers the description of the Cornish written by a visitor to the country in 1775 and weighs it against the fact that in the same year an 82 inch steam engine built by the Carran Company was installed at Chacewater Mine, it is all the more remarkable.

In his note the visitor wrote:

"This county in general has nothing to speak of. The far west of it must be very unhealthy as being but a few miles across from the northern to the southern seas, and is thus always subject to heavy cloud and rainy weather so that those who are usually out of shelter are constantly wet to the skin and over shoes in mud. The natives think little of this but seem very happy when they can sit down to a furze blaze wringing out their clothes and pouring the muddy water from their boots. The common people here are very strange kind of beings, half savages at best."

"Many thousands of them live entirely underground where they burrow and breed like rabbits. They are rough as bears selfish as swine obstinate as mules and hard as the native iron. Those of the lower sort live so wretchedly that poor people in other parts of the country would soon perish if reduced to these conditions. The labourers diet is a form of pasty; potatoes or turnips or leeks and pepper grass rolled up in black barley crust baked under ashes with now and then a little milk. Meat is hardly ever eaten yet the children are healthy strong and looked fresh and jolly."

It seems hardly possible that from such backgrounds a multitude of men should arise capable of great mining works and splendid engineering accomplishments - but arise they did, and made their indelible mark on history, although without the power of steam none of these great works would have been possible.

The interest in this new form of power was awakened by an account of the fire or steam engine recorded in 1663 by the Marquis of Worcester in his "History of Inventions". The description of these engines was so vague and indefinite that little could be gathered from the account that the formation of engines to be worked with steam was practical. The idea being aired was enough to set the minds of mechanical men to work.

Captain Savery, a military engineer, secured in 1698 a patent for his machine intended for the raising of water by the impellant force of fire. At the same time, Thomas Newcomen was working on an engine consisting of a cylinder with piston connected to a large overhead beam which at its further end had a bucket pump connected. By filling the cylinder with steam and then condensing it by means of a jet of cold water, a vacuum was caused which allowed atmospheric pressure to push down the piston giving movement to the pump rod in the mine shaft by the bobbing up and down of the beam. These machines were sometimes known as "bob" engines.

Engine construction continued with variations and improvements being

Richard Trevithick 1771 - 1833

THE FIRST LOCOMOTIVE TRIAL AT CAMBORNE, 24th DEC., 1801.

FROM A SKETCH BY MR. WM. COCK.

Up to Camborne Beacon
Like a little bird.
The engine seen in what is now Trevu Road

contributed by Boulton, Watt and many more, some now forgotten like Cartwright, Hornblower, Murray, Bramah and Woolf.

Before the days of Boulton and Watt the steam engine was used solely to raise water from the mine. Later it was substituted for horses in the working of crushing machines but by far the most important and far reaching was its application to the field of railway locomotion and marine propulsion.

VI

FULL STEAM AHEAD

No mention of the use of steam power can be made without reference to that great son of Cornwall, Richard Trevithick. Much has already been written, but is always worth repeating, especially the story of the first steam locomotive and its trials around the Camborne area.

Richard Trevithick was born in the parish of Illogan, on 13 April 1771, the only son of a Cornish mining engineer and 'Captain'. He grew up during the period when steam power was beginning to be a dominating factor in the mining industry.

Man had always been searching for ways to move things mechanically, ever since the time when he realised that anything round would roll. So it was with steam power; how to use it? Trevithick was among the first to put them both together in practical form, and it was his genius that produced the first locomotive.

The design of the engine is not dealt with here; it is discussed in other books about the great man. What is of compelling interest, is the fact that in Camborne, Cornwall, ran the first ever powered vehicle.

The locomotive was assembled in a blacksmith's shop at Wheal Gerry, near Roskear. It had taken just over a year to complete in the shop of John Tyack, but on Christmas Eve 1801, with darkness falling and rain pouring across the country side, steam was raised, and the marvellous contraption began its journey, from the Weith, up to Camborne Beacon - going off like a little bird.

After a fair run, the engine was turned and brought back to the blacksmith's shop. Modifications and improvements were found to be necessary, and several more runs were carried out before the accident, which on 28 December, destroyed the carriage.

Trevithick and his friend Captain Andrew Vivian had started another run up the Weith when the front wheels hit a gulley across the road, the carriage overturned in a ditch, but was soon pulled upright by the spectators. All this excitement, coupled to the fact that the festive season was not yet over, and that Knapps Hotel was just across the road, was enough to propel all those involved in that direction, to partake of a meal of roast goose and warming drinks. The engine forgotten, its water boiled away, the iron became red hot, and everything combustible suffered irreparable loss.

Trevithick was not too discouraged by all this, and in a short time, both he and Vivian were in London taking out the patent on the high pressure steam engine, in whatever form it might be utilized, for propelling carriages on roads or railways. The great man's imagination was, perhaps, vivid enough for him to have seen the spread of the idea, and the railway system, that would, within fifty years, cover the whole country.

With the varying fortunes of the mines playing an important part in the lives of the mining community, many were forced to move around the country seeking work in new ventures. From the mines in Crowan, Henry Blackwell moved to Gwennap and the great works of Consolidated Mines, Wheal Jewel, Ting Tang and the United Mines where the Bal maidens, those hardy handsome

Through the Lych gate to Kenwyn Parish Church here
Crowan born Henry Blackwell married Eliza Whitford, 1844,
and their son Henry married Eliza Keast, 1867.

Bal maidens and the old Jan, Dolcoath 1890.

Bal maidens receiving cart loads of ore for spalling at Pednandrea Mine, Redruth, nineteenth century.

women who, helped by children, worked in large gangs handsorting the high grade material which could be shipped direct to the smelters from the run of the mine ore. They sang as they toiled breaking up the rocks.

> "I can buddy and I can rocky
> And I can walk like a man.
> I can looby - and shaky
> And please the old Jan."

In 1844, Henry married Eliza, daughter of John and Ann Whitford at the old parish church, Kenwyn, Truro. The Whitfords lived in Whitehall, Scorrier, another rich mining district, where Wheal Busy, Treskerby, Tresavean and other mines were operating.

After their marriage, the Blackwells lived in Whitehall where two children were born, Eliza Jane in 1844 and Henry in 1846.

Life in Cornwall at that time was active especially with the railway planning to connect Plymouth with Truro and Falmouth. Work was started at Truro in 1847, but it was not until 1859 that the line from Plymouth over the Tamar was fully operational.

The very early railways were horse drawn, the first being from Portreath to the mines of Scorrier and St.Day. These were laid down in 1809 and operating by 1812. By 1855 steam locomotives were in use on many of these lines, but with the decrease in mining activities their end was a foregone conclusion, although the line from Redruth to Devoran on the banks of Restronguet Creek continued to operate until 1915.

Passenger services were growing faster than many people realised as the following letter from a traveller to the "West Briton" newspaper of 3 June 1853, reveals.

Chacewater

Sir, Coming from the eastward to Truro, I stopped at Pearces expecting, as I had formerly done, to go by coach to Chacewater but found on making inquiry that old John had ceased running in consequence of the West Cornwall Railway coming so near Truro as to interfere rather considerably with the passenger service over the old trust road. I then availed myself of the opportunity of having a comfortable ride in Pearces "Railway Bus" to the present terminus of the West Cornwall Railway near Highertown, and on a cursory glance at the time table found or rather fancied Scorrier Gate to be the nearest station to Chacewater, whither I had wanted to take myself - got a ticket for Scorrier station and off we go - but lo! After a ride for some fifteen or twenty minutes, came to a standstill.The door opened, 'Chacewater' says the guard, which rather got over me, not reckoning for a moment that there was a station there (which I afterwards learnt had been erected a considerable time but without the necessary conveniences) without being inserted in the time tables. Besides, if I were to give my opinion, I should say that the present station is not at a proper place - I think if it were at a point about half-a-mile to the east of Chacewater, close by the crossing of the turnpike road, it would be a good deal better both for the Company and the accommodation of the public. I have just heard that several other persons in consequence of the non-insertion of Chacewater in the time tables have been similarly or worse served than myself. I hope by thus adverting to the subject by your kind permission through the medium of your journal, the directors will rectify the evil complained of. I am sir your obedient servant,

A.Traveller.

In 1853 preparatory work had started on the stupendous undertaking to bridge the river Tamar at Saltash to allow uninterrupted railway services between Cornwall and England.

These works were prosecuted with great vigour. Extensive workshops and smithies were erected. Steam machinery of every description for planning, rolling into shape, cutting, drilling and punching masses of iron to form parts of the bridge were brought into full operation. The smith's shop contained eight forges working on the principle of exhaustion of what was known as fan bellows, driven by steam. News of this new undertaking soon spread; miners were required for excavation works and blacksmiths were in great demand.

In 1853, at the age of twenty nine, Henry Blackwell was already suffering from phthisis following years of underground work in the Crowan, Gwennap and Liskeard mines. It was from Liskeard that he journeyed to the Tamar, and worked on the construction of the Saltash railway bridge for C. J. Mare, the contractors between 1853 and 1859. During this welcome change of environment, he gained sufficient engineering knowledge to discard underground work, and, returning to Liskeard, was an engineman at one of the mines.

During the 1860's, there was industrial strife in the coalfields of Northumberland, and many Cornish mine workers travelled north to keep the mines operating. Henry Blackwell was among them and it was in the church of the new parish of Sighill near Newcastle-upon-Tyne that his daughter, Eliza Jane, married Richard Symonds, a coalminer, in 1866. Richard's father was a Cornish copper miner, Henry's profession on the marriage certificate was given as Engineer.

In 1871, both families had returned to Cornwall and were living at Polvenna in Perranzabuloe, very near West Chiverton lead mine, where Henry was employed as a mine engine fitter, his son, Henry was the mining engineer's assistant and his thirteen year old daughter, Mary, was a lead ore dresser.

There was no escaping the killer phthisis which was now telling on his health. He tired easily and work became a burden for this man who had laboured all his life and who took pride in relating to his family his experiences when helping to build the great bridge across the Tamar and his venture to the northern coalfields. At the home of his son, Henry, just across the way at Cost-Is-Lost on Sunday, 23 February 1873 he died from phthisis and exhaustion at the early age of 48. He lies buried in the Perranzabuloe churchard.

VII

THE CAPTAINS

With the introduction of steam power and better mechanical equipment, deeper mining became practical and this, coupled with expansion of activities on the surface, made it necessary to plan and organise the running of each mine according to its own special problem.

To describe the manner in which the workings both above and underground were conducted is possible only in the most general terms. The control of its day to day workings was exercised by experienced practical men. The methods used to operate one mine could fail if used in another.

The man chosen to take charge of the mines was given the title of Mine Captain, and once having obtained this position, retained the name for life. With the decline in the number of mines operating over the past hundred years, the title has, sadly, become just a memory, but how much more romantic it sounds, than what is perhaps its equivalent today; the position of Underground Manager.

The duties of the Captains were many, and the responsibilities great. It was their business to inspect the various departments of the work, to see that the miners were properly distributed in the underground workings, to decide on the right direction to take to follow the lode, to see that the men gave a fair day's work, to regulate the price of labour according to the condition of the ground being mined.

It was their business to see the efficient propping up of the more dangerous areas with good timbers, and to make experimental drives for prospecting, or to discontinue a search if thought unprofitable.

The observation of the consumption of candles and gunpowder, the necessity to replace the working tools, to see that the channels conveying water were in good repair, and that the water was properly conducted to the pumping engine shaft from where it was raised to adit and out of the mine.

There is no doubt that Captain Joseph Odgers was physically and mentally designed to carry off to perfection his flamboyant and sometimes reckless way of life, he was usually dressed in black breeches and silk stockings. There was no malice in his roguery, if indeed that is what he was guilty of. The gullible fools who fell for his plans were usually rich and aiming to get richer.

Camborne in the early nineteenth century was the mining mecca ot the world and Joseph came there to see how he could turn things to his advantage, but like most schemes, capital was necessary, especially when it came to operating a mine at Porthtowan, ownership of which he had somehow gained for himself. He had a quick wit and a ready tongue and was always prepared to meet and cultivate the friendship of people who could come in useful, like naval officers who became his means of attending a levee at Greenwich where he was introduced to the Duke of Clarence, the Lord High Admiral of England. All this was no chance meeting; like the good honest confidence trickster that he was, Joseph was well aware of a visit the Admiral had made to a mine in Cornwall when his fleet lay at anchor in Falmouth. The mine was very close to the one operated by Odgers who soon knew of the fascinating effect all the Cornish mining methods and activities had on the Admiral, so completely different from a life on the ocean wave. The memory of what he had seen, together with the blandishments of the fine Cornish Mine Captain, were enough to persuade him and other officers to acquire shares in the Odgers mine. At his suggestion, what better name than Wheal Clarence? The Admiral was honoured.

In 1828, the circumstances of life changed, as Joseph himself describes in the preface to his story, and here very clearly is shown his disarming approach to people in his search for their confidence following his escapades in France.

"To a Generous Public,
My dear friends, for such I esteem you, and such have I found you, through chequered scenes of life, but little thinking, until of late that I should have had so much experience as has fallen my lot. I am a man of humble life, and it is well known to my friends that I am not a man of letters, and therefore you must take and read this narrative of my journey and stay in France in homely phrases. It is not my wish to harrow up your feelings to a high pitch, but in plain language to give you some idea of what it is to be in a strange country, destitute of friends and under false accusations - and how providence will work a deliverance for the falsely accused who can, at his own will, raise up a deliverer in time of need".

Appealing words from the humble man of no letters! In France he was prosecuted by the French Court under two serious charges - Forgery and Swindling and was condemned in a penalty of twelve thousand francs and to be fifteen months in irons at the galleys and to pay all the costs.

It will be asked what induced him to visit France? He was encouraged to undertake the journey by friends for the purpose of finding copper lodes which were supposed to exist in the cliffs in the area around Braage. The story is better told in his own journal, "A Tour To France in Search of Mines, With The Imprisonment Trials, Condemnation and Acquittal of Captain Joseph Odgers of Camborne in Cornwall . . ."

"I left Camborne 28 May 1828 for Falmouth where on the 31st I embarked on board the Bristol steam packet, Captain Ward bound for Plymouth. On 4 June left Plymouth for Portsmouth and on 7th embarked on board the steam packet for Cowes and South Ham, arriving at five oclock in the evening. A change of packet and sailed for Jersey on board the "Harrady" but storms delayed our arrival for two days. The passage to France was beautiful and we arrived at St. Maloes where I was at a loss, not knowing the French language. Being here about three days I found a faithful interpreter and engaged him for a franc per day. We surveyed the cliffs for a great distance and found several lodes and wrote ten letters to the gentlemen who sent me here but received no answer. In this predicament I waited until the 10 June when I met an Englishman who spoke French and by informing him of my discoveries he engaged to raise a company of Frenchmen in which he succeeded.

About the 12 December work commenced and we sunk a shaft sixteen fathoms deep designed for an engine shaft and drove the adit above high water mark as a drain. In July 1829 we cut into an underground stream of water. This necessitated a meeting of the adventurers at St. Maloes in order to raise funds to purchase an engine to take away the surplus water. The Company signed a bond to furnish us with 48000 francs, this bond was lodged as a guarantee between the Company and the lessees but after signing they could not raise the sum and in order to get rid of the obligation, they had me imprisoned, siezed the mine, sold the materials and went to the Notary to destroy the bond which was contrary to the laws of France. The adventurers not coming forward with the needful to prosecute, I left St. Maloes on the 18 July to manage a mine called Pulchitta, about 13 leagues from Brentharbour where I was arrested on the 16th August by gendarmes on a charge that I could not comprehend and committed to prison. I was later conveyed in a cart to a large town about three or four leagues on the north road and imprisoned having nothing but sour bread which I could not eat and water. On Monday 17 August I was removed to another town about four leagues distant and locked up in a small dark room with just a little straw for my bed. Next morning I was removed to another town where I was recognised by a French officer although I had never seen him before. He took me into an inn and gave me proper refreshment. Later in my cell he brought me cider and soup and ordered the turnkey to treat me with some humanity which he did. On the morning of 18 August I was taken out by the gendarmes and they fastened a chain above my elbow and under my arm, then threw it around my neck and fastened it on the point of my right shoulder with a padlock; the same chain was fastened on the point of my left shoulder and under my arm. In this condition I had to walk nine French leagues, that is thirty English miles in a torrent of rain. Here I dropt a silent tear. To the astonishment of the gendarmes I had walked it in eight hours and a half and no one to pity me. There was more travel and different towns on the way back to St. Maloes where I would be tried, but from the place called Doll four of us were put into a cart where I was chained to a madman who began to spit on me and draw much upon my arm to extricate his from mine. I called the gendarmes who threatened to cut the lunatics arm off but this only made matters worse so I formed the resolution to break his arm rather than to suffer further. The gendarmes seeing blood flowing from his arm released me and the remainder of the journey was in peace. At the trial I was addressed by the Judge in the following manner:-

"Monseur Odgers, the charges against you are forgery and bringing stones of copper out of England into France in order to deceive the French people, also by putting copper nails into a crucible stating that the copper was risen out of the mine of Braage. Guilty or not guilty? Not guilty!"

His mining career in Cornwall was explained to the court which was ignorant of mining and its terms. He explained how his brother took him underground at the age of ten and showed him the art of mining such as a barrow boy, a tutworker (contract work) a tributer (whose pay is a certain proportion of the values of the ore they raise) and a mine agent at Dolcoath for seven years.

The court found him guilty as previously mentioned but fate was kind, in the form of a Frenchman Lamooff who owned the land where the mine was to have been developed.

The thirteenth century church of St. Sithney where Captain William Odgers was baptised in 1805.

The Norman Font.

The fifteenth century church in St. Stithians where generations of Odgers were baptised. A grand and noble tower.
Inside the church, a timely reminder. . .
"No state on earth, no pomp may last, no flesh can long endure,
But, being earth, to earth shall turn, of this we must be sure,
Then, since our days be few and ill, and we shall pass the same,
Let us redeem them doing good, not seeking praise or fame".

An appeal was made before a higher court when on the 7th day of November, 1829, judges pronounced him free and justified.

He returned to Plymouth on 23 January 1830. In 1845 at the age of 72 he was found in London suffering from weakness and exposure. He died in St. Bartholomew's hospital in May, 1845.

But other Captains trod the straight and narrow, including William Odgers, who was born in Sithney on 24 March 1805. His forebears had been established in Stithians in the early seventeenth century. He came to the Camborne area as a young man and married Prudence Trevillion, in Camborne church, on 7 January 1828.

A religious man, his upbringing had been guided by parents who were staunch Methodist, a form of worship introduced into Cornwall by John and Charles Wesley.

On Sunday, 15 April 1744, John Wesley visited Stithians to preach, first at Gwennap and later in the day at Stithians. This was not the first time that Methodism had come to Cornwall. It was introduced in 1743, when a Bristol Methodist, Joseph Turner, who was a sea captain, sailed into St. Ives and met people who were members of a Christian Fellowship. He told the Wesleys of this meeting, and they were prompted to come, to preach the Gospel.

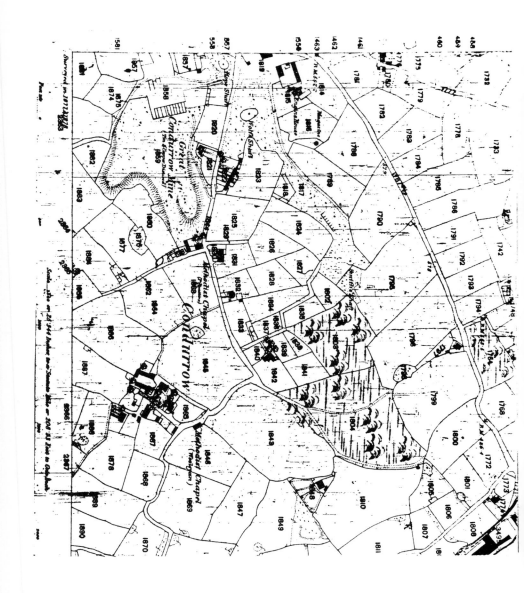

32

Higher Condurrow Chapel, 1888, no longer exists, but services are held at Wesley's Gwennap Pit (below).

Gwennap Pit, 1900.

John Wesley's Tree, Knave-Go-By.

Odgers Villas at Condurrow, built on the site of his original cottages. Sam Ham's house in the background.

34

The memorial was broken by a falling tree.

A virtuous wife, a friend most dear
A tender mother lieth here
In love she lived in peace she died
Her life was crav'd but God denied.

Quick and sudden was the call
When I was taken from you all
Husband and children don't lament
The call to me was quickly sent.

A headstone was then erected.

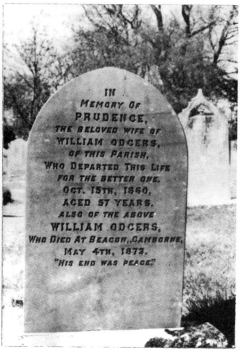

John Wesley was not welcome everywhere he went to preach. A story was told about his visit to the hamlets around Beacon, Camborne areas where heathens chased him down the hill through the place now known as Knave-Go-By. Wesley climbed a tree at the end of the lane and cried out to the knaves to go by. The tree stood for 200 years until, weakened by decay, it fell before the onslaught of a howling gale.

John Wesley's last visit to Stithians was on Monday, 13 August 1750, but in 1762 he was preaching at the Gwennap Pit, which became the focal point of Wesleyans in Cornwall.

The Wesleyan message was a powerful one, and when William and Prudence were living in Condurrow they were holding Primitive meetings in their cottage in the 1850's. This was demolished and William built two cottages at Condurrow and they were known for many years as Odgers' Cottages.

The first Primitive meetings were held in his cottage on weekends, when he returned there on his horse, from Wendron where he was at one time Captain of two mines, Wheal Lucy and Wheal Ann.

The first chapel was built at Higher Condurrow in 1826, at a cost of £25. It was situated to the right of a second chapel, and later served as a Sunday school. By 1866, it had been enlarged, a new floor, pews and pulpit put in, and it seated 150, of which 64 were paid for pews.

All was not peace in the Primitive fold, as it was known and recorded in the circuit's minutes, that one Catherine Prest was not allowed to meet in class until the circuit had proof of her repentance for interrupting the congregation in the chapel, and insulting Thomas Mogg in the lane at Condurrow. The troubles were not confined to Condurrow, as the complaint of the local preacher, Driffield, shows. Much earlier, in 1839, he learnt that his wife's father, Thomas Michell, though perhaps worth £5000, had only left his wife £10 a year in his Will. He wrote..."Can this be true of a man professing religion? One son he has given £500 and another £600 already. Another he is supporting, and I, with my six children, am left . . .Ah well; the Lord will provide!"

There were also divisions in the Condurrow chapel between class leaders, and on 2 February 1888, the foundation stones were laid of a new chapel by Captain W. Richards, Mr. J. Rodda of Carn Entral, Mr. W. Rule, Mrs. J. M. Jewell, Captain W. C. Vivian and Mrs. Prudence Ann Bennett, the daughter of William and Prudence Odgers, born 16 October 1830. Prudence Ann married James Bennetts in 1849, and together they were keeping a grocery shop in Beacon in 1861. To that date they had four children including William John, 11 years.

Shopkeeping was probably not to the liking of James, but it was a source of income, welcome between his trips abroad as an agent for the mining companies, owned by British based adventurers. His wife Prudence was a shrewd business woman who managed the Beacon grocery shop with profit, and who, when her husband died on 18 July 1865 at the early age of 39 from a fever during a visit to Havana, Cuba, used his savings to buy up many acres of good farming land in and around Beacon.

She also built the fine house "Bella-Vista" in Fore Street at the turn of the century. Standing on a corner of the grounds was the first Beacon sub post-office. This old thatched cottage also served as a "dame-school" where young children were taught usually by an old dame for a nominal penny a week per head. Prudence Ann died at "Bella Vista" in November, 1910, aged 79.

The first Beacon Camborne sub post-office.
It also served as a Dame school and stood in the grounds where
"Bella Vista" is today.

The personal effects of James were never returned to his widow. Agents responsible for shipping them promptly stole his trunk and gold pocket watch.

The eldest son, William John, was already working as a mine boy over at the Tolcarne mine, a venture that commenced around 1859, under the management of Captain Joseph Jewell of Redruth, on land owned by Sir R. R. Vyvyan. By 1865 the shaft was 60 fathoms deep, 35 to adit. The pumping and winding engine was 18" diameter. Rock, granite and clay slate made up the land structure, and the workings employed 78 men, 20 females and 22 boys. In 1864, copper ore of weight 834 tons were sold for £3,262.13s.3d. Prospects appeared good, and early dividends were expected, but in the general decline of mining, it followed the trend and closed down. Today the old count house and other buildings remain and are inhabited. The old burrows and fenced shafts are reminders of hopes and energies brought to nought.

Mine Captain William Odgers and his wife Prudence had three other children in addition to Prudence Ann; Elizabeth 1828, William Henry 1841, and John 1843.

William was the landlord of the Railway Hotel, in what was then known as Beacon Road, in 1897.

John, of whom little is known, died at Beacon and was buried in Treslothan churchyard in June, 1874. His headstone also remembers his brother-in-law, James Bennetts who died in Havana, Cuba, on 15 July 1865. James must have been a very popular man; there is another inscription on the headstone of his wife Prudence Ann.

Elizabeth married William Mitchell, a tin miner, in Tuckingmill church on Thursday, 21 June 1855.

The area around Tuckingmill was bustling with activity at this time with mines and an industry now forgotten. Well over a hundred years ago many families in various parts of Cornwall engaged in the home industry of making homespun cloth. This would be brought to what was known as a fulling mill where it was dipped, cleaned and dressed. The old English word Tucker for a Fuller is known. The Cornish for a Fuller or Tucker was Truchier and in Cornish a fulling mill was a **Melyn Druckya**.

The marriage of William and Elizabeth was blessed by three daughters, Ellen Annie, Prudence Ann, and Elizabeth Mary, three women who later became part of the epic Keweenaw copper story which by this time was being written mainly by the Cornish.

James Bennetts, 1826 - 1865.
A photograph taken shortly before his death in Cuba and reproduced in 1899 by his son William John.

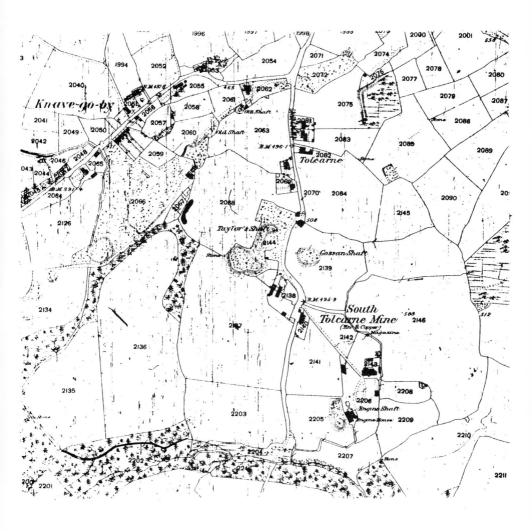

All Saints church, Tuckingmill.
William Mitchell married Elizabeth Odgers, the mine Captain's
daughter in 1855.

VIII

NEW COUNTRY - OLD MINES

Huge copper deposits existed in America, especially in Michigan - deposits so fine that pots and pans could be formed from it without refining in any way. Indeed, from 1843, when the copper rush began, to 1920, it was the only known place in the world where absolutely pure native copper was found in commercial quantities. But all this was at the back of beyond - in Keweenaw, almost surrounded by Lake Superior, the cold lake.

The average American had little ambition to get involved in any activity, mining or otherwise, in what to them was a distant inhospitable and bitterly cold region, almost a foreign land. There were others who saw the tremendous possibilities, mainly financial, of all the shining metal ready to be recovered from the surface or dug out from the depths, but expertise was required - and the sooner the better.

Mining prospects in Cornwall were tenuous and had been throughout most of its history. What better place to recruit a workforce already trained and with an inborn ability to tackle hard rock conditions existing in the north American copper country? So, in the late 1840's the Cornish came to the area and were the first from overseas to work Michigan copper.

By 1854 when the Central Mine opened up its great rich veins enough of them were there to practically take it over. They came and made Central a little Cornwall. The owners were delighted to have them - men from Cornwall made them rich!

They might well have been richer if the Cornish had not been beaten to it by an earlier breed who mined the peninsula many years before.

There were other great mines in the Keweenaw Peninsula, all with their Cousin Jacks, the Atlantic, Cliff, Phoenix, the Pewabic Lode, part of the famous Pewabic and Quincy Mining Companies, and most important of them all, a company claiming to be the richest on earth. It certainly was the most profitable, and in its turn, paid out colossal dividends. By 1930, the total dividends paid by all the copper mines in the area amounted to the staggering total of $325,017,047 of which the Calumet and Hecla Mining Company paid $160,558,398 or 49.4 per cent.

Calumet and Hecla recruited men in Cornwall. William John Bennetts worked there as a young man after leaving Tolcarne Mine during the 1870's.

Many Cornish families set up boarding houses for the miners who had come to America. Most of them were young, and single, and thankful to find a place where their kind of language was spoken and where their way of life and customs could continue, at least in a way, to ease somewhat the pangs of longing for the homeland.

It was in one of these boarding houses in Calumet that William John settled down. Physically, he was a small man, wiry, energetic, and as tough as many twice his size. He was thrifty, and accomplished his goal of making enough money to return to Beacon and set up his own business.

The boarding house was run by a Mrs. Williams, helped by her young daughter Mary. Her husband died, and she married again, this time a man who had little time for the sixteen year old daughter, and his treatment of her left

Places of worship in Calumet seen from the old mine workshops on Redjacket Road.

They came and made little Cornwalls.

much to be desired. William John soon befriended this unhappy soul, and determined to marry her. Consent was given by the girl's mother. Mary was just sixteen years and eleven months when the event took place on Sunday, 9 November 1873. Their child Elizabeth Ann, the first of eleven, was born in the village of Redjacket, one of several clustered around Calumet.

Copper had transformed Redjacket and its neighbours Blue Jacket, Yellow Jacket and Tamarack into boom towns. Money was everywhere.

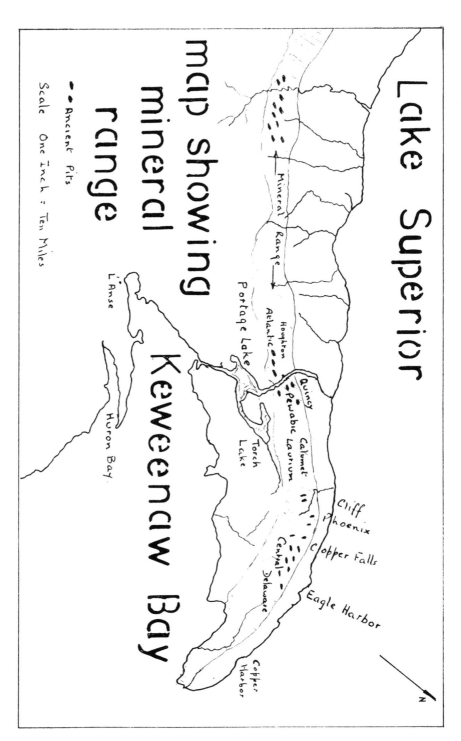

Lake Superior

map showing
mineral
range

Keweenaw Bay

Mineral Range

Portage Lake

Houghton
Atlantic

Quincy
Pewabic Laurium
Calumet

Cliff
Phoenix

Copper Falls

Central
Delaware

Eagle Harbor

Copper Harbor

Torch Lake

L'Anse

Huron Bay

•—• Ancient Pits

Scale One Inch = Ten Miles

N

44

IX

THE ANCIENTS

The origins of mining in Cornwall go back into ancient history, but mining in the Lake Superior region of North America is not only of great antiquity; it is shrouded in mystery.

In the 1840's Cornish miners in the Copper Country were simply giving a new lease of life to a tradition that had perhaps begun 6000 years ago, and, after thousands of years, died.

That prehistoric miners operated throughout the whole of the copper bearing region there is no doubt and the knowledge has given archaeologists, historians and mining men a splendid subject to discuss forever, and men being what they are will do just that. The irritating thing about the whole business is that in spite of the calculated removal of 500,000,000 pounds of pure copper by the ancients, they disappeared, leaving not a solitary skeleton or even a cupboard to hide it in. No dwellings, pottery, household utensils or artistic markings on the rocks - absolutely nothing except thousands of copper bearing pits, in some respects similar to the koffens found in the old tin digging areas of Cornwall, and thousands of hammering stones used to work them. Thousands of years ago man discovered that if rocks were heated with fire and then suddenly doused with cold water they would split open. Large copper bearing rocks were apparantly treated in this way, the smaller pieces then being fragmented using the hammering stones.

The mystery deepens, when consideration is given to the fact that Lake Superior copper was, until the twentieth century, the only known source of the pure metal; yet copper tools and ornaments were seen and noted by all the visitors and explorers to the Americas, including Columbus in Yucatan, Mexico; Cortez, Cartier and Raleigh in the southern parts and Atlantic coasts of the North.

But the most tantalising questions are, where did the bulk of the huge amounts of copper go, and what happened to the miners?

The pits, estimated to number more than ten thousand which had been opened up to recover the metal, had filled with wind blown soil, and by the fifteenth century, were growing a third generation of 200 year old forest. The abandonment of what were great works was sudden and final. Tools were left in positions, indicating that only a brief interruption in the working day was to take place, either for the meal-break or the night's rest. Work, however, had ceased; the legion of miners, indeed the whole community , simply packed their bags and disappeared. Did news reach them of a great disaster in their own homeland, was their presence in the area threatened by the sudden appearance of a warlike tribe, against whom they had no means of defence? In all the centuries, during which they had visited the Lake Superior region for copper, they had probably never contacted other humans there.

When later prospectors searched for copper in the area, they found that others had been there before them, unknown people had, long ago, extracted the metal.

Naturally, it was assumed that the local Indians, or rather their ancestors, had carried out these great works, but when the subject was discussed, they knew nothing of the mines, or the people who worked in them. Their tribal lore made no mention of it in any way.

A more informed study of the whole fascinating story is obtained in a paper written for delivery before the American Association in Cleveland in August, 1851, and published on 1 and 15 November 1852, entitled "Ethnology, The Ancient Miners of Lake Superior" by Charles Whittlesy.

Extensive mining operations had been carried on in very remote periods on the shores of Lake Superior. They were of great magnitude and were found extending over a wide area. The most striking remains of the workings of the ancient mines were on the Ontonagon River extending 15 or 20 miles along the range each way from where it crossed the course of the stream. They were also very apparent in the vicinity of Portage Lake. On Point Keweenaw they were seen extending eastward about 20 miles and across the Lake on Isle Royal abundant remains of mining operations of the very early era were found.

The details concerning the mode in which these ancient mines were worked, the depth and extent of their excavations, the tools and implements used may be seen in the reports of government geologists in the Smithsonian contributions in the United States.

It has been shown in papers written by learned men concerning the history of the copper mines in the Lake Superior region that the Indians had no hand in the discovery of the workings of them. There is abundant evidence that the ancient miners were the Aztecs, a people who entered America from Asia. They had apparently migrated south and then returned to Lake Superior in the summer time to work the copper. They did not permanently reside there, no remains of early settlements have been found. The winters would have been far too severe for them either to work or live in. The copper recovered in the summer time was carried away when the miners returned south to warmer climes. There was no evidence of furnaces or places where copper was refined or melted or where it was crushed in the rock and afterwards separated by washing as is done now.

The works were open cuts and not galleries which would have made them quite impossible to work in the bitter winters of that latitude. The rock was excavated principally by use of fire which softened and fractured the mass. After this a stone maul or hammer was used to break up the wall rock. These hammers were seen in great numbers among the rubbish of the old works and weighed from two to thirty-six or more pounds. They were handled in all probability by putting a withe, the tough flexible branch of a tree, around a groove or grooves cut cut at the middle of the maul and pounding incessantly at the rock on each side of the copper vein. The traces of fire and heat were clearly visible in the remains of charcoal and ashes far down in the wrought veins and on pieces of blackened rocks among the rubbish.

The mines were abandoned at least seven hundred and probably a thousand years ago, and because the ancients were unable to separate copper from its ore they could only use pure pieces. Left in the pits were great masses of metal. They couldn't melt it and had no tools to dig it out. When the white men came in the 1840's these pits were examined and many mines built on them.

After the original miners left the area the whole of the Keweenaw Peninsula reverted back to nature. The Indians, however, had much of it in their possession and they were now the occupiers of the land. Even so, it is doubtful if they would have pursued the matter sufficiently to make an industry out of it. This would be against their nature but what they did was to show a Frenchman a specimen way back in the early seventeenth century. This aroused little enthusiasm, the potential of the metal was not realised, but copper was mentioned with increasing frequency and one French explorer in a journey up the Ontonagon river in 1665 found a vary large solid copper rock lying on the river bank. A piece was sent back to King Louis XIV, but again nothing came of it; gems, silver or gold, were more to his liking.

X

NEW AWAKENING

Eventually, with the defeat of the French in Canada by the British who now took possession of the Keweenaw area, new explorations began to find what resources there might be worth exploiting. News of copper soon reached London. Cornwall was the copper centre of the world so the mining fraternity in the capital knew its value. Some time after 1770 a mining expedition arrived in Michigan and prospected around the Ontonagon river without success. How they could have failed with an abundance of the stuff lying around is perhaps not surprising since the miners were from the coal fields of England and not hard rock men from Cornwall.

Interest in the Keweenaw peninsula and its copper simmered both in America and Britain for years with little or nothing being done about it. Even after the War of Independence the government of the United States did little to get the wheels of the copper industry into lively motion in spite of urging by eager business men but, as is almost always the case, the hour produced the man.

A young physician, Douglas Houghton, had visited the Lake Superior region in 1830, and had seen the big boulder of solid copper beside the bank of the Ontonagon river.

This interested him considerably, and prompted him to reveal his plan to properly explore the region. He approached his friend, Stevens Mason, the first Governor of Michigan, who, not over enthusiastic about the inhospitable backyard of Keweenaw, still saw no harm in trying to find out just what was up there. He created a new office of state geologist, gathered funds together, and in 1840, sent Houghton and his party on their inquisitive way. Just before the year's end, Houghton submitted his report to the State Legislature. There was abundant copper in the peninsula! Huge chunks of it could be blasted out from veins right on the surface.

The copper gates swung open; from a few prospectors in 1841, the number increased steadily, until in 1843, the rush began in earnest, and the boom became incredible.

The nature of this copper country makes it almost impossible to believe that anyone would rush off to such a forbidding place. Roads were non existent. Supplies had to come across a violent Lake Superior, and the winters were a cold hell, when a man could starve or freeze to death, but they came, prospectors, miners, saloon keepers, boarding house landladies, ladies of ill repute, hangers-on, and all the characters in a cast of heroes, because bad or good, that is just what they were, and all held together by that indispensable core of men who, in reality, made it all possible; the Cornish miner. It was reported that some of these were in the Lake Superior region as early as 1840, certainly their descendants are still there today.

But what was it all about? What on earth was this huge amount of copper to be used for?

Certainly the telegraph system employed copper wire, and had done so for five or six years before mining began in Keweenaw. The telephone, and electricity for lighting were still twenty-five years away. Electricity generators, with their stators, and rotors, so intricately and profusely wound, with prodigious lengths of copper wire, were a long way off, but when they did arrive on the scene, created a great new market for the metal.

So, were the markets available in 1843 big enough to sustain the industry? The manufacture of arms, for the purpose of war, shell casings and guns, needed copper.

Pots and pans for cooking were preferred if made from copper. It was used in the making of coins and alloyed to make brass or bronze. The American navy had adopted copper to sheathe the wooden hulls of their warships, and; more peaceful pursuits, it was a valued building material.

Later, technology and industry ensured that Copper Country mines would be employed for a long time to come.

Today, the great roaring mines are silent. A number of circumstances, spreading over the years, caused the death of the industry. One was the failure of the heart of what was once a great living thing - it simply wore out; the copper resources were exhausted.

It may be that there are still large deposits waiting to be found, but for today, the Copper Country is just another Cornwall, relying on the tourist to keep it alive and, like Cornwall, it is fortunate to have so much to offer.

The mines were gathering momentum when William John Bennetts returned to Cornwall with his family, and in 1883, was shown in the local trades directory as a shopkeeper. In that same year, he became converted to Methodism and held regular services in his home in Beacon, next to where the post office, which he and his wife ran for many years, now stands.

Expanding from the shop in Beacon, William John became a successful and widely respected business man. Turning to photography, he operated a studio in the village, and before 1893 opened a shop in Hayle. By 1897 he had bought derelict buildings in Cross Street, Camborne, demolished them, and built new premises for his growing photographic business. An enterprising man, he is reputed to have sold the first camera and the first gramophone record in Cornwall. The records were cylindrical, packed in boxes of six, and were brought by a German commercial traveller.

The business has gone, but memories remain to this day. William John's only surviving child, Mrs. Prudence Bagge, still recalls, with her remarkable memory, those days long gone, days sometimes filled with sorrow, when the long chill hand of death from the far Copper Country, delivered news of the tragic deaths in the mines of two brothers of her mother, the gentle Mary.

The children of William John and Mary prospered reasonably enough, and some settled in foreign lands. Grandchildren are abroad, and one, Constance Stuart Larrabee in particular, has by her own special talents and adventurous spirit, become famous in her own right.

Constance Stuart Larrabee was born in Beacon, Camborne, on August 7, 1914. Three months later she travelled from Southampton to Cape Town. In South Africa the family lived on a tin mine.

In the 1930's she studied photography in London and at the Bavarian State Institute for advanced photography in Munich.

One of her exhibitions was opened in Pretoria in 1944 by Noel Coward who said, "Constance Stuart is a supremely good artist - she has incredible flair".

A reasonable amount of success for William John, seen here with Mary, in Plymouth, 1936.

In World War II she was South Africa's first woman war correspondent, accredited by the South African Director of Military Intelligence for Libertas magazine. She served in Egypt, Italy, France and England, attached to the American 7th Army in France and the South African 6th Division in the Italian Apennines, earning the reputation for always being further up front than the army.

In 1947 Constance Stuart was the official photographer for the Royal visit to the British Protectorates, Basutoland, Swaziland and Bechuanaland.

In 1949 she married in New York, Sterling Loop Larrabee, U.S. Military Attache in World War II, to South Africa, Yugoslavia Government in exile and Greece. Now an American citizen, she has lived since 1950 on Maryland's Eastern Shore.

Internationally known for her work among the tribes of South Africa, she was invited to exhibit "Tribal Women of South Africa" at the Museum of

50

Natural History in New York. The Museum of Modern Art included two of her photographs in "The Family of Man".

In 1979 the South African National Gallery in Cape Town honoured her with a retrospective show of one hundred photographs. It was the first photographic exhibition in the Pretoria and the Johannesburg Art Museums. "Perhaps the first person in South Africa to elevate photography to a serious art form".

In March, 1983, she returned to South Africa with "Celebration" the fifty best photographs by Constance Stuart Larrabee. The director of the National Gallery opened the exhibition in the Stellenbosch Art Museum.

Her grandfather, the well known Camborne photographer William John Bennetts, died in Beacon on 13th December, 1943, aged 93. Mary, his wife, died 24 July 1941, aged 84. They rest in the cemetery over the brow of Greenlane Hill.

A reasonable amount of success attended the affairs of William John, but this was not repeated for his cousin Ellen Annie, grand-daughter of William Odgers. She too became involved in the Keweenaw story, with less happy results.

Lamorran, on the Fal.

51

XI

FROM ST. KEVERNE, ST. MEVA AND ST. ISSEY

Early in 1874 during one of the periods of decline in the fortunes of Cornish mining, a young miner from Tolcarne, Beacon, named Richard Pearce Williams became betrothed to a handsome young dressmaker, Ellen Annie Mitchell, from Beacon.

Richard was born on Monday, 10 July 1854, in an old thatched cottage, now long gone. His father, Walter, was an agricultural labourer turned road maker from St. Keverne, where his forebears had lived since the early seventeenth century. His mother was Louisa Pearce from Mevagissey.

Just why Walter and Louisa were sojourners in the parish of Lamorran is not known but they were married on Saturday, 16 February 1833, in the lovely little church by the creek on the river Fal. A beautiful spot, and lonely with the name suggestive of a Celtic foundation by some saint or hermit who settled there and sanctified the site. There is some history here, as revealed in the cathedral in Truro, where down in the crypt there is a stone with an inscription to Owen Phippen, brother of one of the rectors there who was taken prisoner by the Turks in 1620 and was held for seven years in Algiers as a slave. In 1627, together with ten other Christian captives, he managed to board a Turkish ship and began a cruel fight with sixty five of the enemy which lasted three hours. Five of his companions were killed, yet by the grace of God, he became the captain and brought the ship to Cartagena. The King of Spain sent for him to attend the court in Madrid. He was offered a captaincy and the King's favour if he would turn Papist. He refused and managed to sell the spoils of his fight with the Turks, returning to Cornwall £6000 the richer, to die at Lamorran in 1636.

Lamorran is farming country, and here Walter Williams would have no difficulty in obtaining employment. The land was pleasant and not such a grim place as St. Keverne. Although set in the beautiful Lizard peninsula it was a tragic district, the burial place of many mariners, men, women and children who had lost their lives in the dreadful storms that battered the coast. It also grieved for Cornish heroes.

A slate slab set in the wall near the church gate commemorates in English and Cornish, the martyred rebel hero Myghal Joseph, known as An Gof, the smith, a man of great determination and courage.

Henry VII in his efforts to raise money for the war against Scotland, taxed the poor Cornish to breaking point. An Gof, together with Thomas Flamank, gathered an army and marched on London. At Blackheath, outnumbered and without horse or artillery, they were heavily defeated with the loss of many thousand men. Myghal Joseph and Thomas Flamank were hung, drawn and quartered at Tyburn, acts which have never been forgotten or forgiven by the Cornish.

Smuggling thrived in St. Keverne and was well organised. Underground tunnels have been found in the area and one runs from Godfrey Cove through Trythance and Tregellast Barton across Crousa Downs to the old inn at Zoar.

St. Keverne was probably an Irish saint. The church is situated on the highest ground in the district, having the addition of a spire instead of the

St. Keverne churchyard remembering the servicemen killed by
the wrong enemy.

Sailors and soldiers aboard
H.M. Brig "Primrose" died on
the Manacle rocks, 1809.

Commemorating Cornish heroes on the wall of St. Keverne church.

tower usually seen in Cornwall. The original spire was destroyed by lightning on 18 February 1770. The Reverend Anthony Williams, vicar at that time, related how the spire was rent in pieces. The roof of the church was destroyed, large stones were scattered over the floor and small stones on the outside carried nearly a quarter of a mile. He was rendered insensible and the congregation knocked to the ground but luckily no lives were lost.

Whatever the attractions Lamorran held, they were sufficient to draw Louisa Pearce away from Mevagissey, a doubly holy place named because two saints, St. Meva and St. Issey, combined their names. The word *and* in Cornish is 'ha' or 'hag', hence the name Mevagissey.

The medieval church of St. Peter, Mevagissey.

There were two separate dwelling areas many hundreds of years ago, Churchtown or Lanmoroch and Porthilly, a small fishing village on the east side of the inlet. The parish church of St. Peters is not large, indicating that in the fifteenth century when it was built, the community was not large.

Seine netting, fishing net with floats at the top and weights at the bottom edge for encircling shoals of pilchards was the main industry. There was a large export trade to London by vessels especially after the addition of jetties to the old quay around 1775.

Smuggling was a popular business, especially in the early part of the nineteenth century and special luggers were built to handle the trade of brandy and tea or anything else that would prove profitable. Roscoff in Brittany was usually the port where the Cornish boats delivered their cargoes of anything required on the continent such as tobacco. French brandy was loaded and after crossing the channel the kegs would be lowered overboard in Mevagissey bay or any suitable place for later collection, by what would appear to be innocent fishing boats. In the days when Louisa Pearce was young, smuggling was big business, but declined following the reduction of excise duty on goods. It is debatable that the increase in the number of coastguards was a factor in the decline. The Custom and Excise did take some command at sea when a local shipwright built a fast lugger for them.

Mevagissey, haunt of smugglers.

He went out of business and was fortunate in not being paid for his treachery by being lowered over the side of a boat one dark night. A couple of seine net weights would have done the job nicely. The smugglers were a cunning breed and if the duty on contraband had remained high they would have found ways to outwit the law.

One noted smuggler was James Dunn who lived in Mevagissey in the eighteenth century. In addition to smuggling, he was a man of ill repute, but this did not prevent the teachings of John Wesley from converting him into a stalwart Methodist. This did not interfere with his smuggling activities, after all, was not brandy a necessity of life? His good works must have been many and his trade flourishing with brandy for the parson and baccy for the clerk. He is remembered in a window in Truro cathedral.

Not all smugglers deserved such honour, and although many adventurers were out to make an exciting guinea, there were others who brought the game into disrepute.

In 1768, William Odgers, one of the Customs Officers stationed at

56

Porthleven was murdered in the most barbarous manner by a party of smugglers. £100 reward was offered by the commissioners for the arrest of the killers.

At the inquest, a verdict of wilful murder was returned against Melchisideck Kinsman and others unknown. . . "The controller fears that four of the men implicated are escaped to Guernsey, but later thought to be skulking underground in the tin mines." The next year he reports that the sum of £500 has been offered Hampton, the principal witness for the Crown against the murderers of Odgers, to go out of the country and stay out for two years. This, Hampton refused, and the commission granted him seven shillings a week, as he was afraid to go about his work. Twelve years later he was still receiving ten shillings a week.

Eventually, three of the supposed murderers of Odgers surrendered. They also captured Kinsman and in the struggle one of them was greatly wounded. All four were tried at the Assizes, and contrary to the opinion of the judge and the amazement of the whole court were found not guilty. There is no doubt the jury was bribed by Kinsman's relatives. Three of the jury disappeared after the case.

Coswinsawsin, near Carnhell Green.

Walter and Louisa chose neutral ground to settle down and raise a family. In 1833, soon after their wedding, they moved to Coswinsawsin, near Barripper, in the parish of Gwinear, where Walter was employed as an agricultural labourer. Between 1833 and 1841, four children were born, John, Ester, Elizabeth and Louisa, but the girls all died at an early age. By 1851 three more children had been born, Walter, Thomas and Louisa. The family moved to Tolcarne near Beacon where in 1854 a son, Richard Pearce, was born.

Walter changed his profession and became employed as a road maker. The road network in the area from Camborne Cross to Mount Pleasant and beyond to Mount Pleasure was being extended as was the new connection linking Killivose and Knave-Go-By to Treslothan. The Camborne to Beacon lane was used extensively to haul machinery and materials up to the Condurrow mines and the Grenville mines near Troon and would have been in constant need of repair. Almost on the doorstep of the cottage was the Tolcarne copper mine where Walter junior and Richard gained their experience as miners. The old mine buildings, including the count house , are still there, not as silent as many, but occupied as dwellings. The mine burrows near the shafts are there although parts have been removed to see if modern processes can extract copper in paying amounts. Extraction methods of the nineteenth century were, when compared with those available today, most inefficient. If the sampling process shows this to be true, then we will see the disappearance of many reminders of a bygone mining age.

The migration of the union of the Williams and Pearce families, each with different backgrounds of agriculture and fishing towards the mining industry was now complete, leaving the final step in the great plan of things, emigration to far away foreign parts and their vast and fast growing mining industries. Walter and Richard had dug out the underground of Tolcarne and were ready to pit their strength and skills across the oceans in the continents of North and South America.

Site of the old Tolcarne Copper Mine, the Count House seen centre left with the "Dry" seen in centre.

Removing samples from Tolcarne burrows for copper ex-traction, 1983.

XII

TO THE NEW WORLD

From these backgrounds, Richard Williams left Cornwall, and his future bride, and at the adventurous age of twenty, sailed away to the copper country of Michigan. His final destination, the Pewabic mine, and the township of Franklin, on the heights of Portage Lake, overlooking Houghton, across the water.

Richard was a skilled copper miner, used to the dank, dark caverns of his homeland, and the small thatched cottage in Tolcarne, but stories of better things in America came floating across the green Atlantic, better things made possible by men like himself; and make no mistake; without the men from Cornwall there would have been no miners in Keweenaw (named after the Chippewa Indian word for the short canoe route through Portage Lake, or the 'place-we-go-round') until much later in the nineteenth century.

The Cornishman abroad has at times, been derided and belittled, but again, make no mistake, without their guts, abilities, hard work and sacrifices, too often costing their lives, the mining story of the nineteenth century would never have been written.

Fortunately for Richard, he had arrived in Michigan in early summer and had had time to settle in to his new surroundings before the onslaught of a North American winter.

Cornwall was never cold, in the sense that everyday life was affected. Except for the blizzard of March, 1891, snow and ice in the county were confined to making the landscape beautiful to look at, and the ponds pleasant

Houses built in Franklin Township in the 1870's and once oc-cupied by Cornish mining families.

Houghton County Courthouse. A place to visit if searching for early records.

to skate over, so if a miner arrived in Keweenaw from the Cornish Riviera in winter, the deep snows and bitter cold were, perhaps, unexpected and he would have been happier without them.

There was always the General Store, ready to fit them out with warm winter clothing, and it must have given them some cause for merriment, to watch each other, as they learned to cross the snow on unwieldy skis or clumsy snowshoes. It was something that had to be done - so they mastered the art, sufficiently, to get to where the mines were. On longer distances, a cutter and team would be hired, the Cornish for 'mush' defies print!

At the mine, the most dangerous work was clearing ice from the shafts to keep the skips running.

Newton G. Thomas, in his story about the early days in Keweenaw, *"The Long Winter Ends"* describes the scene:

It was hard, dangerous work, and bitterly cold. . . The men chopped until their bodies steamed beneath their heavy clothes, while their bodies blued and stiffened with the cold.

Talk between the workers was impossible. Candles sputtered and threatened to go out in the showers of ice that flew from the axe bits. Particles fell inside their collars and sleeves to melt and add to the men's distress. The floor on which they stood became slippery and treacherous. But the work went on.

Underground was forever underground. The damp blackness, the dry airlessness and the mute timbers were all the same.

The variations to be found in the miners' search for ore were insignificant parts of their program.

Drifts might be larger, timbered or timberless to the need. The stopes might be overhand or underhand; but the breath of the pit, the blackness of it, the grime of it, the relentless dangers, the heavy labor were forever the same.

It was hard dangerous work. Not all survived the impossible conditions. Many miners had the crossed pick and shovel carved on their headstones like Capt. John Gundry, born Cornwall 12th December, 1812, died Michigan Copper Country 1861.

William Faull, a third generation Cornish American whose forebears left Wheal Rose, Scorrier in the 1850's for the American mining fields, is seen in the background, 1983.

Forest Hills cemetery, Houghton, Michigan, where many Cornish are buried, including Prudence Ann Davey, born in Beacon, Camborne, the daughter of William Mitchell.

There was always the General Store like this one established in 1859, before Lincoln was president.

A giant plough outside the Calumet Museum, was used to remove the snow.

Remains of the engine house at Delaware Mine not far from Central Mine.

What was it in their nature that kept the miners battling, day after day, year after year, in these almost suicidal conditions. Who, on and beneath the earth, were these amazing people?

A race apart, they came from an isolated strip of land, jutting out from the mainland of Britain into the eastern Atlantic. Was it fate, or a plan of the Creator, which drove this tribe from the Ark of Noah, to the deposits of copper and tin that lay in the depths of Cornwall? Was it part of the great plan, that over the years, they should prepare themselves to spread over the world and burrow for the mineral riches beyond the reach of ordinary men? What kept them, generation after generation, agonising their weary bodies down the dark shafts?

Perhaps the answer is given in this further extract from Newton Thomas...

"That was part of their history; It was written in their marrow. Another mine and another until in some dark gut of the earth they found a place for their skill. Every Cornish miner answered the question. . . It mattered not to him what the ore might be that he mined. Mining was his trade. For generations his ancestors had picked and pried, mauled and shoveled, blasted their way by candle light in the Cornish pits. They knew ground, how to break it, to timber it, to channel its water and dispose of it. They knew the whims and veins and followed them as if by scent. . . Given a hammer and a few drills, these men would make passage through anything that steel would dent and powder break . . . Wherever they went, they found that their methods had preceded them; wherever they went, the copy of their work made them feel at home."

There was another thing helping them to feel at home. In the early days, in remote frontiers, their religious faith, as Methodists, enabled them to contend with the miserable hardships of life. Methodist meetings were a feature of life, and if a miner was not a staunch convert on arrival, he soon became, or professed so, through the fervent persuasions of those already saved. The meeting places were sought out by men, hoping to find a friend from home, but once inside the hall, only the brave, or hardened, would escape from seeing the Light.

Singing at these soul-restoring meetings was always loud if not clear and encouraging shouts of approval would be heard when a member of the congregation knelt to receive the blessing. Many similar scenes were witnessed in Cornwall during the revivalist times and memory recalls village chapels in the 1920's ringing to the jubilant cries of the lost sheep now safely back in the fold. A famous gathering place in the copper country of Michigan was and still is the Central Mine Methodist Church.

"Central Mine was organised on November 15, 1854 and finally closed on July 20, 1898. During its forty-four-year lifetime, two generations matured. Central was a leader through Keweenaw - in copper production, in the size of its population (over 1200 at its peak), and in the pride of its citizens in its mine, its cornet band, its handsome schoolhouse and - by no means least - its church.

Long before a church was built worship services were being conducted in the little red schoolhouse on the east side of town at the edge of the north western property. That was in 1856, less than two years after the mine opened. The first services were conducted by the Reverend David A. Curtis who was attached to the Portage Lake Missions. Construction of a church was begun in 1868, and when it was occupied the following year it became the major focal point of religious and social life in the community for all who where members of it and for many who were not. It became a community center in the true sense of the word and offered many services to the townspeople such as planning the Fourth of July picnic for everyone, maintaining a circulating library and sponsoring programs at the school hall which were open to the public. Prior to the building of the new school on top of the bluff, the Central church provided space for public school classes to be held to accommodate the overflow from the original schoolhouse.

It was inevitable that there should be a close feeling among the former residents of Central, who were forced to relocate in other parts of the Copper Country following the closing of the mine in 1898, and the opening of the Keweenaw Central Railroad in January 1907, provided an opportunity for the old-timers to have a "home-coming". Alfred Nicholls is credited with having conceived the idea, and he enlisted the aid of Edward J. Hall and Thomas E. Mitchell. After it had been determined that there was sufficient interest, plans were laid by these three old Centralites, and the first reunion was held on July 21 1907, with both a morning and evening service. However, after the second year, the evening service was discontinued in order to enable those in attendance to enjoy meeting and reminiscing with their former neighbours and friends and still board the early train for home.

The former home of Mrs. Jane Bryant, the milliner and candy store proprietor, standing just east of the church, was used to heat a wash boiler of water so that those attending the "homecoming" could make tea to go with their pasties, saffron cake and perhaps seedy buns or 'eavy cake, all popular Cornish fare.

In those early years close to 200 worshippers would crowd inside the church and others would line the hillside across the road, where they would strain to hear the singing and the message for the day. On several occasions Mrs. Oscar Bruns, a onetime music supervisor for the Calumet Public Schools and later director of the choir that sang in the Hollywood Bowl for the sunrise Easter service, rendered solos, and frequently the organ would be carried to the porch after the service so that she could sing to those who had not been able to get inside.

Central Mine Methodist Church, 1869, 30 miles from Houghton.

As time has thinned the ranks of the old timers, a new dimension has been added to the idea of "homecoming" - the reunion also serves as a tribute to the memory of the hardy pioneers of all faiths from the early copper mining settlements that once dotted Keweenaw County. Central is the last to have its church intact and used once each year, so it is fitting that the Central reunion should remember all those who labored and died here in those early days long ago.

. . . . .

In 1974, it was announced that the Central Mine Methodist Church was listed in the National Register of Historic Places. In 1975, it was included in the Historic American Building Survey, which is conducted by the National Park Service under permanent agreement with the American Institute of Architects and the Library of Congress. Its purpose is to preserve for all time accurate records of buildings surveyed through scale drawings, measurements, pictures and verbal descriptions. It is a source of satisfaction to know that the Central church will, in this way, be preserved in perpetuity regardless of the adverse effects time may ultimately have upon the structure itself.

. . . . .

Traditionally, the Reunion service is held either the last Sunday in July or the first Sunday in August.

. . . . .

"Things change and places and people die, but these hills and blue waters and the beauty of the heavens are everlasting" - George H. Roberts.

With a job secured, Richard Williams sent home to Cornwall asking Ellen Annie Mitchell to join him. In September, 1874, she left Beacon for Michigan. There was little to persuade her not to go, her mother had died in 1866, leaving three young daughters. Ellen was ten and was expected to look after her younger sisters, Prudence, six, and Elizabeth Mary, just two years old. Now, in 1874, her father was planning to marry Mary Jane Curry. This caused some friction and helped her decision to leave. The family bible simply said . . .Ellen went to America 3 September 1874. Her exact route is not known.

The journey was hard, she was just eighteen, but undaunted by the ocean crossing to New York, the train and steamer to L'Anse on the Keweenaw Bay, or the stage coach haul up along the trail by the western shores of Lake Michigan through Milwaukee past Winnebago Lake and places now identified on maps such as Green Bay, Ishpening, Redruth and Houghton, then across the Portage Lake ferry run by John Martin who charged twenty-five cents for the journey. Once across to the Hancock side it was a relatively short journey into the heights above the lake and the township of Franklin, where she married her Richard Pearce Williams, on Monday 28 September 1874.

Richard and Ellen Williams with William John and Florence, in Franklin township, Houghton County, U.S.A., 1878.

William Mitchell, 1828 - 1896, born at Knave-Go-By.

69

Across the Portage Lake ferry from Houghton to Hancock and the Quincy-Pewabic mine near Franklin township.

Now the crossing is made by the new bridge.

Early autumn, before the onset of the heavy snows that blanket the country for most of the winter months, can be very beautiful, and one wonders what thoughts were passing through this young girl's mind as she prepared to build her new world amongst the mines and mining community of Franklin and Pewabic.

She was born and raised in the village of Beacon, and before leaving for America had learned the art of dressmaking;not of necessity; her parents had not been poor, but it was perhaps something a young lady should do.

Her mother was dead, her father was a stern man, perhaps over strict, there was very little of interest in Beacon other than the activities of the local mines over at Tolcarne, Condurrow and Carn Camborne.

The village had only just begun to grow; other places nearby were much older; Tolcarne, Condurrow, Trewoon (Troon) had settlements well established, and Camborne, a barren place known at least in 1181, was now a town. Tolcarne had existed since 1338 and produced a man, worthy of some little remembrance, in John Tolcarn. In his Will, dated 3 July 1558, John, of Tolcarn, left certain properties, real and disposable, naming his two sons-in-law as executors. He had outgrown his native parish of Camborne and became a wealthy merchant in the City of London. Among the bequests was. . ."one cross, with the foot thereof, being silver and gilt, which was 'left to the Church of Cambron in Cornwayle where I was born and christened', for the sake of his own and his wife's soul".

Probably the first house to be built in Beacon was the farm house, still standing, just off the square, and where John Harris, of Bolenowe, the Miner's Poet, used to visit his grandmother Smith. He wrote of his boyhood days in the 1820's. . ."My grandmother Smith, I well remember. For a long time we visited the farm house at Beacon annually, at the Parish Feast, when we generally dined off roast goose - at such times my uncles would tell stories as we clustered around the November log".

There were other cottages with small-holdings in the vicinity, and the village was clearly marked on the 1813 map published by Lt. Col. Mudge.

A public house soon made its presence felt, as the "West Briton", published on 3 May 1833, mentions the death of the wife of Mr. Peter Temby - innkeeper of the Pendarves Arms.

Just why an inn was built, so early in the nineteenth century is not certain. Certainly, Wheal Grenville, on the road leading to Troon was operating. Dolcoath, too, was working and cottages housing the miners would have been built in the area.

There was a great expansion of mining from the early eighteenth century. It was a scattered industry with shafts being sunk, and engine houses built, in widely dispersed areas. Naturally therefore, the miners built their dwellings nearby, with the effect that in the countryside a community would spring up almost overnight. It is evident that many of the houses built for the specific reason of habitation near a mine, would fall into disrepair and eventually disappear after the mine ceased to operate.

Houses of more permanent structure, built in locations where previous habitations still existed, for example, beside a road linking other settlements, would have remained occupied to the present time. These houses would have been built for miners, there were no other activities, industrial or otherwise

71

STATE OF MICHIGAN,

County of _Houghton_

RETURN OF A MARRIAGE.

1. Full name of **BRIDEGROOM** _Richard Williams_
2. Residence at time of marriage _Franklin Township_
3. Age at last birth day _20_ 4. Color of bridegroom* _W_ 5. Birthplace _England_ 6. Occupation _Miner_

7. Full name of **BRIDE** _Ellen Mitchell_
8. Maiden name if a widow _____ 9. Residence at time of marriage _Franklin Township_ 10. Age at last birthday _18_
11. Color of bride* _W_ 12. Birthplace _England_

The parties above named were joined in matrimony by me, at† _Franklin Township_ _____ in the presence of‡ _Edward Sanders_ of† _Franklin Township_ and _William Sanders_ of† _Franklin Township_ this _28_ day of _September_ A. D. 1874

{ _William Dunstone_
Justice of the Peace

I Hereby Certify, That the foregoing is a true and correct transcript from my record of the marriage referred to. _William Dunstone_
Justice of the Peace

Dated this _6_ day of _November_ 1874

* State whether WHITE, BLACK, MULATTO, INDIAN, White and Indian, or other races.
† State the township and county, or city.
‡ Two witnesses.
§ Name and official title of magistrate or clergyman officiating, copied from his records.

72

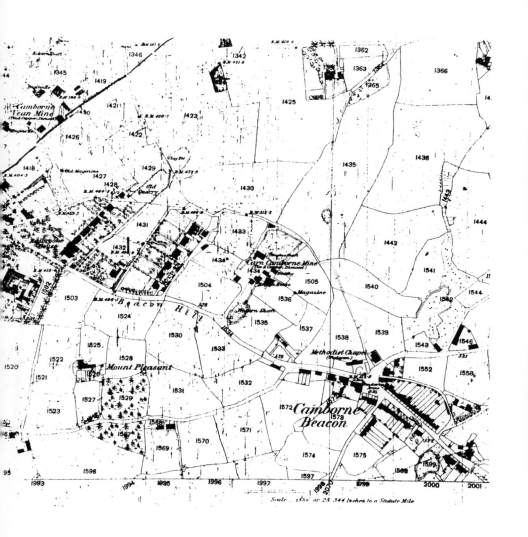

The farm house at Beacon where we dined off roast goose at the Parish Feast - John Harris.

And where the Pendarves family held their Court Dinner at Beacon, 1873.

Beacon Camborne, "The Square".

Centre: "The Pendarves Arms", built about 1830.
Centre left: Miners' cottages of the same period.

Bottom left: The house, Post Office and photography studio built by William John Bennetts after his return from Michigan in the late 1870's.
Bottom: The Sunday School, built in 1895.
Bottom right: The Chapel, built in 1865,

Centre right: The farmhouse where John Harris, the miners' poet, visited his Grandmother Smith in the 1820s.

that would account for their construction. It is very likely therefore that houses to serve a mine, or group of mines, would be scattered in the vicinities, some temporary and some permanent but their purpose would be the same, as Leifchild, writing in the mid nineteenth century observed. . ."If you can get up before the Cornish miners you may see all the cottages scattered over a populous little district near the mines, quiet and dull in the grey morning. Soon however the scene becomes very animated for this part of the country. . . you can see, as far as the eye can reach, men, women, and children of all ages beginning to creep out of low cottage doors. You watch their courses and observe that, after various windings, all begin to converge towards one spot. . the mine and its shaft."

The Pendarves Arms was built before the mid-nineteenth century; the wife of the innkeeper died there in April 1833. The miners' cottages standing nearby were, in all probability, built at or around the same time. The design of these accommodations was typical of dwellings erected for miners at that time. The front door opened directly into a room used as a kitchen and living room. Here, against the far right wall, the oven, and placed before the front window would be the dining table. Immediately to the right of the front door, a screen or partition of board hid the table from view of anyone standing on the threshold and looking in. Straight across the front room from the entrance, was a door leading directly into a narrow passage, to the right of which a door led into the parlour. To the left of the passage, a partition hid the stairs, the foot of which was at the far end of the passage. The stairs led upwards towards the front of the house and a small landing leading into the front and back bedrooms. Attached to these particular houses at the back was a lean-to or back kitchen. Small front gardens protected the terrace from the sometimes boisterous comings and goings of the inn patrons. A gate leading off from Tolcarne road gave access to the back gardens and kitchen doors. Further buildings of this type of housing were continued along the right hand side of what is now Pendarves Street at a later date, but the general design was the same except that the width of some houses had been extended to allow the two bedrooms to be in the front.

The inn was not always a paying business, as Peter Temby who held the lease until 1846, discovered:"...Peter Temby at suit of Ellis Brewers, an old man very infirm and utterly illiterate." Nevertheless, he had kept the business alive for thirteen years after the death of his wife.

The lease was sold to the Abrahams who, in 1857, suffered the loss of a son. Another son, Thomas, married in 1863 and six months later the Beacon Inn, as it was then named, was offered for let because of the impending retirement of Mrs. Susan Abraham. The new tenant, James Stephens, lasted two years, then transferred the business to William Toll, who also had had enough by 1867. Thomas Ivey was the next landlord and on 20 November 1873, was host to the Pendarves family holding their court dinner at the Pendarves Arms. On 18 November 1875, the licence was granted to Oliver Dunstan who had married Elizabeth Ann, sister of William John Bennetts.

The Methodist chapel had been completed ready for worship in 1865 and with the curiosity of youth, Ellen would have watched its building. Did she too, when hearing the Easter hymn, imagine in her innocence that Beacon's Green Lane hill was the very same Green hill faraway where they crucified our Lord?

Other than the inn, the chapel and the crunch of miners' boots on the muddy tracks that served as roads, life had not reached fever pitch by 1874 and, except for a fleeting thought of her young sisters, it was unlikely that the new Mrs. Ellen Annie Williams would allow her mind to wander idly across the many miles that separated them.

America was a violent country with armed gangs on the loose, killing and robbing. Bandits, like the infamous Younger brothers with Frank and Jesse James, were active until their bloodthirsty ways came to an end in Minnesota across the border from Michigan in 1876.

The Indian wars were still being waged when Ellen arrived in America, and Custer's massacre at Little Big Horn was still two years away. The memory

Miners' cottages, Beacon Square, 1840's.

The later, larger houses in Pendarves Street.

The 1873 birdseye view shows, left to right, the Quincy, Pewabic, and Franklin Mines on the hilltop and the Lake Superior smelter and the Pewabic and Franklin stamp mills along Portage Lake. (BCHS HAER)

Quincy, Pewabic and Franklin mines, 1873.
Prosperity seemed assured.

This view of Hancock from the Houghton County Court House was found in the Roy
rier Collection maintained at the MTU Archives and Copper Country Collections
ichigan Technological University, Houghton, Michigan.

A View of Hancock from the County Court House.

of the capture by Commanche Indians of a white settler's daughter, Cynthia Ann Parker, was still fresh in people's minds and the only fear expressed by Ellen during her stay in Franklin was that her children would be kidnapped by marauding bands of Indians active in the Keweenaw peninsula.

Cynthia Ann Parker settled down with the the Commanche tribe and married a chief. They had three children, young braves who grew up to become fierce warriors and thorns in the side of the American army for many years. At the age of thirty-four, Cynthia was recaptured by the Americans but had no desire to adopt the ways of the whites, remaining Indian at heart to the end of her days.

Ellen's fears were unfounded, the famliy grew and by 1881 four children had been born, John, Florence, Walter and Richard.

The prosperity of the Pewabic copper mine seemed assured and the future looked bright especially for the skilled miners who now sent home for their cousins, fathers, mothers, brothers, or sisters, they were all known as cousin Jack or Jenny.

Ellen's sister, Prudence Ann, now felt that she had no place in her father's house in Beacon. Less than four months after his first daughter had departed for America, he had married again.

Prudence was now sixteen, just the right age to follow in her sister's footsteps, except that she had no man waiting for her in the new world.. Ellen was prepared to welcome her and once again, a brief entry in the family bible . . ."Prue went to America on May 22, 1877". She probably stayed with her sister - there is no clear record; but some time later was thought to be working in one of the boarding houses catering for the Cornish miners. Certainly, by 1882, she was managing her own establishment, but that was after the death of her husband.

Alfred Moyle, a mine machinist, had come to Houghton County from Cornwall and worked in the Atlantic Mine about three miles south west of Houghton. He lodged where Prudence worked. He was 24, Prudence eighteen, or so the return of marriage certificate stated. She was actually seventeen years. There are no records available at the time of writing of any children from this marriage, or of the death of Alfred, but on the 27 January 1882, Prudence married Charles Davey at the Franklin Mine. He and his brother John were boarders staying with Mrs. Moyle.

One of the witnesses to the marriage was Elizabeth Mary Mitchell, then eighteen years, and the youngest daughter of William Mitchell. Her presence in America was the result of a tragic accident in the Pewabic Mine, when Richard Williams was caught in a devastating explosion underground that blasted his eyes and ripped off a part of his right arm.

Richard and Ellen had settled in Franklin Township. All had gone well until the disaster which left Ellen with a totally blind and helpless husband together with four young and boisterous children, but she had a dominant will, holding the family until help arrived and the decision to return to Cornwall was made. Ellen wrote home to Beacon and soon Elizabeth Mary was on the way. She was seventeen when the call had come, a beautiful fragile young woman.

RETURN OF A MARRIAGE.

TO THE CLERK OF THE COUNTY OF

Houghton, State of Michigan,

SIR:—On this _30th_ day of _November_ A. D. 187_8_, the following named parties were joined in matrimony by me, at* _Houghton_ _Michigan_

BRIDEGROOM.

1. Full name of **Bridegroom** _Alfred Moyle_
2. Color of Bridegroom † _W._
3. Residence at time of marriage _Atlantic_
4. Age at last birthday _24_
5. Birthplace ‡ _England_
6. Occupation _Machinist_

BRIDE.

7. Full name of **Bride** _Prudence M. Mitchell_
8. Maiden name if a widow _____
9. Color of Bride † _W._
10. Residence at time of marriage _Atlantic_
11. Age at last birthday _18_
12. Birthplace ‡ _England_

The witnesses to this marriage were:§

Mary S. Johnston of‡ _Houghton_ and
Rev. Isaac Johnston of‡ _Houghton_

¶ _C. Milton Johnston_
Minister of Gospel

I Hereby Certify, That the foregoing is a true and correct transcript from my record of the marriage referred to.

C. M. Johnston
Clergyman

Dated at _Houghton_ this _30th_ day of _November_ 187_8_.

* State the township and county, or city.
† State whether WHITE, BLACK, MULATTO, INDIAN, WHITE and INDIAN, or other races.
‡ Give the State and Country.
§ Two witnesses required.
¶ Name and official title of magistrate or clergyman officiating, copied from his records.

Charles and Prudence Ann Davey with their family in Houghton, Michigan, 1902.
Standing centre back row is Walter Williams, killed by a mineshaft rockfall.

RETURN OF A MARRIAGE.

TO THE CLERK OF THE COUNTY OF

Houghton ___ State of Michigan,

SIR:—On this *Twentysixth* day of *January* A. D. 188*2*, the following named parties were joined in matrimony by me, at* *Franklin Mine*. *Franklin Township, County of Houghton*.

1. Full name of **Bridegroom** *Charles Davey*.
2. Color of Bridegroom † *White*
3. Residence at time of marriage *Atlantic Mine. Adams Insp.*
4. Age at last birthday *Twentyfour*
5. Birthplace ‡ *County Cornwall, England*.
6. Occupation *Miner*.

7. Full name of **Bride** *Prudence Ann Moyle*.
8. Maiden name if a widow *Prudence Ann Mitchell*.
9. Color of Bride † *White*
10. Residence at time of marriage *Atlantic Mine, Adams Insp.*
11. Age at last birthday *Twentyone*.
12. Birthplace ‡ *County Cornwall, England*.

The witnesses to this marriage were: §

Joseph H. Richards of ‡ *Atlantic Mine* and

Elizabeth Mary Mitchell of ‡ *Atlantic Mine*

¶ *William Dunstone*

Justice of the Peace.

I Hereby Certify, That the foregoing is a true and correct transcript from my record of the marriage referred to.

William Dunstone

Justice of the Peace

Dated at *Franklin* this *26* day of *January* 187*2*

* State the township and county, or city.
† State whether WHITE, BLACK, MULATTO, INDIAN, WHITE and INDIAN, or other races.
‡ Give the State and Country.
§ Two witnesses required.
¶ Name and official title of magistrate or clergyman officiating, copied from his records.

82

All that remains of the old Pewabic where Richard Williams lost his sight.

The newer No. 2 shaft-rockhouse seen from the worlds largest steam hoist at Quincy-Pewabic, Houghton County, Michigan. circa 1983.

Laborers posed in front of Quincy's rock house. ca. 1880. (QMC/HAER)

Quincy-Pewabic copper mine where Richard Williams worked for seven years, 1874-1881.

Rand rock drills at work in shaft sinking as depicted in the Scientific American of December 25, 1880.

Application Number......5129.........

CERTIFIED COPY of an ENTRY
IN THE MARINE REGISTER

Pursuant to the provisions of the Merchant Shipping Acts 1894 and 1970 and the Births and Deaths Registration Act 1953.

Return of Deaths at Sea, reported to the Registrar General of Shipping and Seamen under the provisions of the "Merchant Shipping Act, 1854," and "Births and Deaths Registration Act, 1874," during the Month of September 1882.

Name of Ship	Official No.	Date of Arrival	Date of Death	Name and Surname of Deceased	Sex	Age	Rank, Profession, or Occupation	Nationality	Last Place of Abode	Cause of Death	Passenger or Member of Crew
Republic	65907	17.9.1882	17.9.1882	Elizabeth Mary Mitchell	Female	19	-	English	-	Acute Pneumonia	Passenger

CERTIFIED to be a true copy of an entry in the MARINE REGISTER of.....DEATHS........
Given at the GENERAL REGISTER OFFICE, LONDON, under the seal of the said Office, this 23rd day of November , 19 82 .

The Births and Deaths Registration Act 1953 (sec. 34) provides that any certified copy of an entry purporting to be sealed or stamped with the seal of the General Register Office shall be received as evidence of the birth or death to which it relates without any further or other proof of the entry, and no certified copy purporting to be given in the said Office shall be of any force or effect unless it is sealed or stamped as aforesaid.

CAUTION:—Any person who (1) falsifies any of the above particulars on this certificate, or (2) uses a falsified certificate: as true, knowing it to be false, is liable to prosecution

NA   4060

Exa Neil
23-11-82

Form A514 Dd 826423J 8/81 200 Msr(2139)

The unmarked grave of Elizabeth Mary Mitchell in Camborne churchyard. A tragic death on board the s.s. Republic in Liverpool, 1882.

Elizabeth Mary Mitchell, 1864-1882. A sad homecoming for all to see.

William Mitchell married his second wife Jane Curry on 2 December, 1874. Black attire was common, but are they mourning the deaths of Elizabeth Mary and their son Joseph Henry Curry Mitchell who died in 1883, aged 7?

XIII

AND BACK AGAIN

The injuries to Richard were so severe, that it was not until August 1882, that the family was able to travel down to New York, and board the steamship "Republic" bound for Liverpool. Another calamity was in store; Elizabeth Mary developed pneumonia and on 17 September, the day of arrival, she died.

Grief knew no bounds, but the tremendous courage of Ellen Williams helped her through the time that followed. The Captain of the "Republic" ordered a casket with a glass cover, to be made for the body of the unfortunate young girl. In his own words 'he could not bring himself to hide so beautiful a face, and that when the coffin arrived at her home everyone would be able to see her.'

Imagine the family arriving by train at Camborne in that miserable year of 1882, Ellen with her shattered husband; four young children and a dead sister. A mournful crowd stood silently around Camborne railway station to greet the tragic family.

On 21 September 1882, Elizabeth Mary Mitchell was laid to rest in Camborne Churchyard. The grave is unmarked, and with her lie her grandfather, William Mitchell, who died in June 1878, and her half brother, Joseph Henry Curry Mitchell, aged 7, who died in July 1883.

The church bells, that tolled so mournfully on that sad Thursday, when Elizabeth Mary was laid to rest, had only a few months earlier, been hung in a new iron frame, and rung in joy to celebrate the occasion. The new peal of eight bells, five old and three new, were hung in the only iron frame in Cornwall and were the first complete peal to be hung in this manner by the manufacturers. This fact, in addition to the knowledge that the weight of the tenor bell was 17½ cwt., encouraged bell ringers from other parish churches to come and estimate the character of the peal for themselves. Of course, chimes were arranged.

> "Easter Tuesday was the date fixed for the first ringing, and a programme of special interest was arranged, including the dedication service led by the Rev. Hedgeland, a public luncheon at 2 o'clock and tea at 5.30 p.m. There was some attractive entertainment in the evening and members of the Devonshire Guild arranged to ring at various times during the day."

Of course, there was now no room in the tower for the old clock. It was not missed in a sense, but several interested persons were thinking whether the workings might not be, in some way, usefully applied. For instance, they might be made to work a machine which, in turn, should so operate upon the chimes, that a series of simple tunes could occasionally be got out of the new bells by clockwork. The outlay would be small, seeing that the workings of the old clock would remain on the premises, and many would gladly subscribe a trifle to defray extra expenses. Memories of the eccentric and erratic behaviour of the clock, the hands of which would sometimes whirl around like a rebellious windmill in a high wind, were sufficient for the idea to be wound up!

Camborne had boasted for many years of having a town clock, but the past carried little conviction according to the following "West Briton" remarks of July 1877....

"For many years past, Camborne, like most other towns, has been able to boast of having a town clock but from its present position and condition the inhabitants generally would be almost as well without it. It is fixed in the tower of the parish church behind the market house and a block of other high buildings. This of course renders it impossible to be seen from most parts of the town - the hands are frequently blown around by the wind."

The arrival back in Beacon presented more problems for Richard and his family. How and where to live? Temporary accommodation with Ellen's father and stepmother gave them a chance to consider the situation.

The most pressing problem was to find their own home, and as vacant possessions were almost impossible to obtain, the only answer was to build. For this purpose land was needed, and money. Compensation had been paid to Richard after his accident at the Pewabic mine and it was sufficient for his idea to build a home with a shop attached and set up in business as a grocer.

The houses in Pendarves Street owned by William Mitchell and a temporary refuge in 1882 for Ellen Williams and her blind husband.

Colonel Sir Courtenay Vyvyan owned land in the Beacon area and was prepared to lease a part of this. On 7 March 1884, Richard Williams leased land and built a house at what became known as 6 Tolcarne Road, Beacon. The house was finished to the stage where in July the business could be carried on from a front room with its entrance from the lane dividing the existing row of houses in the road and number 6. Here too, family life continued with the birth of their first Cornish-born child, Joseph Henry, on 8 July 1884.

The mainstay of the grocery business was the sale of tea and it was the duty of the children to guide their blind father in his door to door sales even as far afield as Tuckingmill. Richard and Ellen had eight children altogether, equally divided between Americans and Cornish. Imagine a pathetic, blind disabled man still in the prime of life, carrying his basket of tea and led by a loving, sorrowful young daughter. Tea sales soared, business was business and every penny counted.

On 30 November 1908, Richard Pearce Williams died at the early age of 53, but before that, in April 1896, William Mitchell, Ellen's father, had died and in April 1908, Mary Jane Mitchell, her stepmother, had also died.

The wounds dividing Ellen from her father had obviously not healed. She received nothing from his estate; the will made this quite clear. To add insult to injury, when Mary Jane Mitchell died, she left the property to her two brothers but they had no desire to do battle with the formidable Ellen who legally challenged the will. In a more or less amicable agreement everything was handed back to her. She now owned three houses and honour was satisfied. Life had taught her how to survive. One thing remained; to purchase the freehold of the property in Tolcarne Road. In 1919 this was done.

Ellen Annie Williams - 1856-1929.
After a lifetime of Trials and Tribulations, now a serene
ancestor.

This Indenture

made the Twelfth day of November One thousand nine hundred and nineteen **Between** Colonel Sir Courtenay Vyvyan of Trelowarren in the County of Cornwall Baronet C.B. C.M.G. (hereinafter called the "Vendor") of the one part and *Ellen Williams* of Number 6 Tolcarne Road in the Town of Camborne in the said County Widow (hereinafter called the "Purchaser" of the other part) **Whereas** The Reverend Sir Vyell Donnithorne Vyvyan of Trelowarren in the said County of Cornwall Baronet duly made his last Will dated the ninth day of June One thousand nine hundred and eight and thereby (inter alia) devised all his manors messuages lands hereditaments and premises known as the Trelowarren Estate in the said County and which included the hereditaments and premises hereinafter described and intended to be hereby conveyed unto the Vendor in fee simple and appointed the Vendor and his Daughter Mary Louisa Vyvyan to be the Executors of his said Will **And whereas** the Testator died on the twenty seventh day of May One thousand nine hundred and seventeen without having revoked his said Will except by a Codicil in nowise affecting the devise of real estate and the said Will was duly proved in the Bodmin District Registry of the Probate Division of His Majesty's High Court of Justice on the twentieth day of September One thousand nine hundred and seventeen by the Vendor alone the said Mary Louisa Vyvyan having renounced Probate **And whereas** the Vendor is now seized in fee simple in possession of the hereditaments and premises hereinafter described subject nevertheless to and with the benefit of the Indenture of Lease or mentioned in the First Schedule of the Schedule hereto by which Indenture the said hereditaments and premises were demised by Sir Richard Rawlinson Vyvyan to the person named in the second Column of the said Schedule for the term of years and at the yearly rent respectively mentioned in the third and fourth Columns of the said Schedule and subject to the covenants and conditions in the said

91

Indenture contained and on the Lessees part to be observed and performed **And whereas** the Vendor has agreed to sell the said hereditaments and premises to the Purchaser subject to and with the benefit of the said Lease at the price of **Thirty pounds** subject to the exception and reservation hereinafter contained **Now this Indenture witnesseth** that in pursuance of the said Agreement and in consideration of the sum of Thirty pounds on or before the execution of these presents paid by the Purchaser to the Vendor (the receipt of which sum the Vendor hereby acknowledges) the Vendor as Beneficial Owner hereby conveys unto the Purchaser **All** that Dwelling house and premises situate at and being Number 6 Tolcarne Road Beacon in the said Town of Camborne now in the occupation of the said Purchaser **To hold** unto and to the use of the Purchaser in fee simple but subject nevertheless to and with the benefit of the said Indenture of Lease and the rent thereby reserved and the covenants and conditions therein contained and on the part of the Lessee to be observed and performed **Excepting** nevertheless and reserving unto the Vendor his heirs and assigns all ores metals and metaliferous minerals in under and throughout the hereditaments and premises hereby conveyed **And** the Vendor hereby covenants with the Purchaser and his assigns to pay and discharge any annuity or any duty or duties which may become payable in respect of or be charged upon the hereditaments and premises hereby assured by reason of the death of the said Sir Vyell Donnithorne Vyvyan and will at all times keep the Purchaser his heirs and assigns indemnified against the same and every part thereof and all actions proceedings costs charges claims and demands whatsoever in respect thereof **And** the Purchaser hereby declares that the determinable Term of Ninety nine years granted by the said Indenture of Lease shall not merge and be extinguished in the freehold reversion and inheritance but that on the contrary it shall be kept on foot until such time as the Purchaser shall execute a Declaration merging the same **And it is hereby certified** that the transaction hereby effected does not form part of a larger transaction or of a series of transactions in respect of which the amount or value or the aggregate amount or value of the consideration exceeds Five hundred pounds **In Witness** whereof the parties aforesaid to these presents their hands and seals have set the day and year first before written —————————

The Schedule above referred to

Date of Lease	Name or original Lessee	Term	Rent
1884 March 7th	Richard Williams	99 years determinable on decease of 3 lives now aged respectively 63. 45 and 42	15/. per annum

Signed sealed and delivered by the fore named Colonel Sir Courtenay Vyan Bart. C.B. C.M.G. in the presence of } Courtenay Vyvyan

Edward J Downing
Trelowarren Maugan
Bailiff

To all people unto whom these presents shall come, I William Mitchell of Beacon Camborne in the County of Cornwall, do send greeting. Know you that I the said William Mitchell, for divers good causes and valuable consideration me hereunto moving, have given granted, and by these presents do give, grant, and confirm unto my beloved wife Mary Jane Mitchell all and singular my goods, chattels, my two houses situated in Beacon, Camborne, in the County of Cornwall now occupied one by myself and the other by Fred Harris, and all other substance whatever, in whose hands, custody, or keeping soever they are or may be found, to have and to hold all and singular the said goods, chattels and substance whatsoever, of me the said William Mitchell unto the said Mary Jane Mitchell, her Executors, Administrators and Assigns from henceforth to her own proper use and uses thereof without any manner of lett trouble, or denial of <u>me the</u> said William Mitchell or any other person or persons whatsoever. Of all which premises I the said William Mitchell have put the said Mary Jane Mitchell in full and peaceable possession by virtue hereof.

In witness whereof I the said William Mitchell have hereunto set my hand and seal this third day of January one thousand eight hundred and ninety six. William Mitchell.

Sealed and delivered,
in the presence of,
William Blewett
Emma Terrill

94

XIV

HAVE EXPERIENCE - WILL TRAVEL

Much has been written, and there is a general awareness in Cornwall about those who travelled to America, South Africa and Australia, but the knowledge of great adventures in other parts of the world is not so widespread.

In the nineteenth century, the influence of the Cornish miners was felt in Brazil and Mexico in particular, where their story is told in "The Search for Silver" by A.C.Todd, author of "The Cornish Miner in America". These are fascinating stories; the Mexican saga, highlighting the power held in the mines and the country by some Cornish families, notably the Rules from Camborne. It was John Rule who took out the first miners in 1824, years before the great flood of Cornish to other parts of the world. He had been chosen for the task of reopening the rich silver mines, by John Taylor, a Norwich man, internationally recognised as a great manager of mines. He held influence in Cornwall, where he recognised the skill of the men, and also the advantage of having them working in his copper mines, from where he could recruit them for Mexico. Many of these miners, eager to travel, sailed from Liverpool. Various trades, all required to operate a mine, were arriving at Vera Cruz to begin their inland journeys on to the properties at Real del Monte and Pachua. Throughout the 1840's miners continued to go to Mexico, usually in small groups. They would board vessels that brought engines and spare parts from Cornwall, sometimes leaving from local ports, as the "West Briton" of December 1840, reported, that- the "Edward Hayes" left Hayle with a new beam engine and then sailed around Lands End to Falmouth to take on two Cornish carpenters, James Pender and Matthew Symons. In September the packet, 'Palestine' was outward bound with seven Cornishmen, Andrew Stevens, blacksmith, John Kinsman, mason among them. Their pay in Mexico was the princely sum of £14 a month.

In May 1842, Francis Blackwell, engineman, boarded the 'Harkaway captained by Charles Hammond and sailed from Liverpool for Vera Cruz. The ship departed from Vera Cruz on August 23, of that same year, on the return voyage to Liverpool. The 'Harkaway' was from Stockton, the highest navigational point on the river Joaquin in California and which feeds into San Francisco harbour.

Francis Blackwell spent many years in Mexico before returning to Praze in his native parish of Crowan. He died at the age of sixty five in October 1866. The death certificate recorded his occupation as a retired engine worker in a silver mine.

His sister Elizabeth, married William Trevarthen, a copper miner in Crowan in 1828. They emigrated to New Zealand in 1839, where William worked on Kawan and Great Barrier Islands. He was accidentally killed by a fall from his horse in Auckland in 1860.

In the 1860's, James Blackwell, a nephew of Francis, left Crowan for the Morrow Velho mine in Brazil, where a son was born in July 1872.

Richard Williams, after his accident in the Pewabic mine in Keweenaw, returned to Camborne, but his brother Walter remained in Brazil, buried next to his young daughter Hattie.

Walter Williams, Cornish miner, born Coswinsawsin, 1846,
buried Brazil next to his young daughter Hattie, who died 1888

Walter, the son of Richard and Ellen, returned to the place of his birth in Franklin Township, in 1901, then travelled down to Arizona, where a short time later he was killed by a fall of rock in a mineshaft.

Finally, the story of Thomas Henry Blackwell, a grandson of Francis. He was born in Camborne, in 1851, the son of Thomas and Hannah. Thomas was a mine blacksmith who had worked in the mines at Troon, Breage, Crowan and St. Just.

In the summer of 1876, Thomas Henry Blackwell, a blacksmith from St. Just, travelled to America and headed for California. With him were his wife's brother and father as companions.

They found work at Eureka Mills and lived through two bitter Sierra winters when the snow was so deep that their only exit from their cabin was through the roof. Here his wife and daughter he had not seen joined him and another daughter was born. Now they were making so successful a living that his wife was able to go back to St. Just with her children, to bring out the remainder of the family. It was while she was there that the news reached California of gold strikes in Colorado, so the men were soon on the move again, this time to the heights of Leadville, where Mrs. Blackwell joined them. Here they battled for five years against the lassitude of an altitude of 12,000 feet until the severity of the winters forced them to search for work elsewhere in the mountains. Mrs. Blackwell's brother was the first to go, leading his family in a waggon over the treacherous 12,200 ft. Independence Pass down to the more genial slopes and streams of Cattle Creek, near Glenwood Springs. They built a log ranch house and hewed and shaped their furniture from the living trees. In due time, by their combined efforts, more land was acquired until the three sons possessed ranches of their own. Thomas Blackwell followed them in the fall of 1886 and at Aspen rented for 25 dollars a month a two room log cabin where twin boys were born, only to die before they were a year old, victims of pneumonia that ravaged the mountain camps in winter. Here he was joined by his cousins from St. Just, James Thomas and his wife, but disaster struck them down almost as soon as they arrived, the husband being killed in the mine, and his distracted wife returned to Cornwall. Almost at the same time his father-in-law died, the companion of all his wanderings, mourned by his widow in St. Just who had resolutely refused to join him in the land so far west of Cape Cornwall.

XV

ALL IS VANITY

There is probably only a hazy conception of just what sort of people these were, who left the poverty of Cornwall, and travelled to new lands, not yet developed. They arrived at their destinations, more often than not with just the bare essentials. They built homes, obtained work and raised families in sometimes heartbreaking conditions. Not many made fortunes, but the majority became respected citizens and had a pride in their being Cornish and looking as good as the next.

Just how did they look, and dress, particularly in America, where so many settled and prospered? Many were proud to be photographed, so that families who had remained in Cornwall could see for themselves that their cousins had "done alright for themselves".

The Cornish had, from the 1840's onward, spread themselves across the continent of North America in addition to the large numbers who had settled in other parts of the world. It is a source of amazement that so small a place was able to sustain such large migrations of people to these countries, settle in so many locations, and still make their presence felt in no uncertain manner.

History tells us that it happened. It is well documented in foreign archives, and visits to cemeteries in far away lands often reveal a predominance of Cornish and their descendants resting after the final journey.

There are other proofs of the Cornish presence, to be found in family albums, of those posing for posterity in Nevada, Hazleton, Pennsylvania; Grass Valley, Houghton, Michigan; Pottstown, P. A; Dover, New Jersey; Virginia and California to mention a few.

The photographs on pages that follow are all from one family album given by a very old Camborne couple many years ago, who had never left these shores. Unfortunately, the subject names were never recorded by them, other than the fact that they were from the Camborne, Helston and Leedstown areas.

There was very little done in the way of photography, where ordinary people were concerned, before the 1870's. After that time, more and more people began to dress in their finery, and, on the odd occasion, their rags, to pose before the box, where a man, strangely hooded in a large black cloth, would suddenly appear, ask for a smile - which he rarely got - operate the lens mechanism, and produce, sooner or later, a likeness of the victim, almost always excellent.

Thousands of portraits were taken over the years, all over the world. Whole families would gather together for group photographs and store them lovingly in ornate albums, built like miniature bank vaults.

Travelling ghouls went from door to door, searching for bereaved families and, playing on their grief, would offer to produce a memorial photograph of the deceased - enlarged, of course - from the family group, if one was available. In fairness to the salesman, the results were usually good and satisfied a need.

Men's fashions appeared to change but little in the period 1860 - 1900 or thereabouts. Morning jackets were worn and after 1858 they sported a breast pocket. Men, in general, wore the same design in clothes; there was a jacket, trousers and waistcoat. Perhaps the cut would vary, but no man would throw a tantrum if he went to a function and saw someone else dressed as he was. He would in all probability congratulate the other on his choice of tailor. Women were jealous of their appearance, and invariably alarmed when confronted with another lady similarly attired. Nevertheless, the fair sex, always, when facing a camera, gave the impression of calm control of the situation, whereas the male, in his vanity, always seemed to be seeking a pose that would show off his masculinity and nonchalance.

Women's fashions have changed as regularly as the seasons, and it is possible for a serious student of design to identify particular periods of time over the centuries.

For example, in the 1870's, dresses became more intricate than previous designs. Skirts became draped, with the arrangements complicated. They also became rather flatter in front and bunched at the back. Sometimes a large bow would be stitched half way down the back of the skirt. Before 1880, gowns took a sheath-like appearance, with long trains behind, with fancy trimmings, ribbons, flounces, frills, lace or any other form of decoration that caught the designers fancy. Anything up to seventy yards of trimming could be used in one skirt alone. Women will, as a rule, put up with much physical inconvenience to be fashionable. The sheath skirt inclined to make them walk like trussed-up chicken, but in spite of its obvious inconvenience, the style remained in vogue until after 1882, when freedom in the form of larger bustles, was thankfully attained. To add a welcome touch of colour, they were almost brought to life by the addition of all kinds of artificial birds and animals. The gentle curves made these skirts attractive in spite of their size, but when, in 1888 or thereabouts, the curves gave way to a bustle that stood out rather squarely at the back, fashion rebelled. The bustle was hustled out to make way for a concept in female attire that first made its appearance as far back as 1878.

Tailor-made costumes had entered the field of fashion to fill a demand for more informal wear and greater freedom of movement.

Skirts too, became much more practical and plainer, but to offset this, bodices became attractive with added decorations. Perhaps the most appealing costume is shown off by the little old lady who was photographed by W. J. Trevaskis, of Leedstown, Porthleven, and Breage.

Young ladies too, were dressed in a kind of fashion in America, and young gentlemen had fashionable hair styles!

The photographs numbered 1 - 12 on the following pages are all of Cornish people who emigrated to America from the 1870's. Photographers and locations are indicated but names of the subjects are not known. It is almost certain that they were all members of related families from the Helston, Leedstown and Breage areas and that those shown on photograohs 13 - 38 are members of that family who remained in Cornwall. The probable exception is the old lady with the stick and bundle. The photographs are included for interest to illustrate the styles of long ago in America and Cornwall.

1. H.Brubaker & Co., Over Washburn's Jewelry Store, Houghton, Michigan.
2. C.H. Ferrand, photographer. Nevada, California.
3. C. H. Ferrand, photographer. Nevada, California.
4. M. M. Hazeltine, photographer. Location unknown in the U.S.A.
5. F. S. Keeler, photographic artist. Boyertown, Pennsylvania.
6. P. Kellmer, photographer, Broad St., Hazelton, Pennsylvania.
7. P. Kellmer, photographer, Broad St., Hazelton, Pennsylvania.
8. P. Kellmer, photographer, Broad St., Hazelton, Pennsylvania.
9. Isaac S. Lachman, photographer, opposite the bank, Pottstown, Main St., Pennsylvania
10. W. H. Pilliners. Enamelled cards, Mill St., Grass Valley.
11. Thomas Taylor, photographer, 233 High St., Pottstown, Pennsylvania.
12. Unknown photographer. ? Arizona.
13. Fred Argall, photographer, High Cross, Truro.
14. - 16 Beringer, photographer, Helston.
17. J. Blampey, St. Mary Church, Torquay.
18. R. Griffiths, Truro.
19 - 20 W. J. Sandry, photographic artist, Chiverton Gate, Marazion.
21 -35 W. J. Trevaskis, photographer, Helston, Leedstown, Breage.
36 - 38 Unknown photographers.

1

2

3

4

5

6

7

8

9

10

11

12

13

14

15

16

17

18

19

20

21

22

23

24

25

26

27

28

29 30

31 32

33

34

35

36

37 38

XVI

THE MINES OF HOME

A certain amount of glamour is given to those who left Cornwall, to work in the mines of America, Mexico and South Africa, but it must not be forgotten that there were many who stayed in the country and by their perseverance, hard work and loyalty, kept the industry alive. No matter where mining is carried out, the story generally remains the same, the dangers still frightening, and the work involved always creating problems which, in the main, were usually overcome.

Defeat came in the end, not because their abilities faltered, but because there was nothing left for them to pit their wits against. Copper and tin, once dug out and disposed of, left only gaping holes in the ground and useless tunnels under it. Sometimes, even with the metals remaining, the price was not worth the effort required to recover it, but, when the market was right, and prospects looked good, the humming of the headgear sheaves, the curtsey of the bob and the thumping of the crushing stamps, told the people in the country round about, that Cornish life was as it ought to be.

In carrying out the work of a mine, there were certain objects of the greatest importance that had to be kept in mind. These were the ways and means of removing the unwanted materials, the necessity and ability to remove the water, which had plagued Cornish mines in particular, and the means of raising and treating the ores.

Mines which were situated at elevated positions had some advantages in their water disposal problems, as drainage, or adits, as they are called, could be cut, leading to low lying areas or even to the sea. Some of these adits were large undertakings and extended some times for lengths of up to two or more miles.

There were disadvantages, too. At elevated sites there were no streams of running water for use in the stamping mills, and these had to be erected at some distance from the mine itself.

Carn Camborne mine stood proudly overlooking the town and the county, from the north cliffs to the south west and Mount's Bay, and across to Carn Brea with its matching castle.

Situated in the parish of Camborne and in what was a first rate locality for minerals, the mine stood where another, known as Heart's Ease, worked in the latter part of the eighteenth century, although Captain Andrew Vivian is credited with having broken the surface as late as 1814.

The mine proper started in 1860. The stack of the engine was built to stand as an ornament of the hill and a beacon for mariners. Its height was about 70 feet, square and castellated. The engine house was also castellated and destined to stand after the abandonment of the mine. Both were most substantially built.

The returns had been gradually increasing, from which it was inferred that the mine would take its stand amongst dividend mines, at a not too distant future. In 1865 the situation was as follows:

The mine in Beacon, Camborne, in 6000 shares.

Secretary: Mr. John Harding of Salisbury;
Purser and Manager: Captain James Seccombe, Menheniot;
Landowners: Sir R. R. Vyvyan, Bart; and J. F. Basset, Esq.
Depth of adit, 25 fathoms; depth below adit, 46 fathoms and now sinking.
Steam engine, pumping winding and crushing, 22''.
Persons employed: 64 men, 15 females and 4 boys.
Rocks, granite, and slate with elvan course. Minerals sold in 1864; Copper
ore 190 tons. 16 cwts, 1 qtr, 0 lbs. for £814.6s.4d.

In 1870, the mine was 110 fathoms deep and employed 54 people. Between 1862 and 1897 it sold 115 tons of black tin, 6310 tons of copper ore, 72 tons of crude arsenic and 40 tons of arsenical pyrites, despite the fact that following the low profit taking, the mine had closed from 1874 to 1880. Dolcoath took over the mine in 1897 and soon after began operating into the Carn Camborne workings from the west section of Dolcoath.

Carn Camborne 1860 - 1897.
Finally wantonly destroyed by dynamite, 1971.

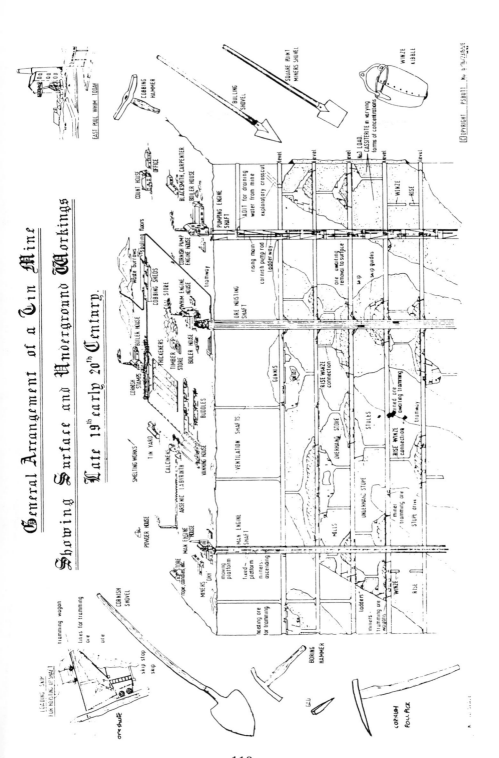

General Arrangement of a Tin Mine

Showing Surface and Underground Workings

Late 19th early 20th Century.

113

DS-I

The mine lay idle for many years, with its stack carrying out its duties as the ornament of the hill and beacon for mariners, until the fateful 23 July 1971, when it was senselessly dynamited to the ground without warning to make way for a housing estate.

The site of the mine being just at the junction of the granite and killas (clay slate) was bounded on the north by a part of Dolcoath, the whole of Stray Park, Camborne Vean and Wheal Francis; on the south by Wheal Harriet and Tryphena; on the west by a part of West Stray Park and West Condurrow; on the east by the southern part of Dolcoath; on the north, part of Wheal Harriet, there it will be seen that the limits were extensive. An adit was brought into this sett at very great expense by ancient miners from the southern part of Dolcoath in which within a distance of forty fathoms four very promising lodes were found impregnated with copper ore. It was thought that if properly worked it would have been one of the great profitable mines of the district.

In 1861 Joseph Watson published 'Cornish Mining Notes' and wrote. . .

"I am writing this on the summit of Carne Camborne. Before me the blue sea and the richest panoramic view in the world. By richest however I do not mean in beautiful scenery, for between the Cornish north cliffs and Carne Camborne I see nothing as far as the eye can reach from east to west but parched and barren ground, little mountains of rubbish and tall dark stacks of chimneys. I see, in fact, the richest mineral district in the world lying at my feet. I am looking upon mines from which scores of families have been enriched and many beggared.

"From up those dark shafts men have come as working miners with stones of ore in their pockets, the fore-runners of fortunes which have made their descendants, in some cases, the largest landowners in the county and in others, men of mark, of rank and title.

"And now as I look upon the apparent quiet scene and watch the heavy beams of the engines work lazily up and down, thousands upon thousands of men burrowing underground like moles some seeking the elusive gain, others seeking by the light of a farthing candle the keenly lode and as they work enriching others if not themselves."

"People may rail at mining as they will but what would Cornwall be without it? It is not only in itself a grand pursuit but there is something exciting and even fascinating in it. The captains when they make a rich discovery are like victorious generals and become at once men of mark and we, the adventurers, become the successful army only somewhat less paid! I said earlier that I was looking upon the richest mineral district in the world and am within the mark when I say that the group of mines before me have yielded minerals to the value of more than forty million sterling. Just at my feet are Stray Park and Camborne Vean, the latter working for 120 years without stop and yielding for copper in early times enormous returns and more than £200,000 in profit."

114

Part of the richest mineral district in the world, 1893.
Camborne-Redruth mining district seen from one of Dolcoath
stamp engines.
Left centre - Old Dolcoath stamp engines and just beyond, the
new Californian stamps.
Right - sinking Dolcoath Valley shaft.
Carn Brea is seen top right.

XVII

THE MISERY OF IT ALL

Mining had its darker side and in the early days, there was misery for many miners and their families.

Doctor Pryce, of Redruth, writing in 1780, in his capacity as a mine surgeon, recorded that he was often called to the home of a poor miner suffering from injuries after an accident at the mine.

Here he would find him, he wrote.."lying in some wretched hut, full of naked children but destitute of all conveniences, and almost all necessities. The whole, indeed, such a scene of complete wretchedness as to defy description."

That which caused the greatest hardship at the mine was the labour of the hand pumps and the toil in climbing a thousand or more feet of perpendicular ladders after working in the hot levels below.

Speaking of the hand pumps, Pryce wrote..."The men work at it naked, excepting their loose trousers, and suffer much in their health and strength through the violence of their labours, which is so great, that I have been witness to the loss of many lives by it."

This hardship was gradually removed by the introduction of the steam pump, the man-engine, and latterly the cage. Some miners had the additional hardship of having to walk five or six miles to and from the mine, yet the patience and skill shown by the men of old towards their work, was extraordinary. They would go anywhere after a bit of tin, the holes and crannies in almost every hill and cliff throughout Cornwall proved how true this statement was. Some miners, caught in this merciless grind of life, heard voices as they struggled to get to the mines in the wet and howling winds of dark mornings, warning them to 'work no more'. These voices, ringing in despair within his poor bewildered head, were enough in many cases, to turn the man about, to retreat in confusion to his hovel, never to work again, at least in the mine.

Medical men and psychologists, studying the science of nature and phenomena of the human mind, could perhaps explain these frightening occurrences as being the result of acute depression and absolute mental and physical exhaustion, causing hallucinations.

Despite the misery generally experienced by the mining working class in particular, there was another side to the picture, shown in the health of other inhabitants of the country and their longevity.

Carew, who lived in the reign of Elizabeth I, observed that eighty or ninety years of age was ordinary in every place, and he mentioned one, Polzew, who died at 106; Prake of Talland, 110; and in the register of the parish of Landewednack the Rev. Thomas Cole who was buried in the year 1683, is said to have been 120. But what was more extraordinary was an instance given by the latter from a manuscript of Scawen... "That in the year 1676 a woman in the parish of Gwithian died at the advanced age of 164 years. She was well known by tradition among the inhabitants. Her name was Cheston Marchant, and she was said by those who remembered her to have grown new teeth and hair in her very old age from which travellers who visited her from curiosity frequently carried off a lock.

"Mr. Polwhele recorded the names of Henry Brenton, a weaver who died in the reign of George I, aged 103, Mrs. Trevannion of Bodmin aged 107, Mr. Richardson of Tregony who died in 1770 aged 102, Mrs. Littleton of Lanlivery, aged 101, a lady of Egloshayle aged 112, Maurice Bingham, a fisherman of St. Just who died in 1780 aged 116, to mention a few."

However, violent deaths like those recorded by Dr. Pryce in 1780, continued to plague the mining industry and through the years that followed, accidents were commonplace; the very nature of the work with its attendant risks made them an every day occurrence. Tired men cannot think properly and are inclined to acts of carelessness. Machinery too gets tired and fails under stress. All too often disasters occurred just as they do today, bringing death to the workers and shocking grief and despair to their families and friends.

The Dolcoath accident of 1893 when seven miners were entombed and the Levant man-engine catastrophe of October, 1919, when thirty one men died, recall but two of the tragedies of mining.

Life in Cornwall throughout almost the whole of the nineteenth century was hard, not only for the mining community but also for the working class in general. Cycles of depression bringing unemployment, hunger, overcrowding and squalor, plagued the county. But who were the working class? Today we visualise the working community as being between the ages of sixteen and sixty five and would view with horror an advertisement appearing in the press similar to one in the "West Briton" of July 1816...

To Manufacturers and Farmers

Wanted for about fifteen or twenty healthy boys and girls from 8 to 12 years of age, masters who will undertake to teach them to get their livelihood. For particulars, application may be made, if by letter, post paid to Mr. Thomas Simmons or Mr. Richard Sampson, overseers of the parish of Gwennap.

Hard times produced hard men, at times ready to improve their lot by preying on those more unfortunate than themselves as was shown in the following "West Briton" report of March 1817....

Camborne Miners Plunder Wreck

On Monday morning last about four o'clock during the fall of snow and in a strong gale from the north, the Brig "Mary" of Ilfracombe, Captain James Bawden, laden with culm was driven ashore at Fassil Geaver cove in the parish of Camborne, a little to the Eastward of St.Ives. On the second evening a party of Camborne miners came down determined for a wreck, they cut the ships cable, carried off her two small anchors, stole all the beef and biscuits on board and even had the hardihood before it became dark to steal some of the seamens cloathes at Gwithian church-town which having been washed by the people of the village for the poor fellows had been hung up to dry. In pillaging the ship they set the watch at defiance by threatening to cut them down with dags or hatchets.

Penalties for wrongdoing were harsh, even for crimes of no great con-

117

sequence, and in Truro in July 1824, two disorderly women named Cleave and Seccombe were committed by William Paul, Esq., the Mayor of Truro, at his petty sessions on Thursday last to hard labour at the treadmill for one month; and a man called Robertson was committed for two months to the treadmill for endeavouring to impose upon the overseers of the parish of St. Mary, Truro, by false representation with a view to obtaining relief as a pauper.

Conditions in the towns, highlighted by the letter which appeared in the "West Briton" on 31 August 1849, were deplorable, little wonder that so many people uprooted themselves to go in search of something better. Surely nothing could be worse.

Public Health in Camborne

That which calls most prominently for reformation in this town is the absence of sewage. I believe that there is not a good sewer in the town. If I err in this belief, I can confidently affirm that there is a general want of sewerage. In many streets, the slops are thrown out on to a surface drain, or water table which conducts the filthy stream in many places to a great distance in front of houses. The drainage of some stables is quite open and the soapy water thrown off by the washer women is seen running a considerable distance. In hot weather, streams of those kinds send forth a pestiferous smell productive of disease. The want of sweeping is also very manifest in the town; vegetable and other decomposing matter being allowed to remain in the streets. In some places, dung heaps containing all description of putrid matter are contiguous to the street. In one place, a stile is a cesspool under a church road. The 'petties' are also in bad condition, where they exist. I should wish every dwelling to have a water closet, but this cannot be enforced.

Conditions had improved but little over the next thirty years as this report in the Royal Cornwall Gazette, of 7 January 1881, showed, concerning life in Camborne.

There are still several cases of fever in this town and during the past week there have been 3 or 4 deaths. The greater portion of the cases is in the Town district. I hear many complaints of the stench arising from the man hole cover of the sewers. The sewerage system appears to a great extent to be ventilated through the man hole covers and while passing these one must either hold ones breath for some seconds or else inhale the noxious gasses arising from the sewers. It is time that some means should be taken to carry these gasses in some other direction, for if they are not harmful to the health of the town they are intensely disagreeable to the passers by.

And was it any wonder that such conditions existed and overcrowding had become such a problem when people were encouraged to have large families. The first meeting of th Penwith Agricultural Society took place at Camborne on the last Monday in June 1824, and was well attended. The ploughing and sheep-shearing were in the very best style and the show of cattle reflected great credit on the farmers of that district, but the prizes were awarded to William Retallack, Illogan, as a labouring man, who has maintained the largest

118

Tragic deaths at Dolcoath Mine, 1893. John Pollard, Charles
White, Richard James, John Osborne, John Henry Jennings, Fred
John Harvey, James Adams

number of children, 19, without periodical relief, £2.2.0, and to John West of Camborne, as maintaining the second largest family, 15, without relief, £1.1.0

Labouring men indeed!

Lawlessness too, was a problem, in spite of the attempts by the Wesleys to install a sense of righteousness into the heathen Cornish.

A lot of young children in the town, full of high spirits, together with a large proportion of adults, indulging in consuming quantities of higher spirits in the kiddlewinks, naturally brought about conditions annoying and sometimes frightening the more staid members of the community, therefore, in consequence of the depredations and disturbances in Camborne and the neighbourhood, a few of the inhabitants raised a subscription and procured a policeman from London who commenced his duties on Saturday. It was hoped that the appointment, in the first week of March 1841, would augur well and that a great improvement in the peace and good order of the town would result. Sad to relate, the presence of a "Bobbie" did not deter all the wrongdoers, and the "West Briton" of 7 April 1843, reported...

Cornwall Easter Sessions; Simon Jury, aged 12 and Thomas Chapel aged 10, were charged with having stolen a smelling bottle, six currant cakes, a pound of raisins and twenty walnuts, the property of William Richards of Camborne. It appears that the two prisoners were seen by the wife of the prosecutor in the shop on Saturday last and on going out, the prosecutrix found the things in question taken. A conviction for felony at the last session was then proved against Jury. Jury, seven years transportation; Chapel to be imprisoned till the rising of the court, be once privately whipped and then discharged.

And what of the apathy of the public when on Wednesday, 14 January 1846, at nine o'clock in the evening, a man sold his wife in the open market at Callington for the sum of 2s.6d. We do not learn that either the authorities or the public interfered to prevent so disgraceful a scene. By not protesting, perhaps other husbands present at the market were mindful that their opportunity to do the same remained open. Perhaps the wives did not protest hoping that it might happen to them.

And how did the reading public interpret the advertisements in the Royal Cornwall Gazette in February 1880. To bootmakers. Wanted, a first class WOMANS MAN. Constant work all the year round! Apply P. A. Renfree and Son, Redruth. W. Rickard of Trispen wanted A SERVANT MAN to work with horses. Twenty years before the cart?

Life went on, the cycle of birth, marriage and death was perpetual and in between these events families lived their lives and created their own private histories peculiar to themselves but which were integral parts of the greater human story.

Mining still held the centre of the stage and many were dominated by its influence either by its prosperity, its decline or the suffering it caused through accidents and deaths.

Towards the end of the nineteenth century miners were becoming increasingly aware of another hazard.

120

XVIII

DREADFUL REWARDS

There was another deadly price the miners had to pay for their diggings. From the time their work took them to the depths, a killer disease wrought havoc amongst the legions of hard rock miners. The Journal of South African Studies, in its notes, made the following records...

B.Ramazzini, writing in his "Treatise of the Diseases of Tradesmen" in 1705, said "this imprisoned air taken in at the mouth for the use of respiration, is loaded with particles very injurious to the lungs, brains and spirits, which, joining in with the mass of blood and spirits, produces all the evils the workmen complain of".

The connection between metalliferous mining and the dreaded lung disease, phthisis, has been known for centuries. In 1556, Agricola, writing in his records of mining, mentioned the high death rate from lung disease amongst miners in the Carpathian mountains of Slovakia and Romania.

In the last quarter of the nineteenth century and the first ten years of the present century, the connections between Cornwall and the Transvaal were particularly strong. Cornish miners and their descendants were the great force on the gold fields.

Conditions prevailing in Cornwall during this period, were of a nature so bad, that the census reports 1871 and 1881 indicated that a large part - estimates put it at at a third of the population - emigrated to different parts of the world, generally to indulge in the killer occupation of mining.

Many returned to Cornwall, broken men, and the sounds and sight of withered men, wracked with the deadly cough and halting every few steps, to lean against a garden wall to disgorge the evil dust clogging their lungs, were common.

The disease has almost disappeared, just as the mines of Cornwall have, with the memories of those who died, recalled by the derelict engine houses standing around like tall, gaunt miners of old, stricken with a melancholy look of death.

How often a miner returned home to his village and family to take to his bed, no longer with the strength to stand, and unable to breathe; and how often the wife, when all was lost, would run across the village square to bring a relative with the anguished cry 'Come, Tom is dying!'

What is this terrible killer that cuts down, without mercy, the ranks of these Cornishmen who in their youth and strength knew that 'it couldn't happen to them', to come, only too soon, face to face with the grey dust of death?

Where mining for gold, tin and copper is carried out under-ground, workers are particularly liable to contract the disease. When the ore is extracted by the use of drilling, which has the effect of reducing to powder the rock, for example, quartz, free silica in a crystalline state is released. This takes the form of fine dust which is inhaled deeply by the labouring driller. Hence the name silicosis, of which phthisis is a form.

Silicosis is a fibroid change of the lung, arising from the presence of these

Stricken with a melancholy look of death, the ruins of Carn Calver's pumping and winding engines near the village of Zennor.

Death spread like a plague. Great Condurrow near Beacon, Camborne, born sometime during the late eighteenth century and died 1914.

articles of dust. Phthisis develops from this change of lung condition by the addition of an infective tuberculosis.

However it would be wrong to suppose that the rock drill alone was the cause of creating the conditions responsible for the disease. Dust created by rock removal is not confined to drilling. Blasting, crushing and shovelling also release dust into the surrounding atmosphere, which need not be underground to be dangerous. Mining is an ancient industry, not merely confined to the search for tin, copper or gold. Thousands of years ago, underground work was undertaken with the sinking of shafts and opening up tunnels for flint for use as arrow heads, axes and implements for the pounding of corn for food, and it has been suggested that the ancient miners engaged in these activities suffered from Silicosis. Flint-knapping, the art of breaking flints with a hammer, or in prehistoric times, with other flints, was a cause of death from phthisis, through flint dust.

Where mining was concerned, in the early days, excavations were made by hand, which, because it was slow, raised little dust and the workings being of no great depth, were well ventillated. For thousand of years, the work remained a laborious process with slow progress in the improvement of tools used. Flint, bronze and iron were used in their turn, and it is known that bronze tools were in use some 6000 years ago, although one method of the breaking of large rocks was by lighting a substantial fire against the face then dashing cold water against the heated rock. This method, known as 'fire setting', was referred to by Agatharchides in the second century B.C. (see Herbert Hoover, The American Mining Engineer 1912). It was in use through to the seventeenth century, when it was neglected in preference to blasting by gunpowder.

A Cornishman, Bickford, invented the safety fuse in 1831, from which time the handling of explosive charges was made much safer. The previous method was to fill straws with fine powder, but this was unsatisfactory and caused many accidents and deaths.

Ancient writers described conditions in mines, before the introduction of mechanical aids, as wretched, noting that dust was a serious problem to overcome and miners made use of animal bladder skins as respirators, to cover their mouths. With the distintegration of the Roman Empire, records concerning mining ceased, but in 1556, Agricola published a great work called 'De re Metallica''.

The leading mining country at that time was Germany, and Agricola carried out an exhaustive investigation into mining practices there. He was a Doctor of Medicine, and saw at first hand, the effects of diseases causing illness and death, amongst the miners. He noted that, 'if the dust has corrosive qualities, it eats away the lung and implants consumption in the body''.

Agricola also made mention of the women of the Carpathian Mountain regions, who had married as many as seven husbands in turn, all of whom had died of consumption, brought about by their employment in the mines.

From the early eighteenth century, the working depths of mines increased considerably, due to the greater use of machinery pumping out the water. The great engineers of that period ensured advancement in the use of steam power, and by the middle period of the nineteenth century mines were worked to a depth of almost 2000 feet. This made ventilation difficult, in addition to the fact that rock temperatures increased with mine depths.

At Poldice Mine, the water from about 1100 feet, was 100 F. This increase in the temperature of water at great depths, is now being investigated practically, with the hot rocks projects, to bring hot water to the surface for heating purposes. One of the problems facing the underground miner was the lack of proper 'dries', or changing facilities at the surface. Conditions were most severe in winter, with men coming up from the great heat, to change in draughty sheds, The clothes they changed into, were often cold and wet and would be worn, sometimes for four or five miles, before reaching home.

Ramazzini has given us an insight into the occupational diseases of the mining industry around 1700. He was an Italian physician, and his first treatise was the start of further study. In his "Diseases of Metal Diggers", he states that in olden days, mining was a punishment for criminals. He suggested that ventilation and respiration should be used to help overcome the problem of dust and metallic elements entering the bodies of workmen.

Perhaps the first real attempt to overcome the dust problem, was the suggestion, in 1832, by the Leeds physician, Charles Thackrah, that there should be a 'common watering' of the surface being drilled. Years were to elapse before his general recommendations were put into practice. The two main causes of dust raising underground, were from the use of the percussive rock drill and dynamite.

In 1849, Couch, of Philadelphia, made the first rock drill. Many more of different design followed, but none were completely successful until about 1870, when Ingersoll and Rand introduced an effective machine, followed by Holmans in 1880 and Stephens, (Climax), shortly after.

Dynamite was introduced by Nobel in 1867. Although this was safer to handle than previous explosives, it was much more powerful and therefore, released far greater quantities of dust.

With the use of machine drills and dynamite, the dust hazard increased considerably and there was little attempt to control it.

From about 1850 to the first quarter of the twentieth century, great mining activities took place all over the world. South Africa, Western Australia and California became large producers of gold. The Americas, Spain and other countries became copper producers, Tin mines were developed in Bolivia. In all these places, it would be true to say, that without the adventurous Cornish miner development and production would have been considerably slower and delayed for many years.

Cornishmen had no fear of the effects of dust and many drilled dry to increase speed. If they came to surface without being covered with dust and looking like ghostly creatures from Hell, it was considered that they had not done their share of work. While all dust-raising activities were harmful, the one thought to have had the most devastating affect, was that of raising shafts. Here the drillers would be constantly looking upwards, with the dust falling like a shroud, covering their sweating faces,

The mortality rate from phthisis, among Cornish miners, was abnormally high and medical investigations into the occupational diseases of miners was carried out, not particularly on behalf of the Cornish, but they did lead to some significant conclusions. Eulenberg, writing in 1876, drew attention to the danger of quartz content of a variety of dusts. Sometime before this Hirt had ivided dust into catagories of organic and inorganic and also into metallic and mineral varieties. He showed that some groups were pointed and sharp. These would damage the lung tissues. Other types of dust were blunt and rounded and was thought that the difference was of importance, especially in view of the fact that the siliceous crystals found in the rocks of the African mines, are needle shaped and that silicosis was a great problem there.

In some other parts of the world where phthisis has not created great problems, it has been found that the needle-like particles are absent.

Just after the Boer War in South Africa, the problem of phthisis became so acute that serious consideration was given to methods of preventing dust. The active life of a miner had been reduced from five to three years. All drilling at this time was carried out by Europeans, who usually remained on the mines, working continuously for years, until struck down by the same disease.

The Miners Phthisis Commission sitting in 1903, advocated that water should be used when drilling and also that ventilation should be improved. But it was not until 1919 that the Prevention Committee in South Africa decreed that dry drilling should be disallowed.

Rock-drill manufacturers, of which only three of any importance remained, now turned their attention to designing machines that would water down the hole.

The Stephens' "Climax" Rock Drill Factory at Carn Brea, in Cornwall, claimed that their patent dust allayer would prevent phthisis, but the surge of interest and active measures to prevent the disease, came too late for hundreds of men, whose lungs were already afflicted by the scourge.

Mainly because of mining, Cornwall and its people were strongly linked with South Africa and especially the Transvaal which, from the 1830's to the early years of the twentieth century, had a more romantic history than any other country in the world.

MINERS' PHTHISIS PREVENTED

125

XIX

THE OLD TRANSVAAL

Twice, since its occupation by white people, the Transvaal had been in the occupation of the Boers and twice under the British flag. From a state of absolute poverty, it had risen to a position of importance, chiefly owing to the discovery and development of its huge mineral wealth, making it one of the richest countries in the world. Much of the credit for the change must be given to the thousands of miners and engineers from Cornwall, who gave their skills and their lives to make it all possible.

Before 1880 the existence of a territory known as the Transvaal was rarely mentioned. The history of the Transvaal began with the great trek, the exodus of the Boers from Cape Colony because of their dissatisfaction with the liberal policy of the British towards the natives.

The Boers moved northwards between 1833 and 1837. Many crossed the Orange River and founded the Orange Free State, but large numbers pushed on to cross the Vaal and reached what is now the Transvaal.

This territory was under the control of a Zulu chief, Moselekatze, whose main kraal was at Mosiga, in the west. To avenge the massacre of some wandering bands of Boers, a force under Maritz and Potgieter, defeated Moselekatze at Mosiga in 1837. In 1838, the Zulu tribe withdrew, crossing the Limpopo River into the country now known as Matabeleland.

The Dutch soon afterwards settled along the slopes of the Magaliesberg. Along the banks of the Mooi River they built a town which they called Potchefstroon, and here the first Volksraad or Council of the Transvaal sat.

While Potgieter explored the Mooi River, Retief with a large section of the trekkers, had discovered passes over the Drakensberg and were the first white people to cross the range.

They descended into Natal with a thousand waggons and were received with apparent friendship by Dingaan, the fierce Zulu chief. To the followers of Potgieter there came the story of Retief's murder by Dingaan and of the attack on the Boer camp at Weenen. Shortly after this, the Boers under Uys, Maritz and Potgieter were again defeated by the irresistible onslaught of the Zulu warriors. The Boers were saved from complete annihilation by the timely arrival of Andries Pretorius, of Graaff-Reinet, at whose hands Dingaan met with his first heavy defeat. On 'Dingaans Day' 1838, the Zulus were driven back with great slaughter and the chief kraal, Unkungunhlovo, where Retief's party had been murdered, was burnt to the ground. In January, 1840, the Zulu army was completely destroyed. Dingaan soon afterward was murdered and his younger brother, the friendly Panda was set up in his place. Natal was proclaimed a Boer Republic, but British settlers were already at Durban and their occupation of the territory in 1843 induced the Boers to retire in two bands across the Drakensberg, some settling in what was known as the Orange River Colony and others moving north into the Transvaal.

Pretorius, the conqueror of Dingaan, proceeded with the Boers into the Orange River area where British rule had been established in 1848. He refused to recognise the British authority and induced many of his countrymen to physically oppose it. The insurrection failed, the Boers were defeated at the attle of the Boomplaats by the troops under Sir Harry Smith and Pretorius led across the Vaal River.

His arrival in the Transvaal was unfortunate for the new country of his doption. He wished to assume leadership, which was naturally disputed by Potgieter. The latter claimed to have been the first to occupy the country north f the Vaal, and naturally looked on Pretorius as an interloper. Pretorius, on he other hand, said that he had defeated Dingaan and besieged Durban as well as having fought at Boomplaats. He insisted that this gave him the right to eadership, while he also reproached Potgieter with being friendly with the British.

The trekkers became divided into two factions and all attempts at establishing an organised government for the Transvaal failed. Civil war eemed apparent but the common sense of the two leaders prevailed and they agreed to the election of a Volksraad and the formation of a central government.

In 1852, Pretorius was instrumental in inducing the British Government to ign the memorable Sand River Convention, by which Great Britain acknowledged the independence of the young republic. It was agreed that the Boers should be free to manage their own affairs, that the Vaal River should be he southern boundary of their territory, and that slavery should not be permitted.

The deaths of Pretorius and Potgieter in 1853 prepared the way for a period of internal peace under the eldest son of Pretorius, Marthinus Wessels Pretorius, who was elected the first president of the "Dutch African Republic" n 1853. The name of the country was later changed in 1858 to that of the South African Republic.

The authority of the government set up by Pretorius, was weak and was not supported by the people. Zoutpansberg, Utrecht, and Lydenburg each formed a little republic of its own, so that there were four parties in the state each declaring the others rebels. To strengthen his position, Pretorius determined to force the Orange Free State into a union with himself and for his purpose he and Paul Kruger, in 1857, at the head of a Commando, crossed he Vaal river and invaded the Free State.

When the news reached Bloemfontein, President Boshof called out his burghers, and, at the head of 800 horsemen, marched to meet the invaders.

The two forces met at the Rhenoster River near Kroonstad, but never came to blows. A few days later a treaty was signed in which Pretorius admitted the illegality of his act and vowed that it would never be repeated.

The disorders produced by the jealousy of the four miniature republics led to several efforts to bring them together to form a strong government; Zoutpansberg and Lydenburg were soon incorporated with the main republic. In 1860, Pretorius obtained six months leave of absence from his post as President of the Dutch African Republic to visit the Orange Free State and soon afterwards wrote that he had accepted the presidency of that country. This caused great dissatisfaction and from 1860 to 1863 the South African Republic was given to lawlessness and strife. These disorders continued until 1864 when Pretorius was accepted by all parties as the legally-elected President of the Transvaal and Paul Kruger as Commandant General or military head.

Troubles continued, especially with the natives, and a general war continued for three years but this did not prevent the discovery of gold and in 1868 Carl Mauch mentioned its existence near the Olifants River in the Transvaal.

In 1870 gold was found in the Murchison Range and Edward Button found it in the Marabastad fields, Zoutpansberg in the Transvaal.

In 1873 gold was found in the Lydenburg district near Pilgrims Rest and in 1882 the De Kaaps Gold Fields were started in the Transvaal.

In 1884 the brothers Struben commenced quartz mining on the farm Weltevreden north of the western section of the Witwatersrand Gold fields and started a five stamp battery.

The value of the Sheba Mine, De Kaap Fields, was recognised and in 1885 the town of Barberton was founded.

In 1886 Johannesburg was founded and by 1892 the deep-level era of mining had begun with the Rand Victoria borehole cutting the Main Reef at 2,343 feet.

Mining continued with great intensity, although in 1895 the stability of the country was again threatened, with the Transvaal becoming the centre of an ill-devised plot to remove the influence of the Boers from the area and replace it with direct British rule.

The ambitions of a number of well-known personalities in South Africa during the latter part of the nineteenth century to increase their personal power in the country and add to the already great British Empire were held in check partly because of the presence in that country of the Boers.

The Transvaal, a Boer republic with Stephanus Johannes Paulus Kruger at its head, was in the middle of South Africa and perhaps would have remained an isolated community but for the discovery of gold around the place later to become Johannesburg.

Incidentally, the mining of gold from the depths in Johannesburg was only made possible at that time by 'Cyanide' James, a Cornishman who discovered the cyanide process used in the recovery of the metal. In 1885 there was no such place as Johannesburg, but with the fever for gold always a driving force, thousands of miners converged upon the area and a shanty town with its shanty dwellers, quickly grew, in addition to the better managed mining complexes.

The Boers, a pious race of people, were alarmed at this presence in their midst, of swarms of hard-living, hard-drinking outsiders, who, in their turn, disliked the Boers.

Certain influences outside the Transvaal felt it necessary that the Republic, and especially Johannesburg, should come under British rule and towards that end, people like Cecil Rhodes and Leander Starr Jameson, allegedly plotted to bring this about.

There have been many arguments about the extent of the involvement of certain other people in what followed, but one thing is certain, that after much preparation, all of it futile, Dr. Jameson actually did invade the Transvaal on 29 December 1895, using Pitsani as his launching site with the intention of liberating Johannesburg and its supposedly long-suffering people, mainly British, from the oppression of the Boers. At a stroke the republic was to become part of the empire and the goldfields a paradise for businessmen and the share market.

On Monday 30 December, the Boers ordered Jameson to leave but he ignored the invitation. The invasion was a fiasco. Bad planning, worse organisation, no luck and the fact that the Boers were much better fighters than anyone had imagined and also knew how to handle the situation, forced Jameson and his four hundred riders to surrender after a noble fight at Krugersdorp on 1 January, and a last stand at Doornkop on the 2nd not far from their goal.

Many were killed and taken prisoner, but many escaped as darkness fell, fearing the punishment that the enemy might inflict upon them.

The only place to hide was among the British community in Johannesburg itself, to mingle with the anonymous crowds who were surging around in a state of great excitement at the events happening in the area. One thing made them conspicuous; their uniforms, in addition to which many still carried rifles. These would only be dispensed with when safety was assured, and one way of achieving this, was to discard their military dress as quickly as possible and obtain clothes that would pass unnoticed in a mining community. This could only be done by finding shelter and sympathetic occupants.

Henry Blackwell, an engineer skilled in erecting great engines and boilers in the mining districts of Cornwall and India, had been advised to live in South Africa and where the climate would be beneficial to his health, rapidly failing because of an infection of the lungs. His abilities were soon made use of in the goldfields of Johannesburg and it was to his room that three despairing soldiers came seeking shelter. Dirty, dishevelled and exhausted, they made a sorry sight as they appealed for a change of clothing in which they could escape. Blackwell could assist only one of the men; the others hid what parts of their uniform which would reveal them to be Jameson's men under a pile of coal in the store together with their rifles. All three disappeared into the African night just as suddenly as they had arrived. Later, when the hue and cry had died

A glimpse of central Johannesburg from the Robinson Mine, 1904

away, the uniforms were removed from under the coal and destroyed but not before a fine valuable gold watch was found in a pocket of one the jackets. The owner was never traced and when Henry returned to Cornwall, before the turn of the century, he brought the watch and one of the rifles home to Zelah as souvenirs of epic events,

War between the Boers and the British on a scale not envisaged when the Jameson raid was planned now soon became inevitable and in 1899 hostilities broke out building up to a major conflict ending in 1901.

During this period mining operations were brought almost to a standstill but in May 1901, three mining companies re-started ore crushing operations and the industry continued to grow, being restrained only by acute labour shortage.

To overcome the problem, a Foreign Labour Department was established on 19 May 1904, when the Labour Importation Ordinance became law in the Transvaal. A new government department was empowered to carry out the arrangements devised for the purpose of hiring Chinese labour for the miners without damaging the social structure of the community or the orientals themselves. Among the many provisions of the Labour Importation Ordinance to ensure that these arrangements were met included the following: No person could import labourers without being licensed and no licenses would be issued until the Lieutenant Governor was satisfied that the accommodation provided was suitable and that proper medical care was provided for the men. Contracts were restricted to three years, renewable.

Labour Department officials had access at all times to the mines, compounds or any place where the labourers were working or living, to inspect their conditions and to see if their treatment was fair or whether there were any grievances. Labourers were allowed to have their wives and children up to the age of ten with them.

They were paid monthly in South African currency, guaranteed a six day working week and granted Sundays, Good Friday, Christmas Day and Chinese Festivals as holidays. Every man had access to courts of law. Only those labourers who had been properly recruited by the agents of the government and who travelled on licensed vessels were allowed to land in South Africa.

The Convention between Great Britain and China, signed by the respective sovereigns in 1860 and renewed in 1904, prescribed that the Chinese labourers for British colonies must be embarked from the Treaty Ports only, and that the local authorities at the ports should take steps to facilitate emigration and appoint officials to be known as Chinese Inspectors to co-operate with the British Consuls in making conditions of service known to the coolies and everyone else concerned. It was the duty of the special identification branch with its staff of five British and two Chinese clerks to identify and register the coolies on arrival. The method of identification used was the finger print system developed by Mr. E. Henry, Chief Commissioner of the Metropolitan Police and at one time adviser to the military administration of Johannesburg on criminal matters. It was noted that the fingerprint system had given excellent results in England and India and was far in advance of any other system of identification.

There were Transvaal Emigration Agents in China at each of the Treaty Ports of Chifu and Chin-wang-tao and at Hong Kong.

On 30 June 1905, there were in transit on the Witwatersrand and at Durban, 41,303 Chinese labourers. A year later the number available for work in the mines had risen to 52,329 and in May 1905, the Chinese Government appointed a Consul General to watch over Chinese interests in the Transvaal. He was Liu Ta-Jen, a man with much Western experience in London and Belgium.

In spite of the interest shown in their welfare, crime was a problem amongst the coolies. The records under the convictions and sentences on Chinese labourers for the year end 30 June 1906, show 13,532 cases of crime. These were listed as desertions, refusal to work and unlawful absence amounting to 7,189, murder 26, assault 708, housebreaking 210, theft 207, and forgery 307.

Other sources of labour were found in Portuguese East Africa but the main coolie strength for a considerable period was Chinese. It was beyond question that the welfare of these people was of great importance to the South African Government. Their food, accommodation and medical care was far superior to anything they had ever known before. Their compounds were spotless. The Chinese had two vices - opium smoking and gambling. Gambling was the greater source of trouble and deeply rooted in their character. Professional gamblers lived in the compounds without doing a stroke of work, their duties being carried out by debtors.

Naturally the Cornish miners came into close contact with the Chinese labour force and soon realised their great value and contribution to the running of the gold mines. There were protests from many quarters both in Africa and Great Britain about the employment and so called slavery of the Chinese, and movements organised to have them repatriated. This was vigorously opposed by many Cornishmen among the 10,000 skilled miners who waited upon the High Commissioner to urgently represent to him the distress and destitution which would ensue amongst the working classes were the Chinese repatriated.

The keenest pleasure of the Coolie (Chinese gambling between the "dumps" on a Mine)

Chinese mineworkers - South Africa, 1904.

132

South African Railways

Many people would be surprised to learn that miners, an industrious lot, were awarded medals for working on the railroads of South Africa and it is probable that even today if some returned miners travelling trunk lying up in the attic should be opened and searched a medal or two would be found.

When the mines of Johannesburg came to a standstill during the Boer War, thousands of skilled engineers and miners were made available to the British authorities who enlisted many to maintain the Transvaal Railways. Railway construction had begun in South Africa in 1890 when under the authority of the Republican Government a single track first known as the Rand Tram was laid to cope with the traffic along the gold reef from Boksburg to Krugersdorp. As the town of Johannesburg and the mines in the vicinity called for increased transport facilities, sections were linked up as rapidly as possible so as to connect the railways of the state then dominated by the Netherlands Railway Company with those of the Free State which were at that time worked by the Cape Government Railways and in 1892 uninterrupted railway communication became effected between the Cape metropolis and Johannesburg.

On the first day of January 1893, the main Transvaal line was finished to the capital Pretoria. A section connecting Pretoria with the Portuguese port on the east at Delagoa Bay was completed in November 1894. On that section a branch line starting from Kaapmuiden junction to connect the De Kaap gold fields and Barberton. A third line from Germiston junction on the main line to the Natal border was put in progress and was in full running order by 1896.

The Central South African Railways at that time therefore comprised main trunks from Norvals Pont on the Cape border through the Orange River Colony and Transvaal as far north as Pietersburg, those connecting Natal with the Rand and Delagoa Bay with Pretoria in addition to other branches subsequently built. The railway lines taken possession of by the British military authorities and then known during the Boer War as the Imperial Military Railways consisted of the following:

1. The Orange Free State Government Railway
2. The Netherlands South African Railway
3. The Pretoria - Pietersburg Railway

These systems were maintained by regular railway staff assisted by engineers and miners from the gold fields who were awarded a special medal struck to recognise the invaluable contribution by the miners to the efficient running of the system during hostilities.

On Friday, 14 June 1878, at the Real del Monte silver mine in Mexico, a son, Thomas was born to Thomas Mayne, a Cornish miner.

At the age of twenty, Thomas was in South Africa working in the gold mines and when the Boer War broke out he was recruited to assist in the running of the railways and given the special medal.

He returned to Cornwall and on Wednesday, 9 April 1902, married Florence Williams at Treslothan Church.

Thomas Mayne worked for many years underground in Dolcoath mine and died on 20 August 1923, from phthisis, at Pendarves Street, Beacon.

133

TYPES OF ENGINES IN USE ON THE C.S.A.R. LINES.

Cornish miners helped keep the wheels turning during the Boer War.

Engines of the South African Railways at the turn of the century.

"Come quickly, Tom is dying!"

Thomas Mayne, 1878 - 1923, Cornish miner, born Real del Monte Silver Mine, Mexico, worked on Johannesburg gold mines and South African Railways during the Boer War. Returned to Camborne and worked in Dolcoath. Died of Phthisis at Beacon, Camborne.

GOLD

It has been shown how the tin and copper industries in Cornwall and the Lake Superior areas developed. It has also been shown how the tinners of Cornwall managed their affairs to the point where they were recognised as masters of the mines with their own parliament. In North America, miners came under the absolute control of the large and mostly benevolent companies.

How then did the gold mining industry develop in the Transvaal from the discovery in 1869 to the period just after the Boer War?

Edward Button found gold in the streams in the Lydenburg district and the first diggers arrived in 1873. There were no laws or administration concerning mining, as the government saw little value in it and were content to allow the owners of the land to consider any findings as their property. However, the success of alluvial gold mining at Pilgrims' Rest in Lydenburg brought large numbers of diggers and it then became necessary to introduce some form of mining legislation although in view of what was considered to be a temporary period of gold recovery this was more or less confined to the keeping of law and order.

For many years before 1906, that feeling had changed and the value of gold recognised. This in its turn, gave rise to recognising the value of the miners. After all, who else could dig it out?

The right of mining for and disposing of gold belonged to the State. The owner of private property could prospect on it without a licence and could allow others to do so on obtaining a licence from an official of the mines department or magistrate. Unless prospecting was done the land could not be thrown open to the public for digging. When private ground was proved payable to the satisfaction of the government and was to be thrown open as a public digging the owner had the right to mark off for himself a mining lease not exceeding one tenth of the ground which he could then hold either at a small rental or a royalty of 2½ per cent of the gross income at the option of the government. He had the right to assign to his nominee a specified small number of concession claims and also to reserve a homestead upon which he obtained exclusive mining rights.

On unproclaimed Crown lands, prospecting could be carried out by anyone in possession of a licence but mining titles were only granted to those who actually discovered gold and had secured formal recognition of their discovery from the government.

When any land was given over to public digging, any person could after taking out a prospecting license from the Registrar of Mining Rights peg out claims not exceeding fifty. If the claims were for underground they measured 150 by 400 Cape feet and the boundary was retained in depth by a plumbline.

If the claim was alluvial the size of each was 150 by 150 Cape feet. 100 Cape feet were equivalent to 103.3 English feet. On private land the prospecting license had to be renewed monthly at a cost of 5s., half going to the State and half to the owner. After pegging his ground, the claim holder had to hand in a sketch of his claims and get his pegs verified by an inspector who would then issue to him a certificate of inspection and assign an official number by which the claim was thereafter designated. Within two months of pegging, the claim holder was required to have his claims surveyed by a Government surveyor and to file his diagrams with the Mines Department. After checking and verification by the department and the Surveyor-General who could certify the claim, the title was completed.

There were many Dutch from the Cape as well as men from the Transvaal and Free State but the main body were of a character and nationality quite different to the local inhabitants. These people were treated as a separate community and subject to special regulations. It is assumed that many were from Cornwall and this is reinforced when it is known that they were governed by a Diggers Committee, a reminder of the Stannary Laws of the Cornish.

The diggers at that time in the gold fields were regarded as sojourners in the land, and that attitude influenced practically all mining legislation in the Transvaal.

In 1883 an important law was introduced taking away the ownership of precious metals from individuals and vesting it in the State. The State allowed a certain share to the owner of the land by way of compensation. There were two main points; the special relations between the State and the alien diggers temporarily occupying land for the purpose of extracting minerals and secondly the adjustment of the proportion assigned by the State to the original owners of the land. In the early days of the industry it is thought that mining legislation was inspired by fear of the newcomers, and a desire to limit their numbers and activities. From these beginnings the Witwatersrand gold industry of the Transvaal quickly grew to mammoth proportions and whereas in 1887 the value of the 19,079 ounces of fine gold recovered was £81,045 by 1905 this had risen to 4,706,433 ounces valued at £19,991,658. The tonnage milled in 1905 was 11,160,422 tons, from more than sixty producing mines some having reached depths of 4000 feet, like the South Randfontein Deep which struck the reef at that level.

The mines were household names in Cornwall which had supplied the core of the work force. It was rare for a Cornish mining family not to have at least one of its members working in the industry.

Even today the names of many mines are remembered by the descendants of the Cousin Jacks; Robinsons Deep, Ferreira, Langlaate Deep, Simmer and Jack, to mention a few.

To understand the nature of gold mining in South Africa during the period under discussion, it is necessary to follow the process from the actual removal of the ore from its place underground and this of course could only begin after shafts had been sunk and the necessary machinery installed at the surface.

The broken ore was removed from the face along the levels, loaded into trucks or waggons and taken to the shaft where it was thrown into bins in readiness for falling into skips holding about three tons. The skips would then be hauled to surface continuing to the top of the headgear and automatically tilted to allow the rocks to fall into an ore bin. Above the bin was an arrangement of steel bars known as a grizzly which separated the smaller and larger pieces.

The finer pieces passed directly to the mill. The coarser ore on its way to the mill was passed slowly over a revolving table or belt and thoroughly washed using a jet of water. Rock recognised as waste was discarded at that

Machine Drill, Robinson Mine, 1904

Miners going on shift, Geldenhuis Deep, 1903

point while the remainder was conveyed to the stone crusher where it would be reduced to a 1 inch size. This broken ore was then lifted on to trams or trucks and hauled up a long incline to above the level of the mill where it was stored in large bins with capacity to feed the stamp mills for a number of hours. The discharge from the bins was regulated by automatic feeders which delivered the ore slowly into what were known as the mortar boxes in which the stamps rose and fell about 95 times per minute, crushing the ore in water until it was fine enough to pass through a screen having from 400 to 1000 perforations to the square inch. This fine ore and water consisting of sands and slimes was known as the mill pulp. After passing through the screens the pulp would flow gently over copper plates, the surface of which were brightened with mercury which caught any free gold and formed an amalgam that, when properly dressed, caught the very fine particles of free gold more readily than would the mercury alone. The amalgam was scraped off the plates each day. The proportion of the gold contents of the ore that was caught in the mill varied with the freeness of the gold but generally 50 to 60 per cent was recovered in this way. Gold that was not liberated was termed bound and was either imprisoned in the grains of sand or so covered with iron pyrites as to be resistant to the action of the mercury. The problem of how to recover the bound gold without great expense had been closely studied with the result that secondary grinding of the pulp was decided upon. Experiments with the tube mill were successful; the ore was reduced to so fine a state that practically all the gold was recovered.

The tube mill was a cylinder of metal about 22 feet long and 5 feet in diameter containing a number of pebbles. When the pulp flowed into the revolving tube the ore was re-ground by the pebbles and passed out in a state of slime. The free gold in the slime was recovered by means of shaking amalgamation tables, a refinement of the prospectors panning shovel. The pulp, on falling from the tables was lifted to a great height by means of a revolving tailings wheel which contained buckets or boxes for that purpose. This allowed the final stages of treatment to be carried out using the force of gravity alone.

After leaving the tailings wheel, a very small proportion of lime was added to the pulp for the purpose of neutralising any acidity that may have been imparted to the ore while still in the mine. The pulp then passed through a series of boxes called "spitzlutten" where it was classified by hydraulic means into three grades, concentrates, the heaviest; sands and slimes, the lightest. The concentrates were sent back to the tube mill. The classification of the sands and slimes was further improved by the flow of the pulp through V-shaped boxes called "spitzkasten" from which they were led to the vats of the cyanide plant. The slimes were treated freely with lime, the action of which causes the impalable powder the ore was now reduced into to settle in a further series of spitzkasten. The clear water was then decanted from the now floculent slimes to flow back to the mortar boxes to recommence its cycle. Both the sands and slimes were treated in their own series of vats with a weak solution of cyanide of potassium or sodium which percolated out the small amount of finely divided gold present in them and after the valueless refuse had been washed to remove the last trace of gold-bearing cyanide solution, it was removed to the refuse heaps that were beginning to form a part of the

139

General view, Jumpers Deep

Tailings Wheel where the gold bearing slimes were lifted to great heights to ensure gravity flow for the remainder of the treatment. At the turn of the century slime pumps began to replace the wheels.

140

landscape of the Witwatersrand goldfields.

The development and application of the cyanide process was successfully established on a commercial scale and was considered to be Johannesburg's great contribution to the industrial mining advancement of the world. The process was based upon the power of cyanogen in the presence of free oxygen to combine with gold into a soluble salt, the cyanogen being usually applied in the form of potassium cyanide or of sodium cyanide.

The origins, brief history and state of the industry at 1906 have been covered and it will be of interest to clarify some of the features of special significance.

Sorting The quantity of ore eliminated in the sorting stations depended on many things, such as the labour available, the adequacy of the sorting arrangements for the stamps and of course the width of the reef. Sorting had fixed economic limitations and to determine the degree to which rejection of poor rock should be carried in order to secure the largest profit, a number of factors, for example, the tonnage at site, stamping capacity and the life of the mine had to be considered.

Conveyance of ore The next stage in operation was the conveyance of the ore from the rock breaker to the mill bins was carried out by mechanical haulage by wire rope, steam or electric locomotives, hoists, conveyor belts and so forth. The conveyor belt had only recently come into operation and at some of the newer mines the ore after arrival at surface was almost entirely handled by that system.

The Gravitation Mill Those stamps weighed from 850 lbs. in the older batteries of the Rand to 1550 lbs. in the latest mills. The quantity of ore crushed per stamp each day, its duty, varied according to the weight of the stamps, the speed at which they were run, the height of the drop and also on the mesh screening used through which the pulp escaped on to the amalgamating tables. An interesting development had been made from the normal practice of driving stamp batteries by steam. The idea was to attach an electric motor to each battery of ten stamps, instead of running them by a line of shafting driven by a steam engine direct.

Gold Precipitation In order to release the gold from the zinc slimes the bulk of the zinc was got rid of by means of sulphuric acid, the slimes were then calcined and finally fluxed and melted in a reverbatory furnace. This bullion was of considerably lower grade than that obtained by amalgamation.

Amalgamation The Witwatersrand practice as regards battery amalgamation and the recovery of gold after leaving the tube mill plates was the same as in other parts of the world. The amalgam collected from the various copper plates daily was squeezed in a canvas cloth and the excess of mercury removed. The product was a hard ball consisting of some 30 per cent of gold. Since the introduction of tube mills, the proportion of gold won by amalgamation had increased the normal percentage of 50 or 60 by at least 2.3/4 per cent. About a quarter of that gold was won from the "black sands" that collected on the copper plates and were separately manipulated. The amalgam was heated in a retort and when some 3000 to 4000 ounces had been collected, the mercury was driven off and recondensed for further use and the gold recovered in a spongy mass. The gold was afterwards melted in a plumbago pot or crucible and cast into a bar of bullion ready for shipment.

141

Beacon, Camborne, Chapel Choir, c.1908.
Outside the village Sunday School before the annual outing
somewhere by the Cornwall seaside.

Back Row Standing:
-, -, Dick Williams (Dicky Tenor), -, William John Williams, -, -, -, -.

Middle Row Standing:
Young girl, Howard Cock, Tom Thomas (organ blower), Arthur
Thomas, John Bartle, Mrs. Cock (Edith Eustice), Mrs. Prideaux,
Emily Rickard, Young boy, -.

Front Row Standing:
Grace Williams (Mrs. Arthur Thomas), -, -, Frances Rickard,
Sam Perry (Boy soloist), Sarah Temby (In mourning), -, -, -,
Beattie Rickard (Mrs. Charles Blight), Lois Temby.

All decked out in their finest array for their annual outing.
William John Williams born 1874 at Franklin Township,
Houghton County, Michigan, standing tall at the back.

It was to this land of gold that many Cornish miners and engineers turned to improve their standard of living. Africa was on everyone's lips, with most mining families having one or more workers either going with hope or returning with pockets lined with sovereigns and a gold watch but all too often with lungs clogged with dusty needles.

Many of the Cornish who left their native land remained exiles; some by choice; others because death offered none. Joseph Henry Williams remained to live and die in South Africa as did his older brother, William John who was born in Franklin, Michigan in the days of the great copper boom there. William John was brought to Cornwall by his parents in 1882. In the early parts of the 1900's he travelled to the gold fields of South Africa but returned to Camborne to work in Dolcoath new shaft. He possessed a fine bass voice and regularly sang in the Beacon Chapel choir, giving solo performances of items popular at the time such as 'Many Brave Hearts Are Asleep In The Deep', a favourite which he sang with great feeling. He married a village girl, Lillie Rickard, who died tragically giving birth to their third child in 1915. In 1917 he was back in Africa, mining for the De Beers Company in Kimberley, Cape Province. Phthisis was beginning to affect his health and in the mid 1930's he came to Johannesburg and worked for Stewarts and Lloyds, retiring in the 1940's. He died in South Africa in March 1955, aged 81; cause of death, phthisis.

His brother, Richard, also an American citizen, born in Franklin in November 1880, was brought to Cornwall in 1882, and, he too, at the turn of the century made his way to the goldfields. A powerful man, he relished a bout of Cornish wrestling as he did on Camborne Feast days in the grounds of the Pendarves Arms at Beacon when as a young man he lived in the village. Boxing, too, was a favourite sport and on one occasion he fought the contender for the heavyweight championship of South Africa way down in an underground level of a Johannesburg gold mine. Why the contest took place there is not known; perhaps there was some illegality about the match that required the absence of the law. From all account, " Richard gave as good as he got".

He returned to Cornwall at about the time of the first World War and when the United States entered the war in 1917 he was called to serve in the American Army as a military policeman.

After the war he farmed for some time from a small holding at Wheal Harriet but was caught in the depression of the 1920's when he decided to try his fortune in the land of his birth. He died in Detroit, Michigan in 1939.

Of the Blackwells, Charles died in Johannesburg in 1941, but his brother, Alfred Ernest, who had sailed to Africa with Joseph Henry Williams in 1909, had left a wife and young family back in Beacon. War with Germany was inevitable, so in 1914 he returned home and had no difficulty in obtaining work in the machine shops of Holman Bros. Ltd. of Camborne. He was soon promoted to the position of foreman and later, was placed in charge of the hardening department, a post he held until his retirement in 1950. Like his father before him, who had placed his three sons with the Falmouth docks firm of Cox and Co. to learn an engineering trade, Alfred Blackwell also sent his three sons to learn trades, this time at Holmans, the world famous engineering works, manufacturers of mining machinery and pneumatic tools, who have played such an important part in the economic life and welfare of Camborne and its people.

William John Williams, 1874 - 1955.
From Michigan Copper Country to Cornwall's tin and South Africa's gold and diamonds.
Cause of death, old age and a touch of phthisis.

Richard Williams, United States Army Military Police, 1918.
Born Franklin, Houghton County, 1880, died Detroit, Michigan,
1939.
"He gave as good as he got."

DS-K

Working on the gold mines of Johannesburg, Alfred Blackwell had left a wife and young family in Beacon, 1911.
Elizabeth Mary (Williams), Charles Alfred Irving, and Marion.

XXI

CAPTAIN COURAGEOUS

Charles Blackwell was born in Cost-Is-Lost, Peranzabuloe, in 1872. He attended the Zelah day school and in 1886 moved to Falmouth, where his elder brother lived, beginning his engineering apprenticeship at the Cox and Co. docks.

In 1892, because of his father's association with the firm, he joined the Harvey engineering works at Hayle, as an improver, gaining valuable knowledge in the manufacture of mining machinery and pumping equipment. The term "improver" was applied to all apprentices who were obliged after the completion of five or six years learning a trade, to work for two years improving themselves before being accepted as skilled men. At this time, Harveys were also engaged in shipbuilding, of which Blackwell had experience during his years at the dockyard in Falmouth.

One of the earliest ships built at Hayle was the 43 ton iron screw ship, "Patmos." Designed as a trawler, she also carried cargo across to France, worked on the London river and ended her days somewhere in South America.

From 1843 to 1893, Harveys built over seventy vessels, including the the steamer "Lyonesse" for service between Penzance and the Isles of Scilly. In 1893, the cargo steamer "Hayle" of 475 tons was built, but by this time Harveys had put the town of Hayle firmly among the builders of iron ships.

In 1846, three steam tugs were laid down for use on the Rhine. These were the "Prussian Eagle," "Dordrecht 1" and "Dordrecht 2." In 1857 they laid down the keel of the "Cornubia," a packet steamer of 411 tons for use on the Hayle to Bristol run. This ship was purchased by the Confederate States, and used by them in blockade running during the American Civil War.

In the 1830's, before the maritime period, Harveys were building engines for the mining industry. This continued, and from about 1843 both activities progressed side by side bringing the firm a sound international reputation. Mining machinery and pumping engines for waterworks were sold to clients in many parts of the world, including Holland and the London water board at Kew, Hammersmith, Hampton and Battersea.

In 1894 Charles Blackwell was living in London and working for the water board on behalf of Harveys, who at this time were facing a decline in the mining industry and shipbuilding which had been depressed from 1892.

In 1894 the foundry was closed down and a large number of men laid off and yet in 1893 Harveys, who until that time had been represented in Johannesburg by agents, decided in August of that year to open a branch for the direct conduct of its rapidly growing business in the Transvaal. Up to that time, out of the Cornish pumps in use on the Rand, 75 per cent had been supplied by Harveys, a fact which spoke volumes for the high regard with which the machinery of that firm was held by the mine owners. Harveys did not confine their attentions to pumps, they were in a position to equip a mine of any size with the most complete plant. They also held the important sole agencies for many manufacturers of machinery, including those of R. G. Ross & Son of Glasgow, makers of Rigby steam hammers, and Gardiner & Sons of

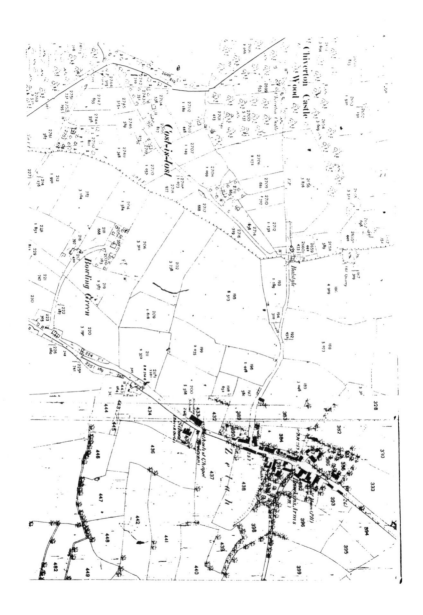

148

Johannesburg offices of Messrs. Harvey & Co. Ltd., 1893. Note the valves, level gauges, pressure gauges and bearings on display.

Compound Single-Acting Pump Engine supplied to the Lancaster West G.M. Co. by Messrs. Harvey & Co. Ltd., Johannesburg. Manufactured in Hayle, Cornwall in the early 1890's.

149

Manchester. Harvey & Company had supplied some of the largest oil engines on the Rand in connection with Gardiners, and one huge store was entirely lighted by two 45 h.p. high speed oil engines made by Gardiners.

Arrangements had also been made with the National Explosives Company of Hayle in Cornwall for Harveys to represent them in South Africa. Harveys' business was controlled from the central offices in the Aegis Buildings, Loveday Street, Johannesburg, but there were large yards and stores at Marshalls Town where a staff of engineers and draughtsmen were kept constantly employed. Another branch of the business was established at Bulawayo and there were ample storage facilities and sidings for the forwarding of goods at East London Cape Colony.

In spite of all that, the home company, once such a force in the international field, faded into insignificance in a relatively short space of time.

There was no longer a future for Charles Blackwell with Harveys, but stories of new ventures in Africa, related by his father Henry, had fired his imagination and he planned to visit there to work. However, war clouds were gathering.

With the outbreak of the Boer War in 1899, Blackwell volunteered his services with the British Army and from that time he led a full and most exciting life. He fought through the campaign, gaining valuable experience for the battle against the Germans in S. W. Africa in 1914-15. In 1902 he returned to Britain and was demobilised, but what he had seen in Africa compelled his immediate return, this time to the goldfields, where he later became chief engineer at the Langlaate Deep Mine.

One of his great passions was the sport of motor racing and he became a well-known driver, winning coveted Certificates of Merit awarded by the Transvaal Automobile Club. In 1910 he became the champion of South Africa, winning the prized silver cup. Where most of the car racing fraternity showed a marked preference for the German Mercedes, Charles refused to drive any but British cars and had many heated arguments with other members of the Automobile Club, roundly condemning them for their unpatriotic attitudes.

Blackwell drove only British Talbots, who made a variety of cars, one to be famous, the 12/16 h.p. model which had been designed around 1904. It is believed that the winning car, owned and driven by Charles, was the first British car of its kind to be made by Talbot, as previous models had been imported from France. It was a 20 h.p. of 1906, designed by C. R. Gerrard, and while still conventional, had an unusually efficient engine of 3.8 litres capacity. This fast car, with speeds up to 60 m.p.h., quickly made a name for itself in competitions. Its slogan was "The Invincible Talbot".

Blackwell voiced his belief that speeds of 100 m.p.h. would soon be reached, and this was accomplished in 1913 when Percy Lambert drove his Talbot at Brooklands.

South West Africa

At the beginning of the first world war in 1914, the Germans had a colony in South West Africa. This was a base to direct hostilities against the British in the south. The south west was a very large area, almost 700 miles from the Orange river up to the Angolan border and some 200 to 400 miles wide from its borders with Bechuanaland Union and the Bechuanaland Protectorate.

TRANSVAAL
MINES DEPARTMENT.

Mechanical Engineer's Certificate of Competency.

ISSUED IN ACCORDANCE WITH THE PROVISIONS OF "THE MINING CERTIFICATES ORDINANCES OF 1903 AND 1906," AND OF THE REGULATIONS FRAMED THEREUNDER.

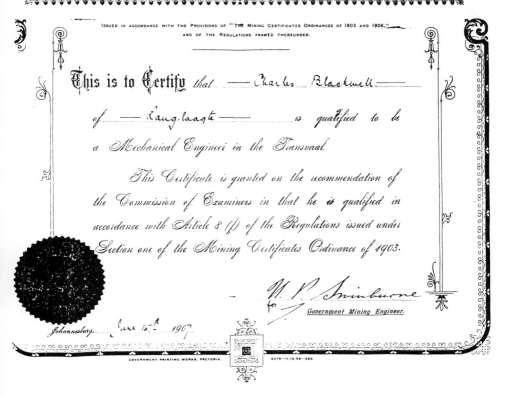

This is to Certify that —— Charles Blackwell ——

of —— Langlaagte —— is qualified to be a Mechanical Engineer in the Transvaal.

This Certificate is granted on the recommendation of the Commission of Examiners in that he is qualified in accordance with Article 8 (f) of the Regulations issued under Section one of the Mining Certificates Ordinance of 1903.

W. P. Swinburne
Government Mining Engineer.

Johannesburg, June 15th 1907

GOVERNMENT PRINTING WORKS, PRETORIA.   5378—11.12.06—280.

151

The southern areas had very little rainfall and there was a desert seventy miles wide inland from the coast. A railway from Keetmanshoop in the south ran through Windhuk (Windhoek) the capital and on to Tsumeb. There were branch lines to the ports of Swakopmund and Luderitzbucht from where, if the campaign had developed into a lengthy affair, the Germans might have received limited help from Germany itself.

The very nature of the territory made it easier to defend than attack. It was very large and in the main inhospitable to an invading force. General Louis Botha, a formidable Boer, had fought against the British in the war of 1899 - 1901 but was now in charge of the South West Africa campaign against the Germans, commanding both the Boer and British forces. Generally the country was a difficult one, especially for cavalry units or the splendid Boer mounted commandos. For the first time mechanised units began to play a part.

For some time early in the war, Charles Blackwell was the personal driver of General Botha who, deciding that motor transport was necessary, wanted a man with expert knowledge of the mechanics of cars in addition to being a champion driver.

Transport was a great problem for the South African forces. The Germans had demolished much of the rail tracks and supplies had to be brought to the fighting units by means of mule waggons. A desert without water wells is a nightmare for an army commander; a desert where the wells had been poisoned was a catastrophe. Mules, horses and men needed water; without it all was lost. The alarming situation was eased and eventually overcome by repairing the rail tracks and the arrival of engines and waggons from the south. Rail lines confine the movements of supplies to the immediate area of the tracks, so the South African Motor Corps was called upon to play a vital role.

The following letter to Lieutenant Blackwell from Colonel C. Berrange and the reference from Major J. S. Hope highlights the role Blackwell played in the successful conclusion of the campaign. The attack against the Germans in South West Africa took the form of three columns movement from the east through Bechuanaland, from the south across the Orange river and from Luderitz along the railway to Aus and the main line. Colonel Berrange led the attack from Bechuanaland.

Mr. C. Blackwell , late Lieutenant of the South African Motor Corps is well known to me. He was one of the senior Officers in charge of the Motor Car Sections attached to the Eastern Force, in the general advance into German South West Africa, and of which I had the Command. - Lieut. Blackwell came very prominently to the front with his excellent knowledge of mechanical transport in all branches; his daring and pluck in running through the desert water and supplies, where lines of communication were open and unguarded and under most trying conditions, I cannot too highly express, - he has an exceptionally good and tactful command of men, - very resourceful and thoroughly good all round soldier, with the capabilities in the working of mechanical Transport of which I have not yet seen equalled. - It was Blackwells services that mainly aided my Column in making such a rapid advance. I feel certain, he will prove his worth anywhere and I shall always look forward to his deserving advancement with interest.

Windhuk, South West African Protectorate
      9th November 1915.

               (Sgd) C. Berrange
                  Colonel
              Inspector General
              Permanent Force.

Union of South Africa

OFFICE OF THE KANTOON VAN DE

DIRECTOR OF MECHANICAL TRANSPORT,
ROBERTS HEIGHTS, PRETORIA.

29th November, 1915.

Lieutenant C. Blackwell,
    P.O. BOX 18,
        Cleveland.

    In Connection with your release from service with the Mechanical Transport which took place as from the 21st September last, I take the opportunity of placing on record my appreciation of the good work performed by you as a Commisioned Officer in this Department.

    The success which the Mechanical Transport has attained during the campaign which has been brought to a successful termination is due in no small measure to the hearty co-operation of, and determination to overcome difficulties shown by, yourself and other officers, who have so worthily upheld the good name of the Mechanical Transport in the Field.

    In your latter position as Officer-in-charge of Workshops, I have to thank you for the manner in which your duties were carried out, and to express the hope that your abilities will be recognised in whatever sphere you elect to serve in at Home.

                   J. S. Hope
                   MAJOR,

        DIRECTOR OF MECHANICAL TRANSPORT
           UNION DEFENCE FORCES.

Captain Charles Blackwell, M.C., 1872 - 1941.
Distinguished service in German South West Africa, 1915.

With the ending of hostilities in South West Africa in September 1915 Lieutenant Blackwell decided to offer his services to the Motherland. Befor his departure from Africa he married Miss Ruby Waldegrave Button, on December 1915. A native of Plymouth, she too was returning home and th newly-weds arrived in that city on 21 December.

On 1 January 1916, Lieutenant Blackwell was awarded the Military Cros for distinguished service in the Field and in connection with the campaign i German South-West Africa, 1914 - 1915.

During 1916 he was engaged in the Chester munitions factory and in 191 was promoted to the rank of acting captain and served in France with the Tan Company.

The mining companies in South Africa employed many thousands (Chinese and during his years in the industry Charles Blackwell had gaine valuable experience in the supervision of these industrious people. When Chinese Labour Company, the 78th Labour Group came to France from th

Pietersburg Commando.

Qr.-Mr. & Capt. John Bernhard Gordon.
Capt. (now T./Maj., S.A.S.C.) Jacobus Johannes Wolf.

Potchefstroom " B " Commando.

Capt. Esasius Renier Snyman.
Lt. Solomon Ignatius Visser.

Rustenburg Commando.

Capt. Joseph Dearlove Hardy Verster.

Standerton " A " Commando.

Capt. Willem Jacobus Van Rensburg.

Standerton " B " Commando.

Capt. Hermanus Bernadus Swart.

Utrecht Commando.

Lt. James John Harding.

Vrijstaatse Schutters (1st Regiment).

Capt. Felix Lutz.

Vrijstaatse Schutters (4th Regiment).

Lt. Ludwig Johan Fredrik Von Maltitz.

Vryheid Commando.

Capt. & Adjt. John Lumsoon Robertson.

Wolmaranstad Commando.

Lt. Lodewikkee Marthinus Wentzel.

INFANTRY.

1st Infantry (Durban Light Infantry).

Lt. (T./Capt.) Charles Percy Norton.

4th Infantry (1st Eastern Rifles).

Qr.-Mr. & Capt. William John Elson.

5th Infantry (Kaffrarian Rifles).

Lt. (now T./Capt., Worc. R.) Theodore Grant.

7th Infantry (Kimberley Regiment).

Capt. (T./Maj.) Thurston James Ford.
Lt. (now Capt., 2nd Cape Corps) Alexander Kidd, 2nd Kimberley Regiment.

8th Infantry (Transvaal Scottish).

Capt. James Alfred William Kerr.
Lt. (T./Capt. & Adjt.) (now T./Lt.-Col., 4th S.A. Infy.) Donald Macleay MacLeod, D.S.O.
Lt. (T./Capt. (now T./Maj.) James Alexander Green, O.B.E., 2nd Transvaal Scottish.
Capt. Allan Herschell, 2nd Transvaal Scottish.

10th Infantry (Witwatersrand Rifles).

Capt. Richard Frederick Cavendish Medlicott.

11th Infantry (Rand Light Infantry).

Capt. & Adjt. (now Maj.) John Washbourn Webber.

12th Infantry (Pretoria Regiment).

Lt. (T./Capt. & Adjt.) Allan Stratton.

1st Rhodesian Regiment.

Capt. & Adjt. Ernest Hope Carson.

South African Irish.

Qr.-Mr. & Capt. Hugh Montgomery.
Capt. Robert McGeown Taylor.
Capt. (T./Maj.) Ernest Walter Woon, D.S.O., attd. from S.A. Police.

ADMINISTRATIVE SERVICES.

South African Service Corps.

Lt. Joseph Richard Adendorff (Supplies).
Lt. Charles Blackwell (Mechanical Transport).
Lt. (T./Capt.) Cecil Stevenson Cameron (Supplies).
Lt. William George Courtenay (Supplies).
Lt. (now Maj., A.S.C.) James Howie (Water Supply) (Supernumerary List).
Lt. (T./Maj.) James Keen (Supplies).
Capt. (T./Maj. (now Maj.) George Herbert Pedler, D.S.O. (Supplies).
Capt. Henry Phipps Valintine, Bde. Train (R. of O.).

South African Medical Service.

Capt. John Edward Briscoe, D.S.O. (R. of O.).
Capt. Guillaume Jacobus Cillie.
Capt. (now A./Maj.) Thomas James William Abram Johnston, M.B.
Capt. James Joseph Lynch.
Capt. Arthur Edward Oakley.
Capt. (T./Maj.) John Pratt-Johnson.
Capt. (T./Maj.) Robert Norman Pringle, D.S.O.
Capt. Frans Karel Te Water, M.B.
Capt. (T./Maj.) James Alexander Thwaits.
Capt. (T./Maj.) Robert Hepburn Welsh.

South African Veterinary Corps.

Capt. Philip Rudolf Viljoen.
Capt. Clement Hamlyn Wadlow.

Chaplains.

Chaplain Capt. the Rev. Mattheus Theodoris Rolwell Smit.
Chaplain Capt. the Rev. Michael Jacob Meyer Van Coller.

South African Field Post and Telegraph Corps.

Capt. Albert Ogden Dayson.
Capt. David Fosbraey.

———

His Majesty the KING has been graciously pleased to award the Royal Red Cross to the undermentioned Ladies of the Nursing Services in recognition of their valuable services in the campaign in German South-West Africa, 1914-1915:—

Awarded the Royal Red Cross, 1st Class.

Miss Isobel Gordon Alexander, Matron, S.A.M.N.S.
Miss Heila Leuria Bester, A.R.R.C., Staff Nurse, S.A.M.N.S.
Miss Mildred Atherstone Fynn, A.R.R.C., Staff Nurse, S.A.M.N.S.
Miss Helena Hendrina Weise, A.R.R.C., Nursing Sister, S.A.M.N.S.
Miss Elizabeth Susanna Wessels, A.R.R.C., Nursing Sister, S.A.M.N.S.

Awarded the Royal Red Cross, 2nd Class.

Miss Evelyn Burgess, Nursing Sister, S.A.M.N.S.
Miss Jane Charlotte Childe, Nursing Sister, S.A.M.N.S.
Miss Jessie Marion Ferguson, Nursing Sister, S.A.M.N.S.
Miss Caroline Jessie Hawkes, Nursing Sister, S.A.M.N.S.
Miss Gwendoline Krohn, Staff Nurse, S.A.M N.S.

Middelburg " A " Commando.
Maj. Jakob Letterstedt Hamman.

Middelburg " B " Commando.
Lt.-Col. Willem Johannes Mouton.

Murraysburg Commando.
Maj. Johan Willem Bergeest.

Philiptown Commando.
Maj. Andrew Meintjes Conroy.

Pietersburg Commando.
Lt.-Col. Piet Willem Moller.

Piet Retief Commando.
Lt.-Col. Petrus Lafras De Jager.

Potchefstroom " A " Commando.
Lt.-Col. George Willem Holl.

Potchefstroom " B " Commando.
Lt.-Col. Pieter François Visser.

Pretoria Commando (Botha's Mounted Rifles).
Maj. Theunis Botha.

Rustenburg Commando (Van Tonder's Horse).
Maj. Pierre Jacques Roussouw.
Col.-Comdt. Roelof Jacobus Petrus Van Tonder.

Utrecht Commando.
Lt.-Col. David Lens.

Vrijstaatse Schutters (1st Regiment).
Lt.-Col. Alfred Lester Thring.

Vrijstaatse Schutters (2nd Regiment).
Lt.-Col. Johan Aderiaan De Necker.

Vrijstaatse Schutters (5th Regiment).
Maj. Christian Joubert.

Vrijstaatse Schutters (6th Regiment).
Lt.-Col. Cornelius Johannes Du Preez.

Vryheid Commando.
Maj. Johannes Andries Kruger.

Wakkerstroom Commando.
Maj. Martin John De Beer.

Waterburg Commando.
Maj. Andries Hermanus Geyser.

Western Transvaal Ruiters.
Lt.-Col. Nicolaas Jacobus Pretorius.

Wolmaranstad Commando.
Lt.-Col. Marthinus Jacob Janse Van Rensburg.

DISMOUNTED RIFLES.
6th Dismounted Rifles (Midlandse Schutters).
Lt.-Col. Johan Robert Francois Kirsten.

14th Dismounted Rifles (Karroo Schutters).
Maj. (T./Lt.-Col.) Willem Herbert Steyn.

INFANTRY.
2nd Infantry (Duke of Edinburgh's Own Rifles).
Capt. Bertram Maynard Woodhead.

7th Infantry (Kimberley Regiment).
Capt. Herbert Francis Lardner-Burke, M.C.

8th Infantry (Transvaal Scottish).
Lt.-Col. John Dawson-Squibb.
Maj. George Charles Fox, 2nd Transvaal Scottish).

10th Infantry (Witwatersrand Rifles).
Maj. Benjamin Young.

12th Infantry (Pretoria Regiment).
Maj. Frank Willoughby Morton.

Rand Rifles.
Lt.-Col. Frederic Hugh Page Creswell.

Railway Regiment.
Maj. Joseph Wilson Carr.
Maj. Ben Cyril Heald (Supernumerary List).

ADMINISTRATIVE SERVICES.
South African Service Corps.
Maj. James Dalgleish Anderson (Transport and Remounts).
Maj. David Hugh Kennard (Supplies).
Maj. Charles Edward Stewart King (Transport and Remounts).
Capt. (T./Maj.) John Thomas Kirwan (Supplies).

South African Medical Service.
Lt.-Col. Servase Meyer De Kock.
Maj. Leonard Guscote Haydon.
Lt.-Col. George Harvey Knapp.
Capt. George Baird Moffat.

South African Veterinary Corps.
Maj. Joseph George Bush.
Maj. George William Lee.

Chaplains.
Chaplain Capt. the Rev. Thomas Henry Jones.

Ordnance.
Capt. (T./Maj.) Morley Humphrey.

South African Field Post and Telegraph Corps.
Capt. (T./Maj.) Robert Taylor McArthur.
Maj. Robert Poole, M.C.
Maj. James Alfred Venning.

———

His Majesty the KING has been graciously pleased to approve the award of the Military Cross to the undermentioned Officers for distinguished service in the Field and in connection with the campaign in German South-West Africa, 1914-15. To date 1st January, 1916:—

STAFF.
Lt. (T./Capt.) Francois Petrus Jacobus Boshoff (Supernumerary List).
Capt. William Ffyner Collender (Supernumerary List).
Capt. (T./Maj.) (now Lt.-Col.) Ewan Christian, D.S.O., Permanent Force (Staff).
Capt. (now Maj.) Thomas Middleton Davidson, Permanent Force (S.A.M.R.).
Lt. (T./Capt.) Maurits Julius Dommisse, 10th Mtd. Bde., Permanent Force (Staff).
Capt. (T./Maj.) Louis Esselen (Supernumerary List).

oldfields, Captain Blackwell was appointed one of their senior officers.

For his outstanding services in Africa and Europe the rank of Captain was conferred on him in perpetuity by King George V. After the war on 16 January 1920, he was demobilised and returned to Africa where he took the post of construction engineer with the firm of Hubert Davies, holding senior staff appointments in the following major engineering projects in that country and Portuguese Lourenco Marques.

In 1920 and 1921, before the time of trouble, he was the construction engineer at the Vereeniging Milling Company and the Mint, Pretoria.

The time was March 1922. A strike by the gold miners had turned into an armed uprising and the Government had to call up troops and summon mounted Burgher commandos from the rest of the country to restore law and order. It was civil war.

The most bloody episode in South Africa's industrial history, it had started off purely as an economic dispute and the fear amongst white miners that the depressed price of gold would cost them their jobs. Among the leaders of the strikers were many extremists and in the background manipulating the strikers, a small cell of the South African Communist party who promptly took advantage of the situation. Within a week they had thrown out the moderate leaders and were in full control. Their aim was to overthrow the Government, sieze the mines and establish a workers' republic. They came to within an ace of turning South Africa into the first communist state outside Russia.

Gradually the Red revolutionaries surrounded Johannesburg and the defence of the power station became the focus of the fight - a grim and desperate affair - the epic defence of the power station had much to do with the ultimate defeat of the revolutionaries. Power was needed for essential services like the hospital, street lighting and the pumping station to ensure the water supply to Johannesburg. The power station staff who joined the strike had sabotaged the plant before they left. It was an appalling mess but volunteers were recruited, and working non-stop got power flowing again after two nights. A few hundred yards away was Fordsburg where the fanatic leaders of the revolt directed operations from the market building. The power station volunteers once they had settled down to a routine, were able to see what was happening outside. They had a detachment of Durban Light Infantry, an armoured waggon and a tank in the yard. The tank went out on patrol every day but one night an S.O.S. was received that it had broken down. Volunteers grabbed guns and, jumping on the armoured waggon, got close enough to the tank to secure a hawser and tow it back to the power station.

There were 56 volunteers, many from scientific and technical societies including people like Sir Spencer Lister, Dr. A. L. Orenstein. Prof. J. H. Dobson and Mr. B. Sansky, general manager of the Gas and Electricity Supply Department. They lived at the power station in a state of siege for three weeks, guarded day and night and sniped at from neighbouring buildings, sleeping where and when they could.

The battle of Fordsburg, which finally broke up the strike, took place right next to the Power Station, and 123 wounded were brought in for treatment. Over two hundred and thirty people were killed during the troubles. Here, some Cornishmen were seen in an unfamiliar and ugly light. Percy Fisher was a member of the Communist Party. He had left Cornwall in 1914 to escape military service and as a militant union member organised a strike at City Deep in 1919. The 1922 revolt gave him his big chance. He began preaching war against the capitalists and his wild speeches roused the men to ugly acts of aggression and violence. Fisher was supported by another Cornishman, H. Spendiff. They both swore that they would not be taken alive and were as good as their words. Fisher died by his own hand after the battle of Fordsburg.

There were others who at that time saw a different future for South Africa and who were opposed to violence and communism. Among them was a Cornishman, one of the 56 volunteers who defended the power station. Captain Charles Blackwell, M.C. had seen service in German West Africa and served in the Tank Corps in France during the first world war. He is seen seated on the tank in the yard.

"And THEY said 'Let there be light' And there WAS light" and the light came from the Johannesburg power station.

From 1923 until he retired in 1938, Charles Blackwell was involved in the construction of the Lourenco Marques power station, the Worcester power station, the installation of printing presses for the Sunday Times and Rand Daily Mail, construction of Vereeniging and Blomfontein power stations. In 1932 he was construction engineer for the Roan Antelope mines, Northern Rhodesia, then at the Phoenix brickfields following which in 1934 he was construction engineer at the Van Dyk mines near Springs. In 1935 he installed the printing presses for the Sunday Times in Durban. His last appointment was as construction engineer at the East London power station.

On 3 October 1941, Charles Blackwell died in Johannesburg and lies buried in Primrose Cemetery, Germiston, Transvaal.

How far was it from the green fields of the little hamlet of Cost-Is-Lost?

This picture is of considerable historic interest and shows the tank ouside Johannesburg power station, 1922. Captain Charles Blackwell, M.C., is seen on the tank, centre, and on right hand of man in shirt sleeves

Front Row Seated L-R: Sir Spencer Lister, A. Rodwell, Dr. Orenstein, E. Sankey, -, Currie, -.
Second Row Standing L-R: -, T. Oates, -, A.H.Davies, V.E. Lewis, L. Ralston, -, -, F.Stokes, Eldson Dew, -, -, Dr. Dobson.

159

XXII

EAST AFRICA

In addition to their presence in South West Africa, the Germans were established in the east of the country. Here too, many men from Cornwall who had gone to South Africa to find employment generally in the gold mines found themselves in uniform fighting for the country they had come to love.

Joseph Henry Williams was born in Beacon, Camborne, in 1884. In 1904, after a brief visit to the copper country around Houghton in Michigan to see his relatives, Charles and Prudence Ann Davey and their children, he travelled down to Arizona and Florida. Gold was the lure in these parts of America, and Joseph Henry spent the next four years prospecting. The story was told that one scorching day watchers in a prospecting encampment saw three horses approaching from a distance kicking up little clouds of dust from the arid desert into the shimmering air. Slung across the backs of the animals were what appeared to be the dead bodies of three of their companions. Joseph Henry was one of the trio long overdue from an expedition into the wastelands. The horses reached the camp where, to the relief of those gathered around, it was found that the men were not dead but almost dehydrated through lack of water, completely exhausted and so badly affected with saddle sores that the only way to travel was the distinctly uncomfortable but less painful way of lying across the horse.

Remembering his days in Arizona, Joseph Henry recalled Geronimo, the great Apache chief. The Apache wars were now over and the last of the Indians had been taken by rail to a prison camp in Florida, where they had been reduced to a scanty living provided by the authorities. They would come down to the prospectors' camp asking for food to break the monotony of prison fare. Joseph Henry met with Geronimo and on occasions shared his breakfast with the Chief while listening to the warrior's memories of a fighting past. Memories were the only things left to help him through his few remaining years until his death in 1909.

Joseph returned to Cornwall but the urge to travel took him to South Africa. Together with his brother-in-law, Alfred Ernest Blackwell, he sailed from Southampton on 9 October 1909, aboard the Union Castle steamer "Armadale Castle", calling at Madeira, Grand Canary Teneriffe, Ascension, St. Helena and Cape Town; the fare, £15.15s.0d.

Alfred joined his brother Charles who was a senior engineer on the Langlaagte Deep Gold Mine. Joseph worked on the mines in the Transvaal until the outbreak of war with Germany in 1914 when he volunteered for service with the South African forces and was sent to East Africa where the ferocity of the fighting took second place to the dreadful physical conditions that were endured.

The men had to fight their way through forest and miles of swamp where the tsetse fly ruled supreme and local supplies were impossible to get. What seemed to be endless millions of flies flitted everywhere around the evil smelling carcasses of draught animals. The heat under those conditions was torture. A high proportion of the troops went down with fever and dysentry. When the rains fell mosquitos declared war and malaria decimated the troops.

On the "ARMADALE CASTLE" bound for South Africa, October, 1909.

The East African campaign was considered one of the toughest and most gruelling tropical wars of history. Joseph Henry Williams was left a complete wreck and there were fears that he would die from malaria as so many did, including Major Herbert Carter, V.C., from St. Erth, but recovery was slow but sure.

He returned to his work as an electrical engineer on the Robinson Deep Gold Mine, retiring in 1955 after 43 years with that great mine. Joseph returned to visit Cornwall in 1956, the first time in forty seven years. He died in 1963.

"In Port Shepstone Hospital there passed away last night a man with whom I was closely associated since February 1915. We worked together on the Robinson Deep Gold Mine for over 40 years until I left at the end of June 1955. During those 40 years we shared some stirring times together, notably during the 1922 miners strike on the Rand, and well do I remember Joe and I queueing up together - two reprobates, cap in hand, to ask for our jobs back after the strike.

We are apt to speak well of a man only after he has passed on, but Joe was a big man in stature and large hearted proportionately - a good friend but a fearsome foe - of whom I retain pleasant memories.

Since his retirement he settled happily in Southport, and I have no doubt endeared himself to such friends as he knew - for he was one of Natures gentlemen.

And so we say farewell to Joe Williams , with a plea that God rests his soul in all eternity."

A tribute from an old friend.

Dave Mocke.

Sea Park, Natal South Africa, April 3, 1963.

SEE BACK OF TICKET.

This Ticket is not transferable and its acceptance by the holder will be considered as binding him to the terms and conditions specified on the face and back thereof.

The Union-Castle Mail Steamship Co., Ltd.

DONALD CURRIE & CO., Managers.

ROYAL MAIL   SERVICE

Between ENGLAND AND SOUTH AND EAST AFRICA,
CALLING AT
MADEIRA, GRAND CANARY, TENERIFFE, ASCENSION, ST. HELENA.

No. **Ax 23492**   **STEERAGE**   INDEX No. *F 3*

PASSENGER'S CONTRACT TICKET.

1.—A Contract Ticket in this Form must be given to every Person engaging a Passage as a Steerage Passenger in any ship proceeding from the British Islands to any port out of Europe, and not within the Mediterranean Sea, immediately on the payment or deposit by such Steerage Passenger of the whole or any part of the Passage Money, for or in respect of the passage engaged.

2.—The Victualling Scale for the Voyage must be printed in the body of the Ticket.

3.—All the blanks must be correctly filled in, and the Ticket must be printed in plain and legible characters and legibly signed with the Christian Names and Surname and Address in full of the person who issues it.

4.—The Day of the Month on which the Steerage Passengers are to embark must be inserted in Words and not in Figures.

5.—When once issued, this Ticket must not be withdrawn from the Passenger, nor any Alteration, Addition, or Erasure made in it.

6.—This Ticket is not transferable.

7.—A Contract Ticket shall not contain on the face thereof any condition, stipulation or exception not contained in this form.

Steamship *"Armadale Castle"* of *12973* Tons Register, to take in Passengers at the Port of LONDON on the ——————, and at SOUTHAMPTON on the *Ninth* day of *October* 190*9* for South Africa.

NAMES.	AGES.	No. of Statute Adults.	
Mr A. E. Blackwell	*24*	*1*	We engage that the Person named in the margin shall be provided with a STEERAGE Passage to, and shall be landed at, the Port of *Capetown* in South Africa in the Ship *Armadale Castle* with not less than 10 Cubic Feet for Luggage for each Statute Adult, and shall be Victualled during the Voyage and the time of Detention at any place before its termination, according to the subjoined scale, for the sum of £*15 : 15 : 0* including Government Dues before Embarkation, and Head Money, if any, at the place of landing, and every other charge, except Freight for Excess of Luggage beyond the quantity above specified, and we hereby acknowledge to have received the sum of £*15 : 15 : 0* in full Payment.
43			
		2	

The Luggage carried under this engagement, whether in excess of Ten cubic feet or not, shall be deemed to be of a value not exceeding £10, unless the value in excess of that sum be declared and paid for. The following quantities at least, of Water and Provisions will be supplied by the Master of the Ship, as required by Law, viz.: to each Statute Adult, 3 quarts of Water daily, exclusive of what is necessary for cooking the Articles required by the Merchant Shipping Act, 1894, to be issued in a cooked state ; and a Weekly Allowance of Provisions according to the following Scale:—

3½ lbs.	Bread or Biscuit, not inferior in Quality to Navy Biscuit.	1	lb.	Sugar.
1	,,	Wheaten Flour.	2	ozs.	Salt.
8 ozs.	Rice.	½	,,	Mustard.
1 lb.	Peas.	½	,,	Black or White Pepper ground.
1½	,,	Potatoes.	1	gill	Vinegar.
	Beef.	6	ozs.	Lime Juice.
	Pork.	1	lb.	Preserved Meat.
	Tea.	6	ozs.	Suet.
		8	,,	Raisins.
		4	,,	Butter.

Mess Utensils and Bedding to be supplied by the Ship.

Henry Ding

For DONALD CURRIE & CO., Managers of
THE UNION-CASTLE MAIL STEAMSHIP COMPANY, LIMITED.
(If signed by a Broker or Agent state on whose behalf.)

October 8th 190*9*

Deposit   £ :   paid ———— to be paid at LONDON or SOUTHAMPTON.

Balance ✱ £ : 00

Total   - £ *15 : 15 : 0*   Balance received on the ————

by ————

NOTICE TO STEERAGE PASSENGERS.

1.—If Steerage Passengers, through no default of their own, are not received on board on the day named in their Contract Tickets, or fail to obtain a Passage in the Ship, they should apply to the Emigration Officer at the Port, who will assist in obtaining redress under the Merchant Shipping Acts.

2.—Steerage Passengers should carefully keep this part of their Contract Ticket till after the end of the Voyage.

N.B.—This Contract Ticket is exempt from Stamp Duty.

✱ The Balance requires to be paid and this Contract Ticket and the attached Counterfoil receipted before the Passenger can embark.

*Joseph Henry Williams, 1884 - 1963, East Africa, 1915.
"One of Nature's Gentlemen".*

XXIII

HOLMANS

There is no doubt that with the closing of many mines in the area, Camborne's future would have been bleak indeed without the stabilising influence of the business of Holman Brothers Ltd. This firm has been operating over the past one hundred and eighty years and until recent years under the directorship of generations of the Holman family and served by thousands of loyal employees.

The business began in 1801 when Nicholas Holman, the blacksmith, founded a boiler works at Pool, near Camborne. He carried out work for Trevithick, including the manufacture of boilers and other machinery for export to Peru. The business grew as mining boomed and Nicholas Holman's four sons became actively engaged in engineering projects. William, Nicholas and John branched out on their own. William at Copperhouse, Hayle; Nicholas established a boiler works at St. Just, and John began another works in Camborne where the No. 1 Works now stand. James continued at Pool.

In the early days the works supplied the mines with a variety of machinery, including pumps, boilers, winches and stamps. When it is known that in 1801 there were seventy-five mines in Cornwall and by 1862 the number had reached three hundred and forty employing some 50,000 men women and children, the reasons for the prosperity of Holman Brothers are plain to see.

By the 1870's the discovery of new tin and copper deposits in other parts of the world where labour costs were low caused a period of depression in the local industry. Success or failure was all a matter of economy. Produce more cheaply and survive or perish.

The introduction of the rock drill and its development saved the day and powered new life into Cornish mining. Jonathan Couch of Philadelphia invented the percussive drill which was steam driven, but in 1851 Joseph Fowle of Boston produced a direct stroke self rotating rock drill. In 1871 a drill of this design driven by compressed air was used in cutting the Mont Cenis Tunnel through the Alps.

In the 1870's Holman Brothers became interested in this form of drilling and in 1881 accepted the design of a new drill developed by a Scotsman, James McCulloch. The drill became known as the "Cornish Rock Drill" and was a first-class machine. McCulloch left the works after a short time and his place was taken by a Camborne man who had joined the firm at the age of twelve. Ben Cock took charge of rock-drill development and held the post of works manager for more than fifty years.

Demand for rock drills grew all over the world and with air now the power source, compressors too were in great demand. In 1877 Holmans were producing these and exporting to the world from the No. 1 works in Camborne.

In addition to compressors and rock drills, other equipment under the general heading of pneumatic tools began to be manufactured after the first world war. Riveters, chippers, grinders, spaders, road rippers and even paint scrapers were produced.

Holman Brothers expanded their business to other parts of the world from Australia to South Africa and Canada with marketing facilities at Takoradi in the Gold Coast and agents in Spain, Brazil, Helsinki, Alexandria, Singapore,

Holmans No. 1 Works, Camborne.

Holmans No. 3 Works, Camborne Office and Works entrance.

To The Memory
of
John Holman
Lieutenant
4th Royal Irish Dragoon Guards
Who Died of Wounds
In France
30th October, 1914
And Rests
In The
British Military Cemetery
Boulogne

And they are still remembered.

166

Holmans Men, 1934.

L. to R: S. Sweet, A. Evans, J. Holman, J. Williams, L. Carveth, A. E. Edwards, A. E. Blackwell, C. Prisk, M. Allen, T. Dunstan. At head Mr. Divers, lecturer.

Post war lectures to the foremen on how to run their departments efficiently.

New Zealand and Sweden, to mention only a few.

In 1951 there were approximately one thousand nine hundred workers employed by the firm, but the numbers have been considerably reduced for a variety of reasons. The days when hundreds of men were to be seen streaming from the foundry gates when Holmans' 'hooter' or whistle blew at five-thirty each evening are gone, perhaps for ever.

Today the Holman families are no longer concerned in the running of the business, although the former directors are still household names in Camborne, and are remembered with nostalgic affection by the many who worked for them, and who, having served the firm, especially during the times of Leonard, Treve, Percy and Kenneth, still recall their years at the works with happy recollections and no small amount of pride.

And not only are the names of the Holmans remembered, many of the workers over the years are often recalled and the managers and foremen are still remembered with a certain amount of awe and affection. Remember Ben Cock, Alf Phillips, Joseph Prisk, Nicky Curry, Mark Trebilcock, Dick Gilbert, Peter Parnell, Alf Blackwell and a dozen more, fine dedicated men who, in a spirit of co-operation made working at Holmans, in the words of one of them, grand old days.

Most of the older generation who formed the backbone of the "Foundry" through the years, until it passed from the control of Holmans, are gone, as indeed, are most of that family, but a visit to the cemetery, at the back of the Centenary Chapel, will revive memories of a great Cornish family to whom Camborne in particular owes a debt of gratitude.

It is believed that a large part, if not all, the historic records of Holmans were needlessly destroyed in very recent times. A person in authority allegedly stated that as far as he was concerned the past meant nothing; the future was all that mattered and in a peremptory manner ordered the destruction of priceless volumes, but not before the surreptitious rescue of time sheets for 1915 and 1935. These indicate little increase in wages over the twenty year period. The author was actually paid ½d. per hour for a forty-eight hour week when commencing his apprenticeship in 1932. With two hundred and forty pence to the pound this was not a princely sum but as the time sheet shows this had risen to one penny per hour in 1935; the affluent years had arrived!

Confident that their experience gained during a long apprenticeship would stand them in good stead, many young men, smitten by the Cornish urge to try their luck abroad, left home for the Americas, Africa and the Colonies, not this time as miners, but as engineers, and many earned respect in their chosen fields, the Royal Navy, the mercantile marine, the gold mines of the Gold Coast and one, at least to the great expanding oil fields of the Middle East, where he became the senior engineer inspector covering installations in Lebanon, Jordan, Syria, Iraq, Bahrain, the Trucial Sheikdoms and Qatar, finally retiring as the construction supervisor for the Qatar General Petroleum Corporation.

It will not be out of place to mention two other members of the same Camborne family. Other Cornish men and women have their own stories of success and ventures around the world, and these too, should be related and recorded - future generations will want to know!

Irving Blackwell, the eldest son of Alfred, began his career as an

168

Department	No.	NAME	Rate	War Bonus	Hours	Overtime	Total Rate with Bonus	Gross Wages			Employees' Contributions		
											Health		Unemployment
		_____	Brought Forward.					889	17	7	13	11 11	15 7 1
3. Machine Shop.	380	H. Berryman	7/	17/	47.		39/	1	19		9		10
	381	H. Rowe	75/6	17/	47.		37/6	1	17 6		9		10
	382	H. J. Gilbert	75/6	17/	47.	35¼	37/6	2	17 10		9		10
	383	J. Negus	75/6	17/	30	18¾ 2¾	37/6	2	3 7		9		10
	384	N. Sowden	75/6	17/	17	28	37/6	1	12 15½		9		10
	385	M. E. Kemp	15/		47.		15/		15		4½		0
	386	H. Combellack	17/6		47.		17/6		18 6		9		5
	387	J. Tregoning	6/		47.		6/		6		9		5
	388	G. H. Mill	40/	17/	30	18¾.	57/	2	13 10		9		10
	389	H. Coombe	40/	17/	30	18¾.	57/	2	13 10		9		10
apprentices.	390	J. E. Day	8/	3 p.hr	47.		8/		8		4½		0
	391	H. E. Blackwell	4/	2	47.		4/		4		9		5
	392	S. J. Dunstan	4/	2	47.	5⅝ e 2	4/		5 4½		9		5
	393	P. R. Hosken	4/	2	47.	5 e 2	4/		5 4½		9		5
	394	J. Robbins	3/	2	47.		3/		3		9		5
	395	O. G. Dyer	2/	2	47.		2/		2				2
	396	G. J. Oxnam	2/	2	47.		2/		2				2
Carpenters	397	E. Glasson	31/	17/	47½	2	43/	2	3 5½		9		10
	398	R. H. Kitto	31/	17/	47.	7½	43/	2	9 10		9		10
(stores)	399	H. J. Roberts	75/6	17/ 41/6	47.	11½	42/	2	13 7		9		10
p. Employment	400	R. E. Coleman	75/6	17/	23½		37/6		18 9		-		-
								917	8 1	14	4 8	15	14 9

Department	No.	Name	Hours	Overtime and Bonus	Rate	Gross Wages		
		Brought Forward				281	9	1
No. 2.	139	Arthur Thomas				5		
MACHINE	140	Johnson Twian	103		30/	2	17	
SHOP.	141	R. T. Keer	84½	8	30/	2	11	1
	142	Hugh Reddick	107	18	30/	3	10	
	143	F. Brown	107		30/	3		
	144	A. Blackwell	101	9	30/	3	1	8
	145	H. Lean	105	18	30/	3	8	1
	146	Geo. J. Bray	105	9	28/	2	19	
	147	Chas. Taylor	107	9	28/	3		8
	148	Robt. White	107		28/	2	16	
	149	E. Chandler	101	9	28/	2	17	
	150	Stuart Rowe	95		28/	2	9	0
	151	G. E. Uren	105	12	26/	2	16	
	152	F. Escott	107	9	26/	2	16	1
	153	Jno. Blewett	-		26/	-	-	
	154	Christ. Rowe	99½	12	26/	2	14	
	155	L. Brown	107	9	25/	2	14	
	156	E. Folkinghome	105	9	24/	2	11	1
	157	F. J. Uren	103	9	24/	2	10	3
	158	R. E. Monk	-		24/	-	-	
	159	R. T. Knight	99	21	22/	2	13	9
	160	J. A. Knight	95		22/	1	19	
	161	J. F. Magor	107	9	21/	2	5	6
	162	J. H. Floyd	107	25	20/	2	9	3
	163	W. H. Hendra	105	9	20/	2	2	
	164	Thos. Brewer	105	8	20/	2	2	3
	165	F. J. Cock	105	13	20/	2	4	1

No.	Name				£	s	d
166	Chas T. Phillips				4	10	.
167	Jno. Powning				4	.	.
168	Jas. Olver	105.	9.	31/6	3	7	7
169	Wm Gilbert	105.	13.	30/.	3	6	1
170	Rd. Gilbert	107.	27.	30/	3	15	.
171	Jos. Blight	105	18.	30/	3	8	11
172	Jo. H Blewett	107.	20.	30/	3	11	1
173	C. Blewett	107	18.	30/	3	10	.
174	W.H. Willoughby	105.	12.	30/	3	5	7
175	H Caple.	99		30/.	2	15	7
176	W.J. Rodda	101.	9.	30/	3	1	8
177	W.G. Burrow	105.	13.	30/	3	6	1
178	C. Euden	107.	9.	30/	3	5	.
179	J. G. Parnell.	103.	1/1. 18.	30/	3	8	10
180	P. Richards	103.	4. 9.	30/	3	5	.
181	F. E. Hotman	105.	8.	28/.	2	19	1
182	A. Kray	99	9.	28/	2	16	6
183	Wm T. Williams.	99	9.	28/	2	16	6
184	Wm H. Jackson.	103.	19	28/	3	3	9
185	Geo. Penquen	60.	4 3/7	27/	1	16	1
186	Wm Tregeagle	70½.		26/	1	14	5
187	H H Taylor	99	7/5.	26/	2	15	7
188	F. Godolphin	90½.	15.	26/.	2	13	8
189	R. J. Trevaskis	107	11	26/	2	15	1
	Carried forward				426	8	10

Holman Bros., Camborne, Time Sheets, 13th January, 1915.
These are believed to be the only surviving Holman records.

171

engineering apprentice at Holmans in 1925. In 1947 the disease, commonly known as itchy feet, caused him to relinquish his post as controller of Jig and Tool Design and Planning Office and Toolroom; destination, the gold fields of West Africa and the Marlu Gold Mine in particular, where he was in charge of the engineering workshops until 1949. In that year he joined Messrs. Bird & Co Ltd., of London and Calcutta to serve in the limestone and dolomite quarries of Birmitrapur, Orissa, India, first as chief engineer and then as manager. Much to the regret of the firm's directors, he left in 1952 after completing his contract and returned to Camborne, where Holmans, eager to obtain his services employed him as the Jig and Tool Designer and placed him in charge of the technical office. During this time, Irving Blackwell lectured at the Cornwall Technical College. Subject - Metrology.

The urge to travel was strong enough in 1954 to take him to Rhodesia where he was employed by the London and Rhodesian Land and Mining Co. London and Salisbury, Southern Rhodesia, as the construction engineer on Rhodesian Mines Group.

In 1958 he was Works Engineer for the Rhodesian Alloys Ltd., in Gwelo. In that year he joined the City Engineers Department in Bulawayo as their Chief Mechanical Engineer.

Well, there were other parts of the world to see and 1961 found him as Chief Electrical and Mechanical Engineer at the Public Works Department Aden and Federal Government South Arabia, a post he held for six years until 1967. History has recorded the years of unrest, bloodshed, and finally, the loss of the colony to Britain. This led to Irving Blackwell's transfer to British Honduras, where the Ministry of Overseas Development employed him in a technical capacity until 1969.

In 1970 another visit to Africa, this time to Johannesburg, as progress engineer for a construction firm; and surely now it was time to settle, but the urge to move was predominant and from 1971, until near the end of 1974 he was, in turn, engaged by the consortium of Kampax (Denmark) and Berger (U.S.A.) who were employed by the World Bank and United Nations Development Projects in the Philippines Highways Department, then by Messrs. Binnie and Partners to work on the installation of an electricity generating plant in the Portuguese colony of Macau, following completion of which he then joined a container shipping company in Hong Kong, ending as the engineer on a 'dead' ship m.v. "Apollo" near Lantau Island, returning to England in 1974 for a short assignment with the Paper Converting Machinery Company of Plymouth before retiring in 1975.

Irving Blackwell, Chartered Engineer, Member Institution of Mechanical Engineers, Member Institution of Production Engineers, lived in frustrating retirement, still with the urge to travel but bound by the knowledge that age was not to be denied and that the time had come to dream, and all too soon in Plymouth on February 4th 1985, to die.

What a splendid adventure it all was

Down to The Sea In Ships.

Couple an industrious nature to a youthful adventurous spirit, add the knowledge that from his grandparents time only four of his close blood relatives from a total of sixteen had not travelled abroad to live, work and sometimes die, and the ingredients for something exciting in life are present.

What inclined Richard Garston Blackwell towards joining the Mercantile Marine instead of an overseas mining concern was his desire to see the world and to turn his mechanical abilities into a worthwhile career. The following documents show the beginnings.

Richard Garston was born in Beacon, Camborne on 24 November 1914, the second son of Alfred and Elizabeth Mary Blackwell. He was endowed with an almost uncanny mechanical ability that is still talked about by those who knew him during his apprenticeship years at Holmans. Rarely known to seriously study he never failed an examination including those for his marine engineer's tickets.

A major shipping company offered him the enviable post of shore-based senior engineer but he refused, prefering to serve at sea. There was an occasion in 1956 when he went to the Sheikdom of Qatar in the Arabian Gulf to work in the power house in the capital Doha, but it was not to his liking. He returned to Cornwall and was approached by the Isles of Scilly Steamship Company and offered the position of Chief Engineer on the new m.v. "Scillonian," then being built in Southampton.

The "Camborne Packet" newspaper publication of the Camborne-Redruth Cameo sums it all up. An interview that was not one at all but a story the newsmen felt compelled to write after a friendly conversation with the Chief during a crossing from Penzance to St. Mary's. It is certain that Gary had no idea that he was being interviewed, otherwise the story would never have been published but fortunately it was...

CAMBORNE-REDRUTH LINK WITH ROYAL VISIT
Chief Engineer of the "Scillonian"

Camborne-Redruth will have a share in Sunday's Royal visit to the Scillies which has not been planned by the organisers. The "Scillonian" makes a special trip to the islands for that day, and when she is inspected by the Duke of Edinburgh at St. Mary's, one of the senior officers to be presented will be the Chief Engineer, Mr. Gary Blackwell, of Beacon Fields Camborne.

His important task will be to conduct Prince Philip around his engine room and, no doubt, answer the many questions which His Royal Highness' own mechanical knowledge, will prompt.

One thing is certain, Naval man though he is, Prince Philip will never have seen a better-kept engine room than that of the "Scillonian". Knowing what the drill was to be, I felt that Garry Blackwell was the obvious choice for this week's Cameo, and equally plainly the place for that interview was in his own spotless, gleaming engine room.

Chief Blackwell has held that position aboard the Isles of Scilly ship that is their lifeline to the mainland, since she was commissioned two years ago. The fact that, apart from weather conditions, she maintains her schedule back and forth with such dependable regularity is due greatly to the care he has given those two 720 h.p. Ruston diesel engines which drive the twin screws.

Knowledge is all-important in getting the best out of a Diesel motor and this Gary Blackwell certainly has, but there is something more behind

173

ANGLO-IRANIAN OIL COMPANY
FORMERLY ANGLO-PERSIAN OIL Cº
LIMITED.

PLEASE REPLY TO
BRITISH TANKER CO.LTD.

TELEPHONE:
ENGNG/C NATIONAL 1212.
EC/BTC. TELEGRAMS:
INLAND: BRITTANKOL,TELEX,LONDON.
FOREIGN: BRITTANKOL,LONDON.

BRITANNIC HOUSE,
FINSBURY CIRCUS,
LONDON,E.C.2.

3rd January 1939.

Mr. R.G. Blackwell,
68, Fore Street,
Beacon,
Camborne, Cornwall.

     The s.s. "BRITISH CAPTAIN" has
been slightly delayed and, provided
you are not advised to the contrary,
please arrange to take up your appointment
as Fifth Engineer at Falmouth on Tuesday
morning, the 10th instant.

     With reference to medical examination
we are pleased to advise you that you are
passed fit for employment in our service
afloat, and we look forward to hearing
that you have taken up duty.

     Kindly acknowledge receipt of this
memorandum by return of post.

BRITISH TANKER CO., LTD.

174

C.2.34.

ANGLO-IRANIAN OIL COMPANY
FORMERLY ANGLO-PERSIAN OIL CO.
LIMITED.
PLEASE REPLY TO
BRITISH TANKER CO. LTD.

EC/ETC

TELEPHONE:
NATIONAL 1212.
TELEGRAMS:
INLAND: BRITTANKOL.TELEX, LONDON.
FOREIGN: BRITTANKOL, LONDON.

OUR REFERENCE
ENC.G./C
YOUR REFERENCE

BRITANNIC HOUSE,
FINSBURY CIRCUS,
LONDON, E.C.2.

30th December 1938.

Mr. R.G. Blackwell,
68, Fore Street
Beacon,
Camborne,
CORNWALL.

Dear Sir,

    Kindly report to Dr. H.V. Deakin
of 1, Grove Place, Falmouth,
on a date and at a time at to be fixed by the doctor with you direc
for medical examination,
in accordance with the Company's conditions of employment.

    If you find you must alter the date and/or the time,
please inform the Branch Medical Officer named above direct
and also the Company.

    Travelling expenses (third-class rail fare allowed),
if incurred, may be claimed by completing the form overleaf
and submitting it to the Company at the above address.

    We do not hold ourselves responsible for any loss of
pay you may incur in keeping this appointment, nor for the cost
of any treatment which you undergo to reach the Company's standard
of medical fitness.

              Yours faithfully,
        For BRITISH TANKER COMPANY, LTD.

B.T.O./M.25

175

ANGLO-IRANIAN OIL COMPANY LIMITED.
FORMERLY ANGLO-PERSIAN OIL CO.

PLEASE REPLY TO
BRITISH TANKER CO. LTD.

EC/BTC

TELEPHONE:
NATIONAL 1212.
TELEGRAMS:
INLAND: BRITTANKOL, TELEX, LONDON.
FOREIGN: BRITTANKOL, LONDON.

OUR REFERENCE
ENGNG/C
YOUR REFERENCE

BRITANNIC HOUSE,
FINSBURY CIRCUS,
LONDON, E.C

30th December 1938

Mr. R.G. Blackwell,
    68, Fore Street,
      BEACON,
        Camborne,
           Cornwall.

Dear Sir,

      With reference to your application for employment, we offer you the under-noted position, and shall be pleased to know whether or not you accept it.

      Your attention is called to the Notes overleaf.

      Food, bedding, linen, soap and matches are supplied without charge.

      Your appointment is subject to Medical Examination in accordance with the Medical Clause contained in the Application Form you completed.

Rank   Fifth Engineer   s.s. "BRITISH CAPTAIN".

Monthly pay effective on taking up duty on board ship is £ 13.10 plus 30/- per month "Service Allowance".

      Provided you are not advised to the contrary, please arrange to take up duty at FALMOUTH on Friday morning, the 6th January. The ship will be repairing with Messrs. Silley Cox & Co., Ltd., Falmouth.

MEDICAL EXAMINATION :- Kindly carry out the instructions contained in th attached letter.

Medical Examination

      Kindly reply by ~~telegram~~/letter immediately.

          Yours faithfully,

          BRITISH TANKER COMPANY LTD.

                      SUPERINTENDENT ENGINEER.

B.T.O/M.13   P.T.O

FOUNDED 1801

BROS. LTD.
Holman

CAMBORNE · ENGLAND
LONDON OFFICE : BROAD STREET HOUSE E.C.2

TELEPHONE. CAMBORNE 2275 3 LINES : LONDON WALL 1036

CAMBORNE

PLEASE
ADDRESS REPLY
Nº3 WORKS

28th August, 1941.

OUR REF. WAGES DEPT. WJR/DV.

TO WHOM IT MAY CONCERN.

THIS IS TO CERTIFY THAT Richard Garston Blackwell served an apprenticeship with us as a Fitter and Turner for a period of five years from 11th August, 1930.

He gained a "Holman" Scholarship and passed through the various Departments of our works.   His Foremens' periodical reports on general conduct, ability and timekeeping during the whole of his apprenticeship were exceedingly satisfactory.

In completing his course he was trained in Fitting, Turning, operating various machine tools (Grinding (precision), Milling, Shaping, Slotting etc) and then passing through our Assembling and Testing Departments.

He remained in our employ until 10th January, 1939, leaving on his own initiative to join the Merchant Service.

For Holman Bros., Ltd., (NO. 3. WORKS),

DIRECTOR.

DS-M

Cornwall Education Committee.

C. D. ALDER.,B.SC. (HONS. ENG.); WH. EX.
PRINCIPAL.

Technical Scho.
Camborne.

18th. May, 1937.

To whom it may concern.

Mr. R. G. Blackwell was admitted to the Mechanical Engineering Course at the above school in September, 1930, and completed the Course in July 1935. He received instruction in Mathematics, Engineering Drawing, Applied Mechanics, Heat Engines Strength of Materials, and Theory of Machines, up to the Advanced National Certificate standard. He made marked progress and was; in every way, an excellent student.

Mr. Blackwell is of splendid physique, and takes a keen interest in games, having played in senior Rugby Football. His character is above reproach, and he has a good personality.

I think very highly of him, and have no hesitation in recommending him as a most desirable candidate for the post for which he is now applying.

Charles D. Alder

Principal

No. **58**   F.1.

ACCOUNT OF WAGES.

(Sec. 132, M.S.A. 1894).

ISSUED BY THE
BOARD OF TRADE

Name of Ship and Official No.
British Captain
146691

Name of Seaman.	Ref. No. in Agreement.
R. G. Blackwell	25

Date Wages began.	Date Wages ceased.	Total Period of Employment.	
		Months.	Days.
13-1-39	4-4-39	2	23

EARNINGS.

	£	s.	d.
2 Months at £13-10-0 per month	27	10	0
23 Days at 9/- per day	10	7	0
Increase of wages, on promotion by £........ per month for........months.......days*			
Overtime E.B. Hours at 1m 6d	4	1	0
Extras 5. Au 2m 23s	4	3	0
TOTAL EARNINGS	45	11	0

DEDUCTIONS EXCLUDING ALLOTMENTS.

Date.	Particulars.	Amount.		
	Reduction of wages, on dis-rating by £.........per month for........months.........days*			
	Advance on joining	3	0	0
	Fines			
	Other Cash Advances, Stores, &c., supplied (*in order of date*) :—			
27-1-39	Port Said	3	10	0
7-3-39	Algiers	3	0	0
17-3-39	Port Said	1	10	0
	S. Ticket		2	6
	Stewards	5	4	0
	Abadan	–	10	0
	Prov. Fund	2	1	5
	Health and Pensions Insur. Contributions for 13 wks.	–	10	10
	Unemployment Insurance Contributions for 13 wks.	–	9	9
	Cash on leaving Ship			
	TOTAL DEDUCTIONS, exclusive of Allotments	19	18	6

	£	s.	d.
TOTAL EARNINGS (as above)	45	11	0
TOTAL DEDUCTIONS, exclusive of Allotments (as above)	19	18	6
● Balance without deducting Allotments	25	12	6
Allotments	12	0	0
FINAL BALANCE £	13	12	6

The above Account of Earnings and of Deductions exclusive of Allotments is correct.

Signature of Master } E. Evans

Signature of Seaman } ....

Port Abadan   Date 4-4-39

ROYAL MAIL LINES, LIMITED

AGENTS FOR
THE PACIFIC
STEAM NAVIGATION C°

ROYAL MAIL HOUSE,
LEADENHALL STREET,
LONDON, E.C.3.

TELEGRAMS:
ROYMAILINE STOCK LONDON
TELEPHONE:
MANSION HOUSE 0522

YOUR REFERENCE ....   OUR REFERENCE ENG/JO   9th May, 1949.

TO WHOM IT MAY CONCERN

        This is to certify that Mr. Richard Garston Blackwell entered this Company's service as a Marine Engineer on the 12th April, 1940 and served continuously as a Junior, 4th, 3rd and 2nd Engineer Officer on Motor ships until 30th April, 1949.

        Whilst in our employ he obtained a 1st Class Ministry of Transport Motor Certificate of Competency.

        He was well reported upon with regard to ability, conduct and sobriety.

        For ROYAL MAIL LINES, LIMITED.

Deputy Superintendent
        Engineer.

JO.

(Later he obtained what is known as an Extra' Chief's Ticket.)

180

two years' trouble-free sea-time for an essential ferry. He has an understanding and feeling for his engines which is shared only by a privileged few among Diesel engineers. To see those engines, hear the Chief describing them, their teething troubles and their gradual nursing into full efficiency of that combined 1,440 h.p. is to realise something of his passion for perfection.

When the Duke descends those steep steel companion ways down into the Chief's domain, he will see something nearing perfection. He will be far removed from the old type of steam engine room for everyday work here keeps this spacious compartment, white-painted, clean and strictly workmanlike. Without a doubt it has also had some special attention in honour of the visit - for instance, the very floor plates of steel will have been highly polished to give them a lustre reflected in the many shining brass pipe lines.

For our Camborne Chief Engineer is not satisfied with paint alone. He likes an engine to be able to gleam with pride in its achievements. Fuel leads, pressure controls, air pipes and valves - wherever possible that fine brass or copper has the burnished finish which is the envy of all who go down there. Even that quieter corner where Bob - one of his assistants - presides over a dozen or more gauges and compressed air controls, has felt the influence and Bob looks after them so well that the Chief has renamed that section the "jewellery shop."

When I went down, Chief Blackwell was deep in the "innards" of an exhaust gland which had been blowing slightly and must be repacked to be just right, for no exhaust smoke is going to spoil the cleanliness of that engine room. Admittedly, it gets hot in the course of the three hours' normal run to the islands, but that happens in every engine room all over the oceans, and by clever development of his ventilating system Mr. Blackwell has improved even this feature.

This business of doing his own maintenance and improvements is one of the things one cannot fail but admire in Gary Blackwell. He wants things right, he knows how it can be done and to make sure it is done he does it himself - everything from a minute valve adjustment to the replacement of a "bottom end," the essential main bearing. A man who can do this and still be a sound Chief is the one who can get a good engine room staff around him and keep them. This he obviously has done and his staff do give that impression of enjoying their work and share his enthusiasm for doing it well.

Well might the representative of Rustons, the firm who supplied those engines, remark to all and sundry, "That's just about the finest engine room I have seen." Gary did not tell me that, for he is quite modest about his work, proud though he is of its effect. It came directly from someone who has known the ship and its working ever since it was commissioned.

Well, that's the ship and its engine room. Now more about the man. A Camborne lad, Gary went from local junior schools to Truro Technical College and then into Holman's. He gives credit for his present knowledge and ability not to himself, but to that firm where he served his apprenticeship, and to one other man whose name I was glad to hear so spontaneously praised.

He is Mr. C.D. Alder, now deservedly Principal at Cornwall Technical College, but at the time of which Gary spoke, head of the technical establishment which preceded even the Dolcoath Technical School. Here Gary went with a Holman scholarship.

"Mr. Alder taught me all I know," he said. "It was his training that made me want engines right. Nothing inferior was ever good enough for him, and he always emphasised the value of precision work in everything".

Our Cameo personality of the week chose a good year for going to sea - 1939! He recalls his first commission began on Friday, January 13 1939 - "A Friday and four 13's to help it," he said. Some people might think it a bad omen but I was one of the lucky ones."

He went right through the war first in tankers, and then trooping, was in some of the fateful convoys which suffered so heavily under "wolf pack" U-boat attacks - in one of them 15 out of 42 survived in the Atlantic crossing.

His position as Chief on the "Scillonian" was accepted only after long persuasion and, strangely enough, it was at a Camborne party that he finally decided to take the job. That was two years ago. Today his cheery grin and good comradeship are as well known in St. Mary's and around the harbour at Penzance and Newlyn as they were when he was second row forward for the Cherry and Whites before the war. Cartilage trouble put him out of the game when he was at his best.

A fine engineer for a fine ship - for that is just what the "Scillonian" is. She is well-founded with everything designed for passenger comfort under all sea conditions. When the Duke boards her on Sunday he will find she compares with the "Britania" in attention to detail and in her up-to-date equipment. And the engine room of the Royal yacht will be no more sparkling or efficient than that of the island boat."

On 5 Febuary 1970, off the coast of Northern Australia the Chief Engineer of the vessel "Crystal Sapphire" trading out from Sydney with a cargo of sugar for Tate & Lyle, was taken ill down in his engine room. Richard Garston Blackwell, a man who loved his home town and his country, lies buried in Darwin. The Church at Treslothan, where in 1944 he had married Avis Williams, was filled to overflowing for his memorial service.

The Call of Mining Still Remains

More than one hundred and thirty years ago, these words were written...

Thou hast, within thy borders, master minds,
Rare spirits, of the modern mining school...

Prophetic poetry from the pen of a Cornish mining man of yore, John Harris; but the vision of a mining school in Cornwall was seen many years before by the Norwich man, John Taylor, whose name became known throughout the mining areas of the world during the nineteenth century. In 1829 he published his "Prospectus of a School of Mines in Cornwall". He saw that as the industry

Richard Garston Blackwell was her Chief Engineer, 1956.
Powered by Ruston diesel engines, the flag is flying from the
mast as she approaches the Isles of Scilly on her maiden voyage
from Southampton.

R. G. Blackwell, 1914 - 1970.
Chief Engineer.

developed there would be need for something more than the intelligent practical miner who could 'smell' copper and drive in the right direction instinctively to dig it out.

The time had come to educate men in the theories and technical aspects of Mining, Metallurgy, Geology, Mineralogy, Surveying and the whole mechanics of the trade concerned with the recovery of stuff from the bowels of the earth, and for this new breed, the elite captains of the industry, to work hand in hand with those traditional diggers who remained the backbone of mining.

Taylor's vision of a Mining School was made reality by the efforts of other dedicated men of the Duchy and, in 1888 the Camborne School of Mines, soon to become famous throughout the world, began its task. Here then was established a base (in Cornwall) to nourish the interests of men from many parts of the world whether or not the industry was declining as it was in Cornwall or booming in the goldfields of Africa or the tin mines of Nigeria and Malaysia. With the disastrous deterioration in the fortunes of Cornish mining, countless miners travelled abroad, and those who remained were forced to find other means of livelihood, not easy when life in general was geared to the recovery of tin; but there was the School, not sufficient in itself to ease the problems of the unemployed miner but at least offering opportunities for those wishing to make mining a career backed by qualifications accepted anywhere in the world.

In Camborne, Holmans and Climax saved the day for many, giving to the apprentices skills that could take them abroad with confidence. This has been illustrated in the story of a Chief Engineer Richard Garston Blackwell, nevertheless, there in the background, remained the call of mining.

In 1968, Garston Blackwell junior qualified as an Associate of the Camborne School of Mines. He is in British Columbia now, a Mining Consultant and Chief Engineer at the Brenda Mine. In 1981, when attending at Queens University, Kingston   , his thesis on mining gained him a Master of Science degree, together with the prestigious Gold Medal awarded for an outstanding paper. This annual recognition had been withheld for the previous three years because standards of submitted thesis were not considered to be of an acceptable standard.

XXIV

CORNWALL

From the early nineteenth century through to the first quarter of the twentieth century, many thousands of Cornish people have left the land of their birth and crossed the rolling oceans to live and work in unfamiliar foreign lands, where conditions were desperate, and at times worse than those existing in Cornwall, but where. in spite of all the agonies, heartbreaks and hard times, there was hope that the future was theirs for the making.

But what of Cornwall? What was it really like, outside the grim picture of mining depressions and threats of starvation? What was it that gave the majority of Cornish exiles a great yearning to go back to the old country?

Even today, the descendants of those early stalwarts, who settled in so many parts of the world, feel a persistent longing to go back home to see for themselves the mysterious country where, in truth, it all really began for them.

Many make the journey, to find the birth places of their ancestors, and to see what Cornwall looks like, but, beautiful as it is today, what was it like, many, many years ago?

Descriptions of Cornwall, written by historians are all that we have to guide us; the rest, we must conjure up in our imagination, to satisfy our feelings about how it all might have been.

How then, did Cornwall and its people appear to the historians?

The county is nearly bounded by water, the Bristol Channel to the north and the British, now known as the English Channel to the south. On the east it is nearly separated from England by the Tamar, so with the exception of an artificial boundary including parts of Devonshire, Cornwall may be almost considered an island, the length of which is 69 miles measured from Land's End to Harwood in the parish of Calstock on the Devon border. Its extreme breadth is 46 miles. The narrowest part lies between St.Ives and Marazion and is about 6 miles.

The air of Cornwall today suffers in parts like the rest of Britain from obnoxious fumes produced in the main by the unrelenting exhausts of petrol and diesel engines. A hundred or more years ago things, according to Fortescue Hitchins the noted historian, were much different. He wrote..."the air of Cornwall though not wholly free from noxious vapours is less impregnated with unwholesome effluvia than that in most other countries. The fogs which occasionally load the atmosphere are of short duration and rarely spread themselves at once over any considerable tract of the country. The air must therefore be esteemed pure and balsamic notwithstanding the saline particles which it acquires from the contiguous seas. In most parts of Cornwall the air is thus impregnated and corrodes iron in a short time but more particularly towards the sea completely devouring the bars and frames of windows and checking in many places the progress of vegetation in plants shrubs and trees. It quickly tarnishes the lustre of any highly polished metals and takes from glue the power of retaining its adhesive qualities.

"But although our rains are frequent, as we have no bogs, lakes or morasses of any considerable magnitude, no noxious exhalations can arise from the stagnant pools, and having no extensive forests which might obstruct the free circulation of the breezes, the air suffers nothing from these impediments or from continuous calms.

The diversity of hills and vales, of bays, projecting rocks and promontories with which Cornwall abounds, cannot fail to intercept and collect every current of atmosphere that moves within the range of its latitude and longitude. Both calms and vapours are therefore prevented from remaining till they produce pernicious effects so that neither the saltness of which the air acquires nor the mineral evaporation by which it might otherwise be tainted are permitted to render it so insalubrious as to be injurious to the life of man. As steams are perpetually arising both from the land and the water and entering the atmosphere from these distinct elements, it is obvious that the air will become more or less humid.

"The uncertainty of the weather in Cornwall has long since become proverbial. The winds by which the clouds are propelled and supported having but a short passage across the county, soon remove these sources of rain and immediately after a severe shower, the sun frequently shines forth with an additional splendour."

The dismal effects of thunder and lightning in Cornwall were such that in or about the year 1681, burned the steeple on the top of the square tower at St. Columb, a lofty, well built structure, about one o'clock in the afternoon on a market day. What was the more remarkable when the accident happened, was that no crack of thunder was heard, only lightning appeared. Of a like nature, was that at Bodmin in December 1699, when the beautiful spire there, esteemed the loftiest and finest in the west, was destroyed too by lightning, by which it sunk down into the tower and yet but one stone removed out of its place which was carried to a Mr. Hoblin's house at Castle Hill near by.

A woman passing by when it fell, was struck double, with what, she could not tell (perhaps the violent concussion of the air) but crawling to a nearby house, she told the people in it that she saw balls of fire thrown at the steeple.

Such an odd effect had lightning in 1684 on the tower of St.Piran-in-the-Sands, out of which was struck a moor stone of very great size near the bottom, and left the rest untouched. The stone was put in again, but loose.

Unusual rain, too, was reported; such was a shower of wheat in 1680 near Rospren Bridge in the Parish of Lanhydrock, which was seen by John Hosken, vicar of St.Piran-in-the-Sands, who had some of it and said that if it was not wheat, it resembled it the most that ever anything did, and had a husk and flour within like it.

Uncertain as the weather has always been, nothing was more unexpected than the frightening experience of the awful blizzard that gripped the west of Britain in its icy hands early in March 1891. In a very short space of time a devastating change came over the whole area.

Cornish butterflies, beautiful and serene in their darting flights in the warm sun, abruptly vanished, making way for other cold white shapes whose flights were directed by shrieking winds of an intensity rarely felt before or since.

Frightening stories of the occurrence told by parents are still vivid and fresh today. Camborne was particularly hard hit by the storm which created a great white world, startling in its appearance and bearing no resemblance to

186

the gentle beauty of a landscape lightly covered by snowflakes that sometimes presents itself to morning viewers after the night's silent fall.

Snow began to fall at about two o'clock on Monday, the ninth and this soon developed into the blizzard. Telegraph wires were blown and lying across the drifts of snow, snared the feet of frightened horses bringing them to the ground. Soon all traffic was suspended, houses were covered with snow to the extent that they were unrecognisable, and many trees were broken down. Fears were felt for the safety of four young dressmakers of Beacon who had left town on the Monday evening to return home. Later it was found that they had reached safety. The horse-drawn bus that usually ran between Camborne and Truro found conditions so bad at Pool that it was left abandoned. Some drifts of snow were recorded as having depths of thirty feet. Soon all communication with other towns was cut off. At the high villages of Beacon and Troon people recalled how they were taken from their bedroom windows by means of ladders and of a funeral where the coffin was tobogganed down over the snowdrifts.

There were surprisingly few human fatalities. A young boy named Wallace, left the Wheal Basset mine on the Monday to walk home. He was found many days later on a snowdrift a short distance away from where he lived.

Losses of cattle were high and hundreds of sheep were buried, in spite of the great efforts of farmers to dig and rescue. Local foundries and mines were unable to operate because their employees were unable to leave home to reach their places of work. Miners coming off shifts found that they were unable to go to their homes. There was also the problem of obtaining supplies of coal to fuel the engines, but the efforts of men who cut ways from the railway siding at Camborne to South Condurrow and Wheal Grenville mines saved the day, although Wheal Grenville and the Newton Mines were forced to stop for a few days.

The railways were badly affected with three trains stopped by the snow. The five o'clock train from Plymouth on the Monday evening took six hours to reach Penzance. Another train which should have been following a quarter of an hour later was lost completely. It was in Cornwall, but exactly where was not known. A train with a breakdown gang was prepared at Penzance to travel up the line in search, taking nine hours to travel the thirteen miles to Camborne, where conditions were impossible with huge drifts blocking the lines. At Camborne it was learned that the missing train had left Redruth at ten o'clock on the Monday night with the storm at its fiercest and the snow driving hard. Looking like a ghost train it made an eerie approach towards Camborne but at Stray Park the battle against the elements was lost and the engine left the rails, ran along for a short distance, coming to rest on its side by a hedge which probably prevented the accident from becoming more serious than it was. The speed of the train at the time was slow and no injuries were suffered by crew or passengers, who, with the exception of five lady passengers, found accommodation in the towns hotels. The ladies were given shelter in the home of Mr. Reed, the Station Master at Camborne.

At sea, conditions were beyond the power of man or ship to control and many wrecks littered the coastline in the aftermath of the fiercest storm ever recorded to batter the shores of Cornwall. The devastation caused by the storm

Beacon, Camborne, March 1891.

THE GREAT SNOWSTORM 9ᵗʰ MARCH 1891.
THE DUTCHMAN FROM PADDINGTON OFF THE RAIL NEAR CAMBORNE.

The ghost train at Stray Park.

of the 9th March defies description. At the time, and in the days that followed, many acts of heroism and unselfish labour were performed, preventing a terrible experience from developing into an even greater disaster.

Other than the occasional freak storm the climate has changed but little over the past hundred and fifty years. It was not injurious to the health of the Cornish except that the damp conditions aggravated those who suffered certain weaknesses of the lungs or joints. Living conditions were much more destructive than the weather, which in general was most beneficial. What a pity therefore that the miners helped to destroy these healthy benefits by their labours in the mines. They also destroyed a considerable part of the natural beauty of Cornwall by their industrial activities, although this ugliness has today, because of a fondness and sentimentality for the old mining story been transformed into a beautiful scene in its own right.

The mining industry of old can be forgiven too for the destruction of the forests, vast areas of which were cut down to fuel the furnaces of the steam engines and for domestic use. Opinion has prevailed that in former years Cornwall was little less than forest and not until these were demolished, thus making it impossible to obtain further supplies, was any consideration given to an alternative which fortunately existed in the coal fields of Wales. In the early seventeenth century coal began to be imported from that country.

The destruction of the forests revealed a beautiful countryside and allowed expansion of agriculture, although the effect of destroying the timber of the country without planting new was deplored by many men.

XXV

A TIME TO PLANT

By the early part of the nineteenth century many of the gentlemen of Cornwall had awakened from the strange delirium of their ancestors and began to plant for posterity. Among those who set an example were Lord Grenville, Lord de Dunstanville, Sir John St.Aubyn and E.W. Stackhouse from Pendarves. The woods now seen around Tehidy and Treslothan are the results of their planting.

The trees of most value and importance to the populace would be those bearing food, and fruit trees of almost every description may be grown in the semi-tropical southern areas. Apples, pears, plums, cherries, peaches can be found as well as chestnuts, walnuts, mulberries and fig trees. More than one hundred and fifty years ago, because of the manner in which the mulberry bushes flourished, it was thought that silk worms might be propagated in the county to some advantage. No trial was known to have been carried out to prove the commercial benefits because of the large amounts of rain that fell during every season of the year.

Sir Walter Raleigh's introduction of the potato into Britain was a life saver, especially in Cornwall where it grew to perfection. Its benefits were and still are enormous.

To produce crops the land itself must be fed, and today a variety of aids to the farmer and small gardener are available. Developed by scientists they have become indispensable, but what were the methods used by the agriculturalist more than one hundred and fifty years ago?

Land must be properly fed to flourish and this is done by spreading of the correct fertilisers or manures as they were once called. In the eastern part of Cornwall near the sea or creeks and rivers, large quantities of limestone were imported from Plymouth and burnt with culm before mixing with manure as a preparation for growing wheat. This was an expensive business and farmers, being thrifty, cultivated barley in the north which did not require the sophistication of the lime treatment.

In all the maritime parts sea-sand, to which old salt and broken pilchards were added, was used by the best farmers in those districts where fisheries were established. Dung of various kinds and rotten earth formed valuable compost and oreweed enriched the composition. The manure produced by broken and decayed pilchards was by far the richest. The next in quality was bay salt which was condemned as unfit for any further use as salt. This, when purchased by farmers, consisted of oil, salt and broken pilchards. It was very rich and was sold from ten pence to fifteen pence per bushel.

It was noted by Carew at about the end of the sixteenth century that the Cornish gave themselves principally to the seeking of tin and neglected husbandry and as a result lived under miserable conditions.

"Their grounds lay all in common or were divided by sticks. They had some little bread corn and their drink was water or at best whey, that part of the milk remaining liquid when the rest formed curds. The richest farmers brewed not more than twice a year. The meat of the ordinary people was a substance called whitsue, being milk, sour milk, cheese, curds, butter and such like as came from the cow and the ewe which were usually tied by a leg at pasture.

"The older folk continued with their legs and feet bare complaining that they could hardly abide to wear shoes because it kept them over hot.

"Their horses were not fully shod and the harness or furniture as it was called consisted of a pad and halter on which the meaner country wenches do ride astride as other English folk used to do before the wife of Richard II brought in the side saddle fashion.

Their habitations and household furniture were exactly suited to their mode of life. Cottages consisted of walls of earth with low thatched roofs, a few partitions, no planchings or glass windows and scarcely any chimneys except a hole in the wall to let out the smoke. Their beds consisted of straw and a blanket.

Concerned wholly with the procuring and refining of metals without agriculture and without other commerce the inhabitants remained a distinct and separate race being almost wholly regulated by the stannary laws until approximately the end of the sixteenth century when the civil jurisdiction that had extended over the rest of Britain was imposed upon the county.

The inhabitants now began to emerge from the barbarisms of their ancestors but even so a Phisicke Doctor, Andrew Borde who visited Cornwall in the time of Henry VIII wrote... "Cornwall is a poor and very barren country of all manner of things except for tin and fish. Their meat and their bread and drink is mard and spoilt for lack of good ordering and dressing. Firs and turves are their chief fuel, their ale is stark nought looking white and thick as pigs has wrestled in it, smoky and ropy and never a good sup. In most places it is worse and worse pity it is them to curse for wagging of a straw they will go to the law and all not worth a hawe playing so the dawe?"

"In Cornwall there are two speeches the one naughty English and the other is Cornish speech. There be many men who cannot speak one word of English."

As to the ready resort to law that he referred to, these law suits were probably in connection with the tin mining industry. The holding of special courts in the county known as the Stannary Courts may have meant a more ready resort to the dispensers of law than obtained elsewhere in Britain. The suitors had faith in the judges and wardens of the courts, otherwise they would not have applied to them so readily,"

XXVI

ROADS AND RIVERS

About one hundred and sixty years ago there were many roads in Cornwall that deserve some mention, but the ones of real note were the turnpikes. These were two, one of which entered at Poulston Bridge and the other began at Torpoint. They both met at Truro then separated. The road that entered at Poulston Bridge was called the great northern road and was more frequently used than the other, passing through Launceston about two miles away and then in a westerly direction through two or three small villages to Bodmin from where it proceeded over the Goss Moors through more villages to Truro. The great southern road stretched from the coast at Torpoint to Truro. Here at Torpoint was the ferry connecting to Morrice Town on the Devon side of the harbour. The road proceeded westward about fifteen miles to Liskeard from which it passed through a small village and part of Braddock Downs to Lostwithiel and so on to St. Austell and Truro, the metropolis of Cornwall. There were branches from this road and between St. Austell and Truro were several which lead to Tregony and on to St. Mawes. From Truro the turnpike road leads to Redruth, Camborne and Penzance, and another northerly road to St. Agnes. Another passed in a south west direction to Penryn and Falmouth through Perran-Arworthal at which place it stretched west to Helston. This branch entered the turnpike road from Penryn to Helston which passed through Marazion to Penzance where it finally terminated. From Penzance to Land's End the public road was not inferior to the turnpike as the following shows from an advertisement in the "West Briton" by the proprietor of the Queen's Hotel, Penzance.

> Penzance - Logan Rock - Lands End. A handsome new four horse brake will run on and after the 14th July meeting the 8.10 a.m. down train and returning in time for the last train up. Fares 2s.6d. Places may be secured by writing to the proprietor Henry Blackwell. Dated 15 July 1875.

There are a number of rivers in Cornwall, of which the Tamar is the largest. Although dividing Devon from Cornwall, its source is in the parish of Morwenstow in the northern extremity of the county. The Hayle river, however, is of the most interest. On entering the northern district the river Hayle is the first that draws attention. It derives its origin from four distinct brooks that unite their streams at Relubbas which may be considered as its head. After taking a westerly course it turns towards the north where at three miles distance it reaches St. Erth or St. Ercy Bridge. This bridge, which is about five hundred and eighty years old, consists of three stone arches and a raised causeway at each end which extends across the valley. Before the bridge was erected a ferry boat was established here and ships of considerable burden came up to discharge their cargoes, but in process of time the sand and earth washed down from the hills obstructed the navigation and rendered the bridge necessary. Since it has been erected a greater accumulation of sand has taken place above it and the haven below has suffered a similar misfortune from the sands driven into it by the north sea. One hundred and fifty years ago only light barges could approach the bridge and then only at high tide. From St. Erth to high water mark at Marazion the distance is just three miles and the possibility of cutting a canal was at one time discussed.

From St. Erth the Hayle river bears due north, passing through an area of sand about half a mile wide and two miles long. It is navigable in the channel at flood tide for small vessels only which proceed about a mile from the sea and approach near the village of Lelant. Not far from its mouth the Hayle river is joined by a brook from the east which makes a branch of this haven near Phillack Church.

But it is not only the harbour that is nearly choked with sand; a bar of sand is also formed at the entrance, over which vessels find a dangerous passage. The bed of the whole is so elevated with the sands which have been accumulating for ages that it admits the tide only when it has been flowing for some time before.

In common harbours and on open shores where nothing obstructs its passage, the tide may be said to flow six hours and ebb six hours, but here the case is different, for the tide must have flowed three hours before it can enter Hayle and it continues to ebb three hours more after it has withdrawn its water from the river. It cannot therefore be considered as affording anything more than a half tide haven so that the season for vessels to enter and leave must be watched with care. Notwithstanding these disadvantages the trade carried on through the medium of this river was very considerable. It was about two hundred years ago a place of great trade for iron and Bristol wares, but more especially for Welsh coals for which there was a great demand for fire engines (steam raisers), smelting houses and home consumption of a populous neighbourhood and often a thousand horses came to carry off the coals for some purpose or other six days in the week.

The Hayle Copper House Company owned considerable land around Phillack creek and at great expense opened a navigable canal through which barges reached their extensive works. At the lower end of the canal, floodgates secured the water when the tide went out. In 1804 a jetty was laid near the mouth of the harbour, while, to collect the water within and to render it usable a dam was thrown across the Phillack creek. This rendered the harbour more commodious and by having a channel laid open through the bar, vessels pursued their course with less danger than formerly.

St. Erth is of great importance to at least one part of the Blackwell family in Cornwall because there in the church in 1596 William was baptised.

There was only one other entry as far as is known prior to this of a Blackwell in the county. In the parish register at St. Neot for 30th November, 1588, is shown the marriage of Robert Bligh and Alse Blackwell.

St. Neot lies about four miles to the north west of Liskeard and twelve miles to the west of the border with Devon. Several members of the Bligh family lived in the area but of Alse little is known. No records have been found concerning her or any members of her family so the arrival on the scene of this lady must remain a mystery and from the moment she married Robert, changing her name to Bligh, she has been lost to us. Where did she come from? Did she cross the Tamar from England at Poulston or at Torpoint or perhaps in from the sea at Fowey? Was Bligh a seafaring man who found the girl later to be his wife in an English port? The mystery remains. Blackwell is an English name and therefore it is possible that she left that country for a particular reason. The sixteenth century was a time of strife in the country with religious persecutions and rebellions. In 1588 the Spanish Armada sailed to its defeat off the coasts of Britain, Francis Drake sailed around the world between 1577 and 1581. Times were exciting.

Church records having been allowed to remain and rot in old wooden chests in older damp churches were in so many instances so badly affected by these conditions that entries of baptisms, marriages and burials became illegible. Many records were completely destroyed during the civil war of 1642 - 1660 by the armies of Cromwell, leaving large gaps in the histories of ordinary people.

William Blackwell married Jane on 17 June 1633, at St. Erth. In 1692, Katherin Blackwell married Richard Barnicoat at St. Budock and in 1695 Lidia Blackwell married John Martin at St. Breage.

In the sixteenth century St. Erth was open to ships trading with other parts of Britain. Roads were almost non-existent at that time into Cornwall. The name Blackwell is supposed to have originated in three places in England, namely Durham, Derby and Worcester, which is not far from the river Severn and the port of Bristol. Ships coming out from Bristol and heading down the coast would naturally look for harbours or havens of refuge from storms and there in the bay of St. Ives they would find the Hayle river along which they would proceed to St. Erth.

The same reasoning would apply for St. Budock with ships coming into Falmouth not a great distance away, and at St. Breage they would have entered where Porthleven harbour now stands. St. Constantine, approached by an inlet from the Helford river saw the baptisms of Robert Blackwell on 6 April 1690, and William on 23 October 1692.

The evidence points therefore to the fact that the Blackwells who became resident in the western parts of Cornwall in the sixteenth and seventeenth centuries first arrived by sea. They stayed, indicating that that normal maritime trading was not the reason for their coming. Their numbers were small, which meant that only an individual family here and there decided to make the journey and it is not certain that they came deliberately to Cornwall. And why did these small groups disembark at different places around the coast? The mystery remains, but consideration should be given to another possibility concerning the arrival of individuals in Cornwall.

Venetia Newall in her introduction to "The Folklore of Cornwall" by Deane and Shaw wrote...

> "Robert Dudley put in to St. Ives in 1595. Later author of a famous treatise on navigation he reached Cornwall in the spring of that year after a privateering expedition to Spain, North Africa, the Canaries and the West Indies. Six months earlier he had sailed from Southampton in the "Bear" and after an exciting but largely unprofitable voyage he paid off at St. Ives at the end of May 1595. His description of how the voyage ended reads well. I made for England where I arrived at St. Ives in Cornwall about the latter ende of May 1595 scaping most dangerously in a great fogge the rocks of Silly. Thus by the providence of God landing safely I was kindly entertained by all my friends."

At least one of Dudley's subordinates settled in Cornwall for, a month after landing at St. Ives, John Underhill, a Warwickshire man like his employer, married Honor Pawley of Lelant.

Is it coincidence that William Blackwell was baptised in St. Erth in 1596? Was his father one of the crew paid off in St. Ives? It is interesting to note that a Mary Blackwell, the great, great, grand-daughter of William, married a William Pawley in Lelant on 30 July 1762.

There is a far more likely explanation concerning the arrivals. In England there are four different parishes called Blackwell. Two in Derbyshire, one in Durham and one in Worcestershire. The Worcestershire name was first recorded in 964, one of the Derbyshire names in 1088, the Durham name in 1183 and the second Derbyshire name in the thirteenth century. Three of these names are recorded well before surnames came into normal use. Etymologically all came from the same source, two old English names meaning Black Stream. Blackwell is a hamlet in Derbyshire which takes its name from the family Blackwell. It is thought that this family came from one of the Derbyshire Blackwells. There were no places of that name in Cornwall in the early middle ages so it is improbable that the Cornish settlements took their name from a topographical feature but more likely as it appears that they were recent arrivals towards the end of the sixteenth century, from the Derbyshire Blackwell family.

Although there is no absolute evidence to show where the Cornish Blackwells came from, if, as it appears, they were sixteenth and seventeenth immigrants into Cornwall they could well have been attracted by mining. It is certain that the Blackwell place names in Derbyshire lie in mining areas. One near Alfreton is a very old coal mining area and Blackwell near Bakewell lies on the edge of the lead mining district.

It is known that in the sixteenth, seventeenth and eighteenth centuries there was much cross migration between Derbyshire and North Wales lead-mines. It is on record that a Cornish mining family came to the lead mines of Derbyshire in the sixteenth century.

The mining fraternity seemed particularly footloose and all that was needed to send a miner on his way in the past was a shortage of work in his area.

Sixteenth century Derbyshire men were very well aware of the south-west and its mining industry. One of the Derbyshire sources of profit in the late middle ages and beyond was the extraction of ores. Local persons engaged in commercial undertakings used two big rivers, the Trent lead to London and the Severn leading to Bristol and the south-west. Medieval man was by no means tied to his native village. He moved probably in lesser numbers than modern man but as far as making a living was concerned for much the same reasons.

If mining in Cornwall had attracted our particular Blackwells it is quite possible that they came from Derbyshire and although this is a matter of concern and disappointment to a family who had hoped to have been Cornish from times of great antiquity, perhaps the fact that residence has been established for almost four hundred years will allow us to be accepted by the more fortunate originals

195

Now Hear The Word of the Lord

Earlier strangers came to Cornwall's shores during the fifth and sixth centuries. The siting of the church at St. Erth, adds credence to the stories of Saints, who came from Ireland, Wales and Brittany.

The Romans brought Christianity to these islands, and in spite of the invasions by the heathen Anglo-Saxons around A.D. 449 the spirit remained alive in the west, aided by the missionaries.

Coming from the Hayle estuary, St. Erth is only a mile or so inland, following the Hayle river towards its source of four brooks, joining to a main stream in the region of Relubbus, at St. Erth was the site chosen by the missionaries, to build a shelter of wood, trees being plentiful. Inside the rude construction, the sanctuary lay with an altar where mass was celebrated. Usually a granite cross would be carved, and set up outside the place of worship. Similar crosses are found in many parts of the county, and are known as Cornish, or Celtic crosses.

All this activity, would attract the local population, who would, naturally, gather around, to listen to the preacher. There must have been a similarity of language at the time, or perhaps actions spoke louder than words! In inclement weather, and there was surely an abundance of that, all who could, sheltered inside. So began the practice of attending church.

The church in St. Erth, like others built around the thirteenth and fourteenth centuries, was, in effect, the centre of life, recording baptisms, marriages and deaths. In the earlier registers, these were usually entered with little detail. For example, an entry in 1633 states simply "William Blackwell married Jane."

The church in St. Erth is pleasantly situated amidst agricultural country which produced wheat, barley and oats, as shown in the will of Thomas Blackwell, in 1719.

The building is in the perpendicular style of architecture and has a nave; the body of the church from the inner door to the Eastern part reserved for the clergy and choir, aisles, and tower porch with three bells. There are brass monuments of considerable interest of the ancient Davies, Giddy and Gilbert families.

The churchyard revealed no memorial to any of the Blackwell family, but there is a headstone to the memory of Major Herbert Carter, V.C., son of a former vicar. The Company he commanded during the Jidballi campaign in Somaliland was driven back by a troop of Dervishes who outnumbered them thirty to one, leaving behind a badly wounded Indian Sepoy who had lost his horse. Major Carter rode back alone four hundred yards, charged the Dervishes and after three attempts got the wounded Sepoy on his horse and brought him to safety. Major Carter died of fever in East Africa while preparing to attack the enemy at the beginning of the first world war.

By 1633, the year in which William Blackwell married his Jane, the St.Erth Church was about three hundred years old. From this marriage, three sons were born, John baptised 20 January 1633, William in November 1635, and Thomas in 1645. Some pages in the register are difficult if not impossible to read. At that time too, troubles were stirring in the country culminating in the civil war of 1642 - 1660 between King Charles I and his royalists and Oliver

Remembered in St. Erth Churchyard, Major Herbert Carter, V.C. and his father the Vicar. Major Carter, serving with the 101st Grenadiers, led a column to the relief of Mwele and Mdogo in Tanganyika, January 1916, sacrificing his life.

St. Erth Parish Church where William Blackwell was baptised in 1596 and where in 1633 he married Jane.

Cromwell's parliamentarians.

Many records were destroyed, mainly by Cromwell's forces and many old institutions were forbidden to continue, for instance, the church register of marriages which were now to be carried out by civil clerks. Confusion reigned. The year 1660 saw the return of the monarchy with Charles II as King. The Church of England was re-established and again became the centre of registering baptisms, marriages and deaths.

In 1672 Thomas Blackwell married a lady named Sidwell. The name occured in the sixteenth and seventeenth centuries for Cornish girls after St. Sidwell, the patron of Laneast Church near Launceston. Little or nothing is known about her, just as nothing more was mentioned about the wife of Thomas in spite of the fact that she bore five children, James 1672, Thomas 1676, Richard 1679, Margaret 1686, and Lidia 1688, all of whom were baptised in the church at St. Erth.

One interesting document remaining from that period is the inventory of the possessions of William 1635 - 1666. Born in St.Erth, he died in Phillack. How he earned his living is not known; his tools are not described, but the footnote shows his 'relicte' or widow to be named Edithe.

An inventory of all the goods of William Blackwal (1) of the Parish of (sic) in the Countye of Cornewall. Appraysed by Edward Ripper of Breage and Rich (ard) Harford of ye parish of Phillacke the 2nd day of May 1666:

Imprimis	his Apparell		5s	0d
Item	His bedding & bed (clothes)		6s	8d
,,	2 flaggons & 1 pinte		2s	6d
,,	5 pewter dishes		8s	0d
,,	2 pewter saltes & 1 pewter cupp		1s	0d
,,	1 Cubberte		2s	0d
,,	2 old keeves 2 barrells & 1 tubb		2s	0d
,,	1 Iron krocke & 1 brandise		2s	0d
,,	1 old bras pan & 1 old skillett		1s	6d
,,	his working tools		2s	0d
,,	1 table boord farme & forme		2s	0d
,,	dishes spoones & trenchers			6d
,,	for 2 Coffers		1s	0d
,,	for things for-gotten		1s	10d
		suma £1	18s	00

IN WITT (NESS)
ED: RIPPER
RICHARD HARFORD

PHILLACK

HELSTON 4 May 1666

INVENTORUM BONORUM WILLIAM BLACKWALL, DEF
SSA EST EDITHE EIUS RELICTE

From the third known generation of Blackwells in St. Erth, Thomas, who was baptised in 1676, married Priscilla Williams on 21 June 1698. He was a successful husbandman who, in addition to working hard at his calling, spent many happy hours frolicking in the hay, both before and after his marriage. Eight children were born by 7 March 1710. Thomas, the husbandman died in 1719, leaving a Will, dated 15 January 1719/20. The date is shown in this manner because prior to 1752, a year was calculated as beginning on 25 March and not 1 January, so that for example, a marriage on 20 February 1624 according to the ecclesiastical year, would have been in 1625 according to the civil year. To make matters clear, the date would be shown as 20 February, 1624/5.

The will of Thomas is of great value, showing his profession, his wealth, his children, more or less proving the continuance of the proper line of family descent in that particular instance and also his attitude toward his wife and family.

It reads:

In the name of God Amen the 15th day of January in the year of our Lord 1719/20. I Thomas Blackwell of St. Earth in the County of Cornwall husbandman being very sick and weak in Body but of perfect mind and memory thanks be given to God therefore calling unto mind the mortality of my Body and knowing that it is appointed for all men once to die I do make and ordaine this my last will and Testament that is to say princably and first of all I give and recommend my soull into the hands of God that gave it and for my body I recommend it to the Earth to be buried in Christian Like and decent manner at the discretion of my executors nothing doubting but at the general resurrection I shall receive the same again by the mighty power of God and as touching worldly goods whereof it hath pleased God to bless me with in this life I give devise and dispose of the same in the following manner and form.

Imprimes I give and bequeath to Priscilla my dearly beloved wife the sum of twelve pounds of good and Lawfull monys to be paid unto her if she mary or not mary, my executors are to pay her the sum aforesaid when they doe com of age If she goes of to live from them or at any time after if she goes live not with them

Item. I give to my well beloved sons John Blackwell and William Blackwell whom I likewise constitute and make and ordaine my only and sole Executors of this my Last Will and testament and all singular my goods and chattels movable and unmovable by them to be possessed and enjoyed and I do hereby utterly disallow revoke and disanull all and every other Testaments wills and Legacies Bequests and Executors by me in any way before this time above named.

Item. I give to my son Thomas Blackwell the sum of twenty shillings of good and Lawfull moneys to be paid by my executors

Item: I give to my son Richard Blackwell one shilling of silver to be paid to him by my executor

Item: I give to my daughter Lidda the sum of twenty shillings of good and Lawfull money to be paid by my executors

Item: I give to my daughter Mary Blackwell the summ of five pounds of good and Lawfull money when she comes to the age of twenty

Item: I give to my daughter Elizabeth the sum of five pounds of good and Lawfull monys when she comes to the age of one and twenty

Item: I give to my son Ambrose Blackwell the summ of five pounds of good and Lawfull monys when he comes to ye age of one and twenty and be kept to school to larn to Read and write and Sifer by my executors this and no other to be my last will and testament in witness whereof I have hitherto to set my hand and seall the day and year above written signed sealled published pronounced and declared by the said Thos Blackwell as his last will and testament in the presence of us the subscribers. Thos Hill Anne Hill. Follows a true and perfect Inventory of all and singular the goods and chattels Debts and Credits of Thomas Blackwell of the parish of St. Earth in the County of Cornwall labourer lately deceased taken and appraised by William Davies and Thomas Hill this 18 May 1720

two oxen	06-00-0
Two cows and three heifers	08-00-0
Two young bullocks of one year old and one of two years old and three rearing Calves	04-10-0
Five nags and Mares and three colts	14-00-0
Fifty small sheep and twenty lambs and some piggs	10-00-0
Five acres of wheat in the ground	05-00-0
About seven acres and a half of barley in the ground	10-00-0
About an acre and a half of oats in the ground	01-00-0
About two bushels of barley and some wheat in the Mowhay	03-10-0
Gees Ducks and other poultry	00-10-0
Husbandry Implements	01-10-0
His wearing apparel	01-00-0
One old feather bed and Rugg & blanketts	01-00-0
Two old soft beds and bed clothes	01-00-0
Some old pewter, two tables boards and some other houselod goods	01-00-0
Total	68-10-0

William Davies
Thomas Hill

Thomas was a farmer. In his will he was mentioned as a husbandman and also a labourer. He was not a poor man according to the inventory of his goods and chattels. He tried to ensure that his youngest son Ambrose attended school which must have been established in St. Erth at that time. The boy gained benefit from his education, becoming a yeoman in nearby Phillack where he possessed free land. Yeomen were middle-class farmers, many of whom joined the volunteer cavalry force ready to serve the country in time of war.

Thomas, an elder brother of Ambrose, was a husbandman who in 1730 moved to Crowan to marry Jane Webster. They raised eight children, among them the eldest boy, Thomas, born in 1732.

Copper mining was now establishing itself as an alternative source of employment and in the area the Crowan Downs mine was active, yielding rich copper as it had done for years. There was a demand not only for miners but also for men with mechanical ability such as blacksmiths. The result was that men were drawn away from the land to attend to the mechanics of the business. Thomas Blackwell became a mine blacksmith, beginning the line of men who progressed to engine fitters and mechanical engineers down to the present time.

His grandson, Francis, however, began his working life as a miner, given as his occupation at the baptism of his first children to 1836. He was obviously mechanically minded and was an engineman at Breage by 1840, but also worked for some years as a miner.

Francis Blackwell was born at Crowan in 1802. In 1822 he married Jenifer (Jane) Champion and their first children, Francis, 1822, and Henry, 1825, were born in the village. Later, the family began moving around Cornwall, dictated by the varying fortunes of the mines. Their progress can be charted by studying census returns from 1841 which showed Francis senior working at the St.Agnes tin mines and living at Rosemundy village. In 1842 he left there for the silver mines of Mexico where he was employed for many years as an engineman.

In 1841, his wife and seven children were living at Breage; housing problems would no doubt have prevented them moving to St.Agnes, but after Francis had gone overseas, she lived at Scorrier, near her son, Henry, who resided at Whitehall nearby, and mined at Gwennap before moving to the mines of St.Neot in the late 1840s.

The 1851 and subsequent census returns showed occupations and birthplaces. Children of Francis and Jenifer were born at Wendron 1827, Gwennap 1831, 1834 and 1836. In 1840, a son, Matthew, was born at Breage. This information was most important, because with the introduction in 1837 of a central office maintained by the Registrar General to record all births, marriages and deaths, a birth certificate was available giving his father's occupation and his mother's maiden name. This latter information was not usually included in church records, causing much confusion, for instance where there were two families, each with parents' and childrens' names being the same, and recorded at the same church in the same period of time.

This is highlighted by the fact that Francis Blackwell had a cousin in Crowan bearing the same name and who in 1818 married the seventeen year old Jenifer Rodda, with her parents' consent, and had a son, Henry, born in 1824.

Little wonder that Francis sailed off to Mexico and Jenifer called herself Jane and moved to Scorrier!

The Crowan family remained in the area and in the census returns of 1861 and 1871 Jenifer (Rodda), widow, is entered as the schoolmistress.

Alongside the growth of mining in the early nineteenth century, there appeared the "Royal Cornwall Gazette" and "West Briton" newspapers giving information increasingly concerned with everyday life, showing that much more was happening to the people than the births, marriages and deaths recorded in church registers around which the local population seemed to revolve. There were no record books for hunger, misery, hardship or pleasure but now, from the pages of these weeklys, glimpses of life in the early years are revealed.

During these years the familiar spectre of hunger was always present in

St Earth

19º Maij 1720º

Testamentum cum
Inven[tario] Bonorum de
Cujusdam Thoma
Blackwell nuper
de S¹ Earth in com[itatu]
forma coram m[agist]ro
Joh[ann]e Furs[ma]n Cl[er]o
officii &c

A true

Tho⁵ Blackwell

203

In the name of god Amen the 15th day of January in the
year of our Lord 1719 20 I Thomas Blackwell Earth
in the County of Cornwall yeoman being very sick and
weak in Body but of perfect mind and memory thanks
be given to god, therefore Calling unto mind the mortallity
of my Body and knowing that itt is appointed for all men
once to die doe make and ordaine this my Last will and
Testament that is to say primeably and first of all I give
and recommend my soull into the hands of god that gave it
and for my Body I recommend itt to the Earth, to be Buried
in a Christian Like and decent mannar, at the descression of
my Executtars nothing douting but at the genarall resurection
I shall receave the same againe by the mighty power of god
and as touching such worldly goods wherewith it hath pleasd
god to bless mee with in this life I give devise and dispose of
the same in the following mannar and form —

Imprimes I give and bequeath to priscilla my dearly Beloved
wife the summ of twelve pounds of good and Lafull monys
to be paid unto her if they marry or not marry my Executors are to pay her
the summ a fore said when they doe come of age if they goes of
the summ a fore from them or any any time after if they be nott with them
Item I give to my well Beloved sons John Blackwell
and william Blackwell whom I likewise constitue and
make and ordaine my only and solo Executors of this my
Last will and Testament and all singular my goods and
Chattels moveable or on engagge by them to be possessed and Enjoyed and soe hear
by utterly desallow, revoake and desanull All and every other
Testaments wills and Legasies Bequests and Exectors by mee
in any ways before this time named —

Item I give to my son Thos. Blackwell the summ of twelve
shillings of good and lawfull monys to be paid by Exectors
Item I give to my son Rihard Blackwell tone shilling of Silver
to be paid to him by my Executors
Item I give to my daughter Lidda the summ of twenty shi-
of good and Lafull monys to be paid by my Executors
Item I give to my daughter mary Blackwell the summ
five pound of good and lawfull mony when she comes to age
Elizabeth to be paid by my Exectors
of one and twenty Elizabeth the summ of five pound of good and
Item I give to my daughter to ye age of one and twenty the summ of
Lafull monys when she comes to ye age Item I give to my son Jno Blackwell
five pounds of good and lawfull monys when he comes to ye
age of one and twenty and to be kept to scool to Larne to
Read and write and Liser by my Execotrs other to be my Last will
and Testament in witness where of I have hether to set my
hand and Seall the day and year above written.
                                    Thos. Blackwell

Signed Sealled publshed
pronounced and declared by the
said Thos Blackwell as his last will
and Testament in the presone of us
the Subscribers. Thos. ffill Ann ffill

204

A true and perfect Inventory of all and singular the goods
and Chattels Debts and Creditts of Thomas Blackwall of the pish
of St Earth in the County of Cornwall Labourer lately deceased
taken and appraised by William Davies & Thomas Hill the
18th May 1720.

Imprs Two Oxen	06 = 00 = 0
Two Cows and three heifers	08 = 00 = 0
Two young bullocks of one years old and one of two years old and three wealing calves	04 = 10 = 0
Five Naggs and Mares and three Colts	14 = 00 = 0
Fifty small sheep and twenty Lambs and some piggs	10 = 00 = 0
Two acres of wheat in the ground	05 = 00 = 0
about seven acres and half of barly in the ground	10 = 00 = 0
about an acre and half of Oates in the ground	01 = 00 = 0
about two bushells of barly and some wheat in the Mowhay	03 = 10 = 0
Geese Ducks and other poultry	00 = 10 = 0
Husbandry Implements	01 = 10 = 0
His wearing Apparell	01 = 00 = 0
One old Featherbed and bead Rugg & Blanketts	01 = 10 = 0
Two old Dust beds & bedsteeds	01 = 00 = 0
some old pewter two table boards & some other houseild goods	01 = 00 = 0
Totall	68 = 10 = 0

Wm Davies

Thomas Hill

205

Fifthteenth Century Crowan Church where Eliza, first of the Crowan Blackwells, was baptised in 1702

Cornwall, and the scarcity of flour in 1812 prompted the Easter Sessions of the associated attornies of the County held in Truro…"to propose and unanimously resolve that during the present scarcity of corn - "We will not permit pastry or puddings of any kind of which flour shall form an ingredient to be made use of in our respective families, and that we will, in every other respect, as far as we possibly can, contribute to lessen the consumption of flour".

In Crowan in 1825, Thomas Rodda 20, a relative of Jenifer, was killed in the act of blasting a rock in his field, which he was clearing for the purpose of cultivating. It being dark when he began his work, it is supposed he applied the fire to the touch paper too near the hole.

By 1828 life took on a more cheerful appearance when it was announced that on Monday 12 May the following prizes would be rung for on the bells of the Parish of Crowan.

1) Six gold laced hats;
2) six white hats;
3) six silver laced hat bands.

Each set of ringers had to bring an umpire, and all questions were to be decided by the majority of umpires, but should they not agree, three others would be chosen by the parishioners of Crowan, whose decision would be final. The ringing was to commence at nine o'clock in the morning.

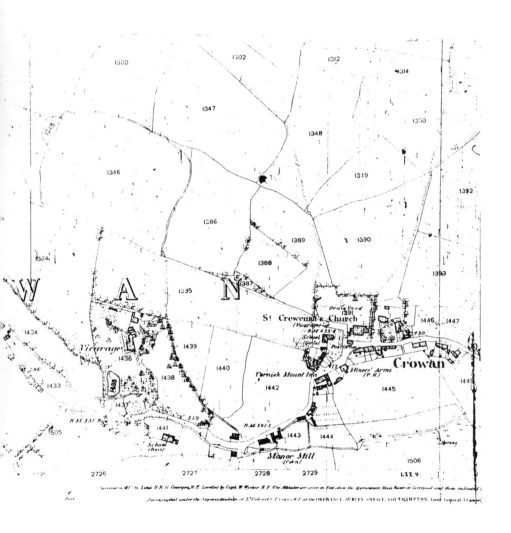

207

To Sᴿ. John Sᵗ Aubyn Barᵗ. this Western view of *Clowance* in the parish of Crowan̄,
Cornwall, engravd at his expence, is most gratefully inscribd by
WᵐBorl

Clowance

"Marriage solemnized in the Parish of Crowan in the County of Cornwall in the year 1818 Francis Blackwell of this Parish and Jenifer Rodda of this Parish were married in this Church by banns with consent of Parents this 30 day of November in the Year One Thousand eight hundred and 18 by me John St. Aubyn
Marriage solemnized between Francis Blackwell
and Jenifer Rodda - her mark in the presence of
John Davies and John Goldsworthy."

The great family of St. Aubyn lived in Clowance House near Crowan for 300 years. In the eighteenth century the Prime Minister said of Sir John Aubyn M.P. for Cornwall; "I know the price of every member of the house except the little Cornish Baronet".

XXVII

THE PEOPLE - WARRIORS

In the time of King Egbert, A.D. 835, the Cornish challenged the honour of leading the van in the day of battle; an honour which they had enjoyed in the days of Arthur.

In Canute's reign from 1016 to 1035, we find the Cornish bringing up the rear, which John of Salisbury attributed to their distinguished valour. The danger in the rear was then greater upon some remarkable retreat of Canute's army. The writer Lluyd calls the Cornish "the stoutest of the British nations" and says they "were deemed the most valiant in warlike affairs."

An anonymous writer in an eloquent and stirring poetical appeal to Cornishmen in November 1803, to resist to the death the threatened French invasion -

> "Chosen race! revolve the hour
> When to the foremost ranks your fathers ran
> And, amidst the arrowy shower,
> Flushed with indignant ardour, claimed the van
> Struck by the mailed gleams from glorys track
> All the Saxon tribes flew back;
> And where the chieftain strode
> Hail'd other Kaliburns that down a million mow'd
> Yea, the warriors' generous blood
> Hath mantled in your veins thro' every age
> Witness they whose might withstood
> In Cromwell's ominous days the rebel rage!
> Witness the trophied field where Granville bled
> Where, as knightly spirits fled,
> I mourned your falling sires
> And saw, yet undecayed, Cornubia's ancient fires."

Prince Arthur, son of King Henry VII, was a great admirer of the Cornish, and before his death at the early age of 16 in 1502 is said to have entertained so high an opinion of their prowess as always to place these chosen bands in front of his army and to have invariably found in their known character a sure presage of his own victory.

Alluding to these effects of their ferocious courage, independence, combination and perseverance, the causes of which he distinctly saw, Haivillan, a poet who flourished more than 650 years ago, thus described the giants of Cornwall -

> "Of Titans monstrous race
> Only some few disturb'd that happy place
> Raw hides they wore for clothes; their drink was blood,
> Rocks were their dining rooms, their prey their food
> Their cup some hollow trunk, their bed a grove
> Murder their sport and rapes their only love
> Their courage, frenzy; strength; their sole command

Their arms what fury offer'd to their hand
And when at last in brutish fight they died
Some spacious thicket a vast grave supplied
By such vile monsters was the land oppressed
But most the farthest regions of the west
   of them then Cornwall too
Wast plagued above the rest."

It cannot be said that outside their hours of toil and industry the lives of the Cornish were spent in listlessness and inactivity. Few were more active, enterprising or persevering. Their appearance has been remarked upon through the centuries... "The Cornish men are very strong, active and for the most part personable of good constitution of body and very valerous. They are masters of the art of wrestling, and this, written before the introduction of Olympics - so that if the Olympic games were now in fashion, they would come away with the victory. Their hug is a cunning close with their fellow combatants the fruits whereof are his fair fall or foil at least".

Richard Carew writing about the sport at the turn of the fifteenth century said...

"Wrestling is full of manliness. The continual exercise of the Cornish in this play has made them so skilfull that none can deprive them of their laurels. Spectators form a ring calling it a place into the middle of which two champion wrestlers step forth stripped to their doubtlets and untrussed that they might make better command of their limbs, and first shaking hands in token of friendship they fall presently to the effects of anger for each striveth how to overcome and take hold of the other with his best advantage and so to bear his adversary down, wherein whosoever overthrows his mate in such sort as that either his back or the one shoulder and contrary heel do touch the ground is accounted to give the fall.

If he be endangered and make a narrow escape, it is called a foil. Wrestling has its laws of taking hold above the girdle, wearing a girdle to take hold by, playing three pulls for the trial of the mastery, the fall given to be exempted from playing again with the taker and bound to pulls for the trial of the mastery, the fall given to be exempted from playing again with the taker and bound to answer to his successor. Many sleights and tricks appertain hereunto in which a skilful man will soon get the overhand of one that is strong and ignorant. Such are the trip, forehip inturn, the faulx forward and backward, the flying mare and many others."

Today wrestling is an almost forgotten art but it flourished in South Africa with the arrival of Cornish miners in the latter part of the nineteenth century. Interest in the sport continued into the years before the first world war. The redoubtable Sam Ham who hailed from Condurrow reigned as undisputed champion of the South African miners. There appeared no one experienced or strong enough to throw him until the arrival in Johannesburg of a young man still in his teens, named Alfred Williams, from the village of Beacon. Born 13 January 1889, he was the fifth son of Richard and Ellen who had returned from Michigan's copper country in 1882.

Alfred (Barney) Williams (1889 - 1943), Cornish miner and wrestler. (centre). Jagers Fontein Orange Free State, 1912.

Known affectionately as Barney to the Cornish community, he took up the challenge to wrestle Sam for the championship, The challenge was dismissed with scorn by the champion but to everyone's surprise, not least Sam's, after a long and hard-fought match when all the tricks of the trade, and a few more besides, where used, the crown changed hands. Barney emerged from the gruelling battle as the new Cornish wrestling champion amongst the miners of South Africa and was presented with a fine silver cup.

The former champion was not satisfied and had no intention of letting the youngster deprive him of his laurels for very long. A second match was arranged but the result was the same and this time Sam Ham conceded that he had met his master. Alfred Williams returned to Cornwall in time to serve his country in the Royal Navy where he continued wrestling whenever the opportunity presented itself. Barney was also a very useful rugby forward and played for Camborne before the first world war. Cornwall was a stronghold of the game and had been, almost from its inception in the nineteenth century. The Cornish excelled at the sport which had fired their imagination and produced many great exponents, some of whom became internationals of repute. There were many others equally worthy of an England cap but fortune could not favour all the brave.

The story of Cornish miners exporting their skills to the world is well known, but less so is the story of how they brought the game of rugby with them to fascinate the curious locals who, like the South Africans, soon became brilliant and a dominating force on the field.

Around the turn of the century, many miners made their impact on the African rugby scene and names including those of G. Bailey, J. Peters and S. Hosking who played for the Crown Reef team that won the Blane Cup in 1899, and T. Richards. A. Edwards, Fred Rodda, B. Thomas and W. C. Beckerley were members of Randfontein United when they won the Dewar Cup and Shield in 1909. And how many hours were spent in the bar of the Plough Inn, Camborne, during the 1930's by men long returned from the goldfields living again

Hovering, with eagle eye,
Sticklers circle straining men,
Then swoop to prod the vanquished
When shoulder, back and heel
Are by the victor pressed to earth

212

Founded 1930 - Chicago Southerns Rugby Club.
Front Row - Walter Mayne, Captain, with ball.
Standing - Second from end on right, Romney Timmins, known
as the giant from Camborne.

the great games played there. Who better to keep those memories alive than Bert Rodda, the landlord, a splendid character, rugged player and gentleman of the old breed whose like will never be seen again.

In the United States where large numbers of Cornish have lived over long periods, the game failed to kick off in spite of determined attempts by some very fine players, among them Walter Mayne. He did succeed to some extent and gathered the Cornish in Chicago, to form the club known as Chicago Southerns in the 1920's. The eldest son of Thomas and Florence Mayne, he was born in Beacon, Camborne, on Wednesday 21 January 1903. He played for Camborne and Cornwall in the twenties and in 1926 was chosen to play as a forward in an England trial game. In that year he was offered employment in Chicago and had no option but to decline the rugby invitation.

There were attempts to encourage the game of cricket in the States, but these were confined to a few English and Cornish lovers of the game. Cricket and rugby football have thrived into national games in almost every country and colony where the British made their presence felt with the exception of North America. Today there are exponents of the games in the United States and Canada but they are by no means the national pastimes.

Copper Country miners at the Pewabic mine were playing cricket in 1908, as the photograph seen in the Quincy hoist house shows...

C. Simmons, scorer; W. Brewer, long off; F. Nancarrow, long on;

213

Lillian Timmins, Cornish born daughter of Richard and Ellen Williams, baked a huge pasty in the form of a rugby ball. Everyone had a tasty piece.

215

(Previous Page)

The Randfontein United Rugby Football Team
1909
Winners of the Dewar Shield and Bailey Cup

Record: 218 points against 27

Insets: R. Eathorne, A. Difford, J. Cough.

Top row: L. to R. A. Edwards (sec.), W. T. Varker (VP), W. Walker, W. D. Hearne, T. Richards, A. (Fred) Rodda, E. P. Whelan, W. C. Beckerley, W. Pearce, A. Tippett, A. Lithgow (VP)

Middle row: J. B. Andrews (VP), C. Rothman, W. Pearce, C. A. Ferguson (President), R. Davey (Captain), B. G. Hambridge, A. E. Hosking (VP).

Bottom row: E. Thomas, mascot, T. M. Noll.

Fred Rodda, who was known as 'Doctor' to his friends was considered to be the finest forward in South Africa and when a member of the Camborne Club, played in a 1900 England International trial.

Below:
Fred's brother Herbert who also played for the Randfontein Club is shown seated second from the left in the 1902 - 3 Camborne Football Team.
Their brother Nick played for Cornwall on four occasions during the 1918/19 season and in two England trials in 1919.

Camborne Football Team, 1902 - 1903.

E. Pascoe, mid off; F. Nancarrow, sen., Umpire; A. Hooper, mid on; M. J. Commons, cover point; William Taylor, square leg; A. Curnow, point; J. Osborne, slips; P. Hoare, wicket keeper; Richard Menear, capt., bowler; W. Easterbrook, long stop.

The Detroit side of the late 1920's came from the Camborne, Cornwall area....

Jack Williams, R. Trevithick, J. Williams, Richard Williams, W. Toy, E. Williams, Joe Kitto, L. Sullivan, Pat Selwood, T. Tresidder, Sam Davies, Trewhella.

Impact - Cornish Style

In Carson City, Nevada, on Wednesday, 17 March 1897, cheered on no doubt by many Cousin Jack miners, a Cornishman, Bob Fitzsimmons, the blacksmith from Helston, delivered his hammer blow to the heart of 'Gentleman' James C. Corbett, laying him low in the fourteenth round and thus gaining the world heavy weight boxing crown, an accomplishment never equalled by a British boxer. Bob Fitzsimmons, with his spindly legs, was a phenomenal fighter and the only man ever to win world boxing titles at three different weights; all the more remarkable when taking into account his slight build. The power in his left hand which had only to travel six inches before impact, was devastating, and the rushing noises in an opponent's head and ears must have sounded like an anvil's ring.

There are times when an exile feels the call of home which will not be denied, and nothing can describe the feelings of a returning Cornish traveller when crossing the bridge over the Tamar, sighting Carn Brea and at long last drawing into the home railway station, be it Camborne or Redruth or any other in the Duchy.

Not all returned but among those who did and relived the heady days of a fine sporting past was a great rugby forward.

Camborne - Redruth Cameo...

Former Rugby Football Forward Returns

Walter Mayne's Visit Home

'Camborne's all right, thank goodness. The town and its people have not changed at all.'' Nothing fulsome about this compliment, but it is a sound, sincere one which goes to the heart of things, and if an exile can come home after 35 years' absence and make this comment quite sincerely, then there cannot be much wrong with the town or its people.

For this was the verdict of stalwart Walter Mayne at the end of his brief three weeks' stay - the first in this country since he left Camborne for Chicago, U.S.A. in 1926. He had brought over his American wife to visit his folks, quite a few of them, including his mother, now 84, in Beacon. And Walter is a man well-qualified to discuss his home town - he was very close to the centre of its sporting and social life before he emigrated to the States.

So close, indeed, that after he had seen his old team play Teignmouth a week ago, his former team mates put on a "smoker" for him at the White Hart. For Walter Mayne is still remembered for his hard sporting work as a back row forward for Camborne and Cornwall in the earlier 20's. In those days he was developing the winging forward technique so popular today and was

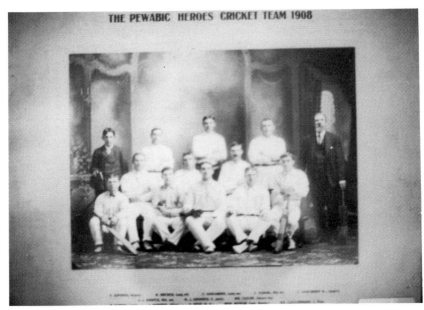

THE PEWABIC HEROES CRICKET TEAM 1908

Cousin Jack cricketers, Copper Mines of Quincy, Pewabic.

Detroit, Michigan in the 1920's. From mining to the motor industry. Standing far right of back row, Richard Williams, born Franklin, Copper Country, 1880.

218

making a particularly good job of it.

"What a pleasure it was to spend Saturday evening playing those old games over again," he told me the day before he left to return to Chicago. "I don't reckon any other town than Camborne could have kept almost the whole of that team together after 35 years. The same spirit is there and they are as fine a bunch of boys as when I left them for the States."

Those "boys" included some of the well-known names in Camborne's football history. They had staged the evening for Walter's benefit to remind him how much they appreciated his play and companionship in the old days. he had been a brilliant fast forward and played 11 games for the county - just missing his county blazer by one game. From what he told me he did not forget the game when he crossed the water. Chicago was just beginning to think of playing rugby football at its university, and with several other amateur clubs starting up they wanted men who could show them just how the game should be played. Walter Mayne helped to show them as other Cornishmen - notably George Jago - showed the handling code to other parts of America. Jago helped introduce the game to Yale, Walter told me.

The Reason Why

Walter became captain of one of the Chicago clubs - another good instance of Cornishmen knowing the reason why and illustrating it effectively in distant parts of the world. It was probably this Cornish determination with its Camborne pride in not giving up that kept Mr. Mayne in the States during the depression from 1929 onwards. He kept working - with the valve engineering firm he has stayed with to the present day and where he now holds a responsible position which sends him to many states and may well bring him back to England in the future.

Those depression days were not easy, and Mrs. Mayne explained that those who kept working maybe only two days a week were often worse off than their neighbours on relief. But they saw it through, even though they were then raising a young family of son and daughter. "It taught us and them the value of money," she said.

Walter agreed. He had heard a great deal in recent years of the British Welfare State ideas, but had not realised what they meant to the ordinary working man and his family. Now he does, and it had surprised him and in a way, made him somewhat envious of our way of life.

"You people are now growing up with the idea of security as a certainty," he said. "We don't have that in the States. Folks either spend too much time worrying about the uncertainty of the future and old age or they just do nothing about it and then it suddenly hits them and hits them hard. Home here you don't have to worry about your retirement or sickness. Doctors' bills for the family just don't mean a thing to you. And again, over here, or around Camborne anyway, there is far less of this 'keeping up with the Joneses.' Looks to me if your neighbour has an automobile and you haven't you just say 'Good Luck to him'. Over in the States you feel you just have to have one that's bigger and better."

Warm Welcome

Mrs. Mayne, an American, said "I could not have had a better welcome. What struck me so much was the warmth of it. Sometimes when you go some

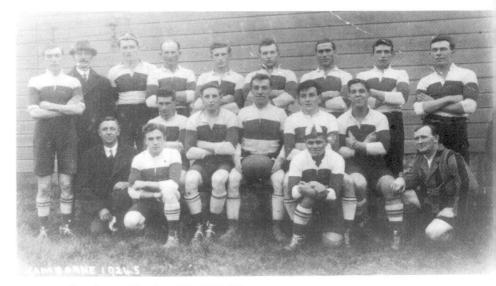

Camborne Rugby XV, 1924-25:
R. Hunt, Dick Holman, W. T. Biddick, T. Harvey, J. Carter, Bob
Warren, H. Wakeham, F. Selwood, W. Mayne.
Seated: F. Barnard, R. Parnell, G. Thomas, P. Collins, C. Rogers.
Front: Hodge, B. Tremelling, Darkie Rogers, Visiting referee.

place for the first time you get an over-hearty greeting just meant to give a good impression. In Camborne and everywhere we've been in Cornwall they really mean it."

And what did our exile think of Camborne's changes? "There aren't many," he said. "I miss the old Commercial, and the Tyacks Hotel corner is opened out but apart from that the town hasn't changed at all. And I can tell you something that hasn't changed, though some of your townsfolk today don't seem to appreciate it. I watched Camborne play football on Saturday and I can say from my own experience that they are just as good as ever we were. They have the speed and the courage and the will to play good football. But they want encouragement, and if you don't give them that then you can't expect a winning record. So I say to Camborne folk 'Get down there and give the lads some support. They deserve it."

Though a visitor for the first time, Mrs. Mayne knew of one change. "Walter used to take pride in the fact that he could run all the way home up Camborne hill," she said. "Now he has to walk it."

Our one-time brilliant winging forward agreed ruefully. "To tell the truth, there are times when I think of taking a rest on the seat half-way up," he said. "But I've managed to resist it this trip."

Retirement may come in the next few years, and then we can expect to see more of Mr. and Mrs Walter Mayne in Camborne-Redruth. In the meantime they are taking back happy memories and will be just the same as other exiles going back to the U.S.A. after a Cornish visit - monopolising the conversation among fellow Cornishmen they might meet in talking about "home."

The Twenty Third Psalm

The Lord is my shepherd: I shall not want. He maketh me to lie down in green pastures: he leadeth me beside the still waters. He restoreth my soul: he leadeth me in the paths of righteousness for his name's sake. Yea though I walk through the valley of the shadow of death, I will fear no evil: for thou art with me; thy rod and thy staff they comfort me. Thou preparest a table before me in the presence of mine enemies, thou anointest my head with oil; my cup runneth over. Surely goodness and mercy shall follow me all the days of my life; and I will dwell in the house of the Lord forever.

In Memory of

WALTER L. MAYNE Sr.

BORN	**PASSED AWAY**
Jan. 21, 1903	Feb. 25, 1981
England	Chicago Heights, Il.

SERVICES AT

Steger Memorial Chapel
Friday, Feb. 27, 1981
10:00 A.M.

OFFICIATING

Rev. Earl Ferguson

INTERMENT

Skyline Memorial Park
Monee, Illinois

221

The People - The Intellectuals

The Cornish, in addition to their physical bravery and prowess, were, in many instances, people of remarkable intellect and learning. Many too, had abilities and gifts in the arts and science. Their names are well known, among them Borlase, the historian, Neville Northey Burnard, the sculptor; a great master of his craft; Sir Humphry Davy, the inventive scientist, Richard Lander, the explorer from Truro, John Opie, the Cornish Wonder, who painted the portraits of the great and the vain.

There were others, equally as brilliant, but lesser known to most, such as John of Cornwall, a student at Rome and other universities in Italy who wrote about the Incarnation of Christ, dedicating it to Pope Alexander III, by whom he was highly favoured.

The Archbishop of York and Chancellor of England, in the reign of Edward I, was William de Grenefeld, and another Cornishman, Michael Tregury, was the Archbishop of Dublin, in the time of Henry VI. He was so famous for his learning, before he was raised to this exalted post, that he had previously been appointed Governor of the university at Caen, in Normandy. In the time of Henry VII, John Arundel, became Bishop of Coventry and Lichfield. Sir Jonathan Trelawney was Bishop of Winchester, and Simon Thurnay, who having obtained to a great eminency in learning at Oxford, went and studied Divinity at Paris, and became one of the most celebrated Doctors of the Sorbonne.

The translation of the Bible in the reign of Richard II owes much to John Trevissa, Edward VI library keeper, and Dean of Chicester was Bartholomew Traharon while finally, Charles Herle was Prolocutor of the Assembly of Divines and Rector of Winnick in Lancashire, the greatest parsonage in England. It is obvious from these brief mentions that Cornwall had the ability to produce sons of genius in the field of learning and the arts. It also produced men of perception able to utilise the natural tin and copper resources of the county and to apply mechanical knowledge in its production. All this casts doubt on the verdicts of some historians and writers who portrayed Cornwall in a much more primitive and savage light, or is it, that over the centuries until comparatively recent times there were several sides to the lives of the people of the county and that divisions of culture were indeed very sharply defined.

School for all

Towards the latter part of the nineteenth century, education was becoming available, and indeed compulsory, for all children. More villages and towns were being provided with schools for infants from the ages of four to eight, at which time they would progress to the elementary school. There were some schools where children would be educated from infancy right through to the age of fourteen, this was free but compulsory. At many board meetings instructions were issued to send letters to parents requesting them to send their children to school. Sampson Keast was **requested** to send his children to school by the Chairman of the board of St. Allen school at Zelah in 1878.

In February 1880, the school board advertised in the 'West Briton'..."Wanted, a Certificated Mistress for the board school (mixed) at Zelah. Accommodation for 110 children. Application in the handwriting of the candidate, stating age, experience, and salary required, accompanied by testimonials, to be sent on, or before, 24 March to Fras Truscott, clerk."

Punishment at school varied in its application. One lady teacher was reprimanded for making children, who fidgeted in class, to sit, precariously balanced, on a mantlepiece where any further fidgeting or swinging or dangling of legs, would cause the poor unfortunate to crash to doom in the fireplace below. How many burnt offerings were made, before the practice ceased, we are not informed.

Many of the pupils at the Zelah school were from the farming community, although the village was recognised as a township and had many houses. It was, and still is today, a farming area. Crops of wheat, barley, oats and turnips were the mainstay of the area in the mid-nineteenth century, from an acreage of about 3200. There were some mining families in the area, and these too, maintained smallholdings, especially when a mine opened up in the vicinity and one of the miners married a farmer's daughter, the pair would combine their skills for the benefit of the family.

When the Zelah school opened its doors in the 1870's, the population catered for was probably nearing a thousand. The township was and still is in the Parish of St. Allen with its own village on the river of the same name. St. Allen has a church, dedicated to St. Alleyn, but in 1859, Zelah also settled for the Wesleyan Chapel.

There were few activities involving the use of the school after normal hours, but in 1899, it was proposed and resolved that the school should be granted to Mr. Thomas for two nights a week, for the purpose of practising for a Fyfe and Drum Band about to be started in September.

The school no longer exists but the building has been converted into a dwelling house.

Among the first to attend the new school were the three children of Henry and Eliza Blackwell, Annie, Henry and Charles.

Henry senior was born in Whitehall, Scorrier, in 1846, the son of a miner working at Gwennap. Before 1851, the family moved to St. Neot in the Liskeard mining area, where the boy was brought up surrounded by mines, miners and great engines. He entered the industry when very young, becoming involved in the running of the engine houses, probably helping the greasers, fetching tools and gradually absorbing the knowledge and practical experience to operate, maintain and install the great pieces of machinery. By 1861, after his father had returned to Liskeard and mining after working on the Saltash railway bridge, they were both employed as engine men. The boy was just 14.

In 1859 the West Chiverton lead mine at Perranzabuloe began operating and in the 1860's, Henry came to live at Allet, nearby, and worked as an engineman at the mine. By 1870 he was the mining engineer's assistant, and in 1875 became mine engioneer.

Eliza Keast also lived at Allet; she was a daughter of James and Maria, farmers from St. Allen. In 1867 Henry and Eliza married at Kenwyn Parish Church and moved to the nearby hamlet of Cost-Is-Lost, about two miles to the north from Allet. There were only three or four homes in the vicinity and these were occupied by farmers or smallholders. Eliza managed the smallholding and Henry carried on working in the mine. This was not an uncommon practice in Cornwall. Four of their children were born in Cost-Is-Lost. In 1879 the West

No.	Year	Month	Day	Child's Name (Christian and Surname)	If Baptized (When)	Parent/Guardian Name	Address	Occupation
1	78	7	1	John Borlase		John Borlase	Zelah P. Hill	Carpenter
2	78	7	1	Eliza Borlase		"	"	"
3	78	7	1	Chas Henry Hore				
4	78	7	1	Edwin Saundry		Henry Saundry	Zelah	Bootmaker
5	78	7	1	Chas Henry Saundry		"	"	"
6	78	7	1	Lilley Nance		John Nance	"	Carpenter
7	78	7	8	Agnes Arthur		Jane Hosking	Lane	Shop keeper
8	78	7	1	Matilda Ann Rowe			"	
9	78	7	8	Edith Lampshire		Fanny Lampshire	"	
10	78	7	1	William John Tremayne				
11	78	7	1	Emma Jose		John Jose	Zelah	Carrier
12	78	7	1	John Jose		" "	"	"
13	78	7	1	Ellen Jose		" "	"	"
14	78	7	1	Catherine Flamma				
15	78	7	12	Georgina Rawlings		John Rawlings	Zelah	Bootmaker
16	78	7	1	Alfred James Seymour		Alfred Seymour	"	Grocer
17	78	7	1	Elizabeth Letcher		John Letcher	"	Smith
18	78	7	1	Kate Letcher		" "	"	"
19	78	7	1	John Letcher		" "	"	"
20	78	7	1	Charles Letcher				
21	78	7	1	Laura Jane Coom		James Coom	Hendra	Miner
22	78	7	1	Mary Eliza Coome		" "	"	"
23	78	7	1	Elizabeth Ann Coome				
24	78	7	1	Sydney Cock		James Cock	Tolcarne	Farmer
25	78	7	1	Ellen Cock		" "	"	"
26	78	7	1	Henry Blackwell		Chas Blackwell	Zelah	Engineer
27	78	7	1	Charles Blackwell		Chas Blackwell	Zelah	Engineer
28	78	7	1	Annie Blackwell		"	"	"
29	78	7	1	Ellen J Lampshire		Fanny Lampshire	"	
30	78	7	1	Stephen Lampshire		" "	"	
31	78	7	1	Edith Chapman		Richard Chapman	Downs Hill	Miner
32	78	7	1	Ada Chapman		" "	" "	"
33	78	7	1	Richard H Chapman				
34	78	7	2	Bessie Lean		John Lean	Bolitan	Labourer
35	78	7	2	Susan Lean		" "	"	"

224

No.	Date of Admission Year	Month	Day	Child's Name (Christian and Surname)	If Baptized (when)	Child's Parent or Guardian Name	Address	Occupation
348	89	7	1	Gregory John	✓	Thomas	60, Acres	Labourer
349	89	7	15	Tresail Elizabeth Jane	—	Charles	Hosken's Moor	Labourer
350	89	7	22	Arthur Richard Henry	—	Richard	Rose Hill	Farmer
351	89	8	19	Sandry George Fred	—	Thomas Henry	Lane	Shoemaker
352	89	10	7	Gill Richard Phillips	—	William Nicholas	Terise	Farm
353	89	10	21	Gregory William	—	Thomas	60, Acres	Labourer
354	89	11	26	Gill William	—	William Nicholas	Terise	Farmer
355	89	11	25	Gill Reginald	—	"	"	"
356	89	11	12	Tamblyn Beatrice	—	John	Tregard Farm	"
357	89	9	12	Curtis Samuel	—	Samuel	Place Barton Arms	Miner
358	90	2	3	Downell Joseph	—	James	Rhuan	B.Smith
359	90	3	25	Parker Alice Mary	—	Samuel	St. Allen	Gardener
360	90	4	14	Hamann R. Albert Vici	—	George Henry	Lane	Miner
361	90	4	28	Hamann R. Alice Clara	—	William John	"	Labourer
362	90	4	29	Tremayne John Henry	—	William	St. Allen	"
363	90	5	7	Lawer James Hy.	✓ —	Charles	Lower Down	"
364	90	12	7	Lawer Ernest	—	"	"	"
365	90	5	7	Lawer Syaney	—	"	"	"
366	90	5	7	Lawer Arthur	—	"	"	"
367	90	15	19	Hoskin Louie	—	William	Lane	Carpenter
368	90	5	20	Benny Fanny	—	John	Downs Hill	Hind
369	90	6	2	Tamblyn Clara Maud	—	John	Tregard Farm	Farmer
370	90	6	2	Lanyon Albert Cornelius	—	Albert Cornelius	Lower Down	Farmer
371	90	6	2	Lanyon John Henry	—	"	Trevalso	"
372	90	6	9	Symons John Thomas	—	John	Wheal Francis	Labourer
373	90	6	9	Lanyon Louisa	—	Sarah	Newlyn	Shop Keeper
374	90	6	16	Ball Jethro Molesworth Rogelly	—	James	Lane	Labourer
375	90	7	7	Blackwell Alfred Ernest	—	Harry	Zelah	Engineer
376	90	7	9	Ball Lilian Harriet	—	William Thomas	Two Bors	Miner
377	90	7	14	Bunt Fred John	—	Frederick	Little Water	Farmer
378	90	10	20	Lanyon Mabel	—	Sarah	Newlyn	Shop Keeper
379	90	11	17	Jewell Janie	—	John	Lane	Butcher
380	90	11	17	Jewell Ada E	·	John	Lane	Butcher
381	91	1	5	Jewell William J	—	"	"	"
382	91	1	5	Heard Ann Maria	—	Samuel	Zelah	Labourer

Zelah Board School Admissions Register, 1889

Ladock Churchyard - burial place of Henry and Eliza Blackwell.

Chiverton mine closed down and shortly afterwards the family moved to Bowling Green a short distance away and very close to Zelah in the parish of St. Allen. Bowling Green farmhouse was reached through a lane leading off from the left of the main road from Redruth that passed through Zelah and on to Bodmin.

After the closing of the West Chiverton mine, Henry Blackwell worked on other mines, installing engines, and in connection with these activities, he spent some time at Harveys engineering works in Hayle during the time that they were constructing the boilers and other machinery for Cornish and overseas mines.

Some time before 1884, Henry had gone to India to install mining machinery and boilers. Large mineral resources had been discovered in the southern parts of India, including vast quantities of copper. Gold had also been discovered in the Neilgherry Mountains and at least fifty-seven localities had been found in the Assam and the western provinces of the country. Because of his association with Harveys at this time, it must be assumed that the equipment was supplied by them. It is known that Blackwell and four other Europeans made the journey with the machinery and were involved in hauling it, including the steam boilers, to the mine site using oxen and elephants. During the time it took to reach the location, three of the men died from the dreaded cholera. Blackwell himself suffered an attack of the disease and lost the sight of his right eye.

Returning to Cornwall in 1884 by steamer, the ship called in at Aden to take on coal. The captain, knowing of this particular passengers discomfort, advised him to go ashore to see the local doctor. This one, an Arab gentleman,

Allet Common looking towards Zelah and Chiverton Mine. In a
hundred years the scene has changed but little.

Cost Is Lost today. Almost as it was in the beginning.

Zelah Day School opened in the 1870's, is now a dwelling house, 1982.
Carved over the window "St. Allen Primary School 1878."

Zelah Chapel still going strong since 1859.
Where the Blackwell and Keast families worshipped.

whose qualifications were better suited to witchcraft, solemnly advised that he could cure the sickness by taking sight from the good eye, and by the will of Allah, make it shine from the evil eye. The good eye, being strong, would suffer no ill effects and all would be well.

How he proposed to perform this optical miracle he did not reveal. Henry's one good eye was sufficient for him to see through the doctor's dubious reasoning. He returned to the ship and sailed home to Cornwall.

In September 1885, after an interval of ten years, Henry and Eliza had their last child, Alfred Ernest. In July 1890 he was admitted to Zelah school. In June 1900 his mother fell ill and the family moved to 4, Railway Terrace, Grampound Road, where Eliza died on 31 July 1900 in the home of her daughter Annie Warne from the effects of typhoid fever. She was buried in Ladock churchyard.

Being the younger child and the only one now at home, Alfred had a close and loving relationship with his parents. This was revealed in the pathos of the story told when his father, because of a serious lung infection, was advised to leave the damp Cornish scene and live in the beneficial climate of South Africa. When Henry was about to leave, the young boy in misery 'ran out into the fields of Zelah, lay down and cried'.

Although the nineteenth century had seen great improvements in the mechanisation of the mines and the extensive use of steam power enabling greater depths to be worked, it became increasingly apparent that the great days of Cornish mining were doomed to shorten and, with few exceptions, die. Some people clung desperately to the hope that all would be well continuing to occupy themselves in the industry and directing the energies of their families to working in the mines. One advantage of this was that a large work force was available to man the growing industry in other parts of the world when the local mines closed down.

There were others who saw the precarious situation and diverted their sons into other activities. Henry Blackwell arranged for his sons Henry, Charles and Alfred in their turn to be indentured with Messrs. Cox and Company at Falmouth dockyard as engineering apprentices, and he too became employed as an engine fitter.

In 1901 Alfred began his apprenticeship and lived at No. 10, New Street, Falmouth with his brother Henry and his wife Jane but on finishing his time at the docks in 1907 decided to work as a journeyman at the Carn Brea works of R. Stephens and Son, makers of the famous "Climax" rock drill.

In Camborne he lodged in Dolcoath Road and soon after met and became engaged to Elizabeth Mary Williams from Beacon. She was the daughter of Richard Pearce and Ellen Williams who had returned from the copper mining area of Keweenaw in 1882. The wedding was planned but before the happy event in 1908 Cornwall won the rugby championship of England by defeating Durham at Redruth, celebration postcards telling,"from every town in England crowds came to witness the famous victory".

Among them was Henry Blackwell, a personal friend of the Jackett family of Falmouth. E. J. Jackett the famous international full back was playing that day. Henry was a rugby enthusiast, a sober mild-mannered gentleman, whose only vice was to enjoy a glass or two of ale on a Saturday evening in one of Falmouth's hotels.

Falmouth Docks with Pendennis Castle on the hill, 1890.

Falmouth No. 2 and No. 3 dry docks. Steam and sail, 1900.

Henry Blackwell, 1846-1911. Returned from India with a fevered eye.

His wife Eliza, 1844-1900. Typhoid victim.

This Indenture made the twenty third day of December in the year One Thousand Nine Hundred and Two *(hereinafter* **Between** Alfred Ernest Blackwell *referred to as "the said Apprentice")* and Henry Blackwell of the one part and **COX & COMPANY**, of Falmouth aforesaid, Engineers, Founders, Boiler Makers, and Iron Ship-builders *(hereinafter referred to as the said Masters)* of the other part **Witnesseth** that the said Apprentice of his own voluntary accord and by and with the consent of the said Henry Blackwell his Father testified by the said Henry Blackwell being a party to and executing these presents **Doth** put and bind himself apprentice to and with the said masters to learn the art, trade, or business of

An Engine Fitter & Turner Co the

and to serve the said Masters in the same until the full end and term of 5 years 1 month to be computed from the ninth day of September One Thousand Nine Hundred and One and fully to be completed and ended **And** the said Henry Blackwell and the said apprentice do hereby for themselves jointly and severally and for their respective heirs, executors, and administrators, covenant with the said masters in manner following — **That** during the whole of the said term the said apprentice shall and will faithfully serve the said masters as an apprentice in the said art, trade, or business of

An Engine Fitter & Turner Co the

and shall and will be true just and faithful to the said masters, and shall not absent himself from the service of the said masters unlawfully, nor shall he without the previous consent of the masters make or cause to be made for his own use or for the use of any other person than the masters any copy, tracing, abstract or extract of or from any plans, drawings, specifications or documents of the masters, but will cheerfully and readily obey all the lawful and reasonable commands of the said masters and every of them and in all things as an honest and faithful apprentice shall and will demean and behave himself towards the said masters and every of them during all the said term; **And** that the said Henry Blackwell shall and will provide the said apprentice with board and lodging, clothing, and all other necessaries during the said term. **And** the said masters in consideration of the premises and also in consideration of the sum of _____ pounds on or before the execution of these presents paid to the said masters by as and by way of premium (the receipt whereof the said masters hereby acknowledge) covenant as well with the said Henry Blackwell as with the said apprentice that they the said masters shall and will during the term of the said apprenticeship teach and instruct or cause to be taught and instructed the said apprentice in the art, trade, or business of

An Engine Fitter

paying him as wages One shillings per week for the first year Two shillings for the second year and so on rising one shilling per week for each succeeding year of the said term, **Provided always** and it is hereby expressly agreed by and between the said parties hereto that if the said apprentice shall at any time during the said term wilfully disobey any lawful and

reasonable command of the said masters or either of them or shall unlawfully absent himself from the service of the said masters during the regular or ordinary times or time of working without their consent or shall commit any breach of any other of the covenants on the part of the said apprentice hereinbefore contained then and in any or either of the cases aforesaid it shall be lawful for the said masters either of them or any person authorised by them or him in that behalf to dismiss the said apprentice from their employment and to cancel and determine these presents and the contract hereby created without returning any part of the said premium of _____ pounds which shall remain the property of the said masters.

And it is hereby agreed mutually by and between the said parties hereto that in case the said apprentice shall at any time or times during the said term be absent from his work by reason of sickness, accident, or any other cause, then and in every such case he the said apprentice shall not be entitled to receive any wages for or in respect of any day or days or part thereof during which he shall be so absent from his work as aforesaid. **And** further that he shall after the expiration of the said term serve such additional time as he shall during the said term have been absent from his work as aforesaid and shall only be entitled to receive therefore such wages as he would have been entitled to have received in respect of the days or respective days or part thereof for which such additional time shall be substituted. **And** further that in case the said apprentice shall be required at any time during the said term to work for his masters after the usual hours at which the workmen leave work in the afternoon he the said apprentice shall be paid for such overtime at the rate of wages &c. as provided for in the printed Rules and Regulations of the Firm.

Provided always that the said apprentice shall not be entitled to be paid for any such overtime unless and until he shall have worked and made up his full number of hours during the current week it being the intention of the said parties that any deficiency in the regular or ordinary times or hours of working may be set off against such overtime as aforesaid until such deficiency shall be made up. **And** further that the said apprentice shall be allowed the usual hours for meals allowed to the workmen engaged in the factory. **Provided always** and it is hereby lastly agreed that where the context allows the expression "the said masters" includes the survivors and survivor of them and their or his assigns and future partners or partners or other the persons or person for the time being carrying on their said Trade or Business.

In Witness whereof the said parties to these presents have hereunto set their hands and seals the day and year first herein-before written

Signed sealed and delivered by the above-named
Alfred Ernest Blackwell
Henry Blackwell
in the presence of
Henry Blackwell Junr
10 New Street
Falmouth
And by the above-named Cox & Co.
in the presence of
W. S. Reginald Phillips
6 Killigrew Street
Falmouth.

Alfred Ernest Blackwell
Henry Blackwell
Cox & Co.

232

URES

CONTRACTORS BY APPOINTMENT TO
ADMIRALTY & WAR DEPARTMENT.
FALMOUTH DOCKS IRONWORKS
ENGINEERS
COX & Cº
FOUNDERS
BOILER MAKERS & SHIP BUILDERS

GRAVING DOCKS. ADJOINING ABOVE WORKS.
T X 71 FT X 22 FT DEEP & 350 FT X 50 FT X 14 FT.

ALL LETTERS TO BE ADDRESSED TO THE COMPANY.
TELEGRAPHIC ADDRESS ——" COX."
NATIONAL TELEPHONE Nº 18.

Falmouth.

13th. April 1907

We have pleasure in stating that
Mr Alfred E. Blackwell has served
with us as an apprentice Fitter & Turner
for over 5 years, and during the last
six months as a journeyman.
We can recommend him as a steady
and good workman, and we understand
he is leaving us to better himself

Signed Herbert H. Cox
M I. Mech. E.
Engr. Manager
Cox & Co

CODES USED:-

BROOMHALL.

WESTERN UNION
TELEGRAPH.

MOREING AND
Mc CUTCHEON.

MOREING & NEAL.

A.B.C. 4TH EDITION.

A.B.C. 5TH EDITION.

AGENTS:-

SOUTH AFRICA.
Wm HOSKEN & Co
JOHANNESBURG
BOX 667.

WEST AUSTRALIA.
GEO.ALEX.BURKETT.
WELD CHAMBERS.
St GEORGES TERRACE.
PERTH. W.A.

R.STEPHENS & SON,

MAKERS AND PATENTEES OF

THE CLIMAX ROCK DRILLS.

(13 PRIZE MEDALS.)

LONDON REPRESENTATIVES:-
WILFLEY MINING MACHINERY Co.
SALISBURY HOUSE.
LONDON WALL, E.C.

CARN BREA, 2nd Octr. 1909.
CORNWALL.

TO WHOM IT MAY CONCERN.

This is to certify that Mr. Alfred Blackwell has been in our employ since the 29th May 1907, as Lathesman, and during that period we have found him to be a good time-keeper, sober and industrious, and we have pleasure in recommending him as a first class workman.

We understand he is leaving our employ, for a position abroad, and he has our best wishes for his future success.

H.W.

R. Stephens Son.

234

Falmouth Docks Apprentices, 1907, and others.
Photo by Anthony Belleti who had a photographer's business
just outside the dockyard gates.
Alfred Blackwell, centre front row.

1908 - Rooms in Dolcoath Road after serving his engineering
apprenticeship at Falmouth Docks.

The gateway to Bowling Green, near Zelah.

Bowling Green farmhouse where Alfred Ernest Blackwell was born, 2nd September, 1885.

He chose the day of the great game to visit his son Alfred and Elizabeth Mary by first setting out very early in the morning and walking from Falmouth to Redruth. After the match he walked to Beacon to spend the night at Tolcarne Road in the home of his future daughter-in-law. On Sunday he walked back to Falmouth.

The wedding of Alfred and Elizabeth Mary took place in the Wesley Chapel, Camborne, in 1908 with the Cornish Post and Mining News telling the story in the quaint style of the day...

"A very pretty wedding was solemnised at the Wesley Church, Camborne, on Saturday last. The contracting parties were Mr. Alfred Blackwell and Miss Elizabeth Mary Williams, second daughter of Mr. Richard Williams, of Tolcarne Road, Beacon. The Rev. W. N. Briggs officiated. The bride who was prettily attired in a creme blouse with a navy blue skirt and hat to match, was given away by her brother (Mr. W. J. Williams). The bridesmaid was Miss Lillian Williams (sister of the bride), who was tastefully attired in a dress of white, with hat to match. After the ceremony a large number sat down to luncheon at the residence of the bride's parents. The bridal party subsequently went for a drive and several places of interest in the district were visited. The happy couple were the recipients of numerous costly presents. Mr. and Mrs. Blackwell have the best wishes of their numerous friends for a long and prosperous future."

The housing situation was difficult and finding a place to live was a problem, especially after the arrival of their first child Marion in 1909. The answer, as so many had discovered before, was to go abroad. His brother Charles was chief engineer of the Langlaagte Deep Gold Mine in South Africa and Alfred joined him in the later part of 1909, to be given the traditional welcome by the native mine workers. In reality it was not a welcome but a trial to see how strong the newcomer's nerves were. The natives, in their tribal warrior's dress, rushed at Blackwell, swinging their knobkerries around their heads until the lethal heavy ball at the end was within an inch of his head. He had been warned what to expect and he must not flinch even the fraction of an inch or show any sign of fear. To have done so would have lost him the respect of the men who would be working under him.

It was true that the natives who worked for the Europeans were jealous of their own standing in the community. There was a distinction between having a master or boss who held a better position, drank more or who entertained on a more lavish scale than others. To be able to boast about the "boss" was a fine thing, it gave a feeling of importance. It was also a fine thing that the new boss showed no fear. He could be relied upon in an emergency to remain calm therefore he deserved respect and loyalty. Blackwell stood his ground.

Education Catches On

The nineteenth century saw the beginning of an extensive school building programme in Cornwall. Properly organised classes and the lessons taught came at the right period for the growing number of children, especially boys, whose future looked black with the decline of the mining industry, which in the

Camborne Wesley Chapel 1902

238

Alfred Ernest Blackwell 1885 - 1968.

Elizabeth Mary Williams 1886 - 1962.

Married in the Wesley Chapel, Camborne 1908.

Warriors with their knobkerries - the thing was not to lose one's head.

past had absorbed so many without the necessity of a formal education. Hammering at the ore face, shovelling, climbing up and down slippery ladders in shafts, and getting wet and miserable required little in the way of reading, writing or arithmetic. Common sense and a natural instinct for mining got most through their working lives.

The Board School at Zelah opened in 1878 and gave the sons of Henry Blackwell sufficient knowledge to begin apprenticeships and to develop into engineers.

Farther west in 1893 a school was built in Basset Road, Camborne, for boys and girls from the age of eight. At the Camborne Beacon an infant's school for 112 children from the age of four to eight was opened in 1890. The first headmistress was Miss Maud Mary Richards.

Both these schools have now ceased to function as educational establishments; the one at Beacon changed its role in 1979 to village hall and a variety of activities are carried on in the Basset Road building.

At Beacon, the children of Alfred and Elizabeth Blackwell began their education under the eagle eye of the schoolmistress of the day, Miss Jessie Mary Pengilly, who, as all the youngsters knew, had a stone in her belly. She was ably assisted by the kindly Miss Spurway from Troon and the glamorous Miss Keast. There were few problems in these initial stages of learning.

It soon caught on that if twenty-six strange strange scribbles known to the wise as the alphabet were with constant repetitive dronings absorbed into a fairly fertile young brain and then laboriously and squeakily chalked on to a slate it was possible, sooner or later, to form words then sentences which, as if by magic, were understood. Numbers, too, were quite interesting to count, but soon became a nightmare when fiddled around with as "sums" and quite

Beacon Camborne infants school, 1984.

1903

Waiting for the teachers outside the school gates, Elizabeth Mary Williams (1885-1962) in the garden of the house built by her father the blind miner, Richard.

1

2

3

4

243

5

6

7

impossible when one and two transformed into x and y.

With basics mastered, most of the other requirements for a sound education, such as surreptitiously tormenting the girl who sat in front by pulling her hair, came naturally. Even today, sixty years on, when meeting someone from the scholastic past the greeting, usually with a grin, is, 'Yes, of course I remember you; you're the one who used to pull my hair in class' What pleasant memories!

Soon it became the vogue to have group photographs of teachers and pupils taken. How did they appear, those children of sixty or seventy years ago? They seemed to have questioning looks when facing the camera but none of them could have known the problems and advances in technology that were about to engulf them. Electricity, radio, cars and aeroplanes were still in their infancy and the seeds were being sown for a second world war that all too soon engulfed them. Wherever they are, do they look back longing for an age that, although hard, was uncomplicated? Many school photographs taken years ago are still available to us.

Beacon Infants, 1917, group 1 shows Irving Blackwell standing fourth from left, second row. Garnold House is far right, second row - a young daredevil who feared neither man nor beast and who played wing threequarter for Camborne rugby team and fourteen times for Cornwall, 1929 - 1933. He died in a motor crash in Southern Rhodesia. Standing next to Irving Blackwell is Andrew Curnow who, just a year or so before the second world war and without the slightest knowledge of anything airborne, attempted to pilot a home-made aeroplane taking off briefly from a field out near the light-house farm Carn Entral. Headlines on the news stands announced "Secret plane in a barn in Cornwall". This was built by a local carpenter from plans drawn up by a Beacon boy, Garfield Johns, and powered by a motor cycle

245

engine donated by Howard Bennetts who lived in Beacon Square. There was great excitement; we Cornish were in the forefront of technology and if war came would soon be shooting the Germans out of the sky. It crashed, fortunately without loss of life, and that was the end of that!

Tom Wake, third from right, back row, was a very good cricketer who, after many years working in the goldfields of West Africa, died of blackwater fever.

The 1921 photo (group 2) shows Richard Garston Blackwell standing fourth from left in the middle row. Standing third from left and seated second from right are the Hocking boys who emigrated to Canada with their parents and sisters in the late twenties.

Seated far right, Telfer Kent, pinned down by sniper fire after the Normandy landings and losing a leg. Standing third from right is Donald Andrews who became the well-known secretary to the Camborne School of Mines, a position he held with some distinction for many years. Group 3, seated second from the right, is Ronald Dean who joined the Royal Navy before the second world war and was believed to have been killed during an air raid on Glasgow. Group 4, standing third from the left on the back row, is Ernie Eva, who joined the police force. Seated third from the left is Ella King who lived in the Tolcarne mine 'dry' for many years and whose grandfather had been mine captain of the Great Condurrow Mine. Group 5, of 1923, the author is seated third from the right. Group 6, in sailor suits, are the Kitchen brothers who mined in West Africa and the Far East. Standing far left in the middle row is Howard Bennetts whose motor cycle engine powered the ill-fated secret plane. He was killed in tragic circumstances in Camborne's Cross Street. Seated far right is Jack Medlyn whose parents kept a shop in Fore Street and whose father delivered paraffin door to door from his horse-drawn waggon, keeping the homes of Beacon in light from oil lamps. Jack joined the Air Force, became a rear gunner and was killed in North Africa.

Time has dimmed the memories of happy days at Beacon School and many of those seen in the Basset Road Group 7 are hard to recall. Garfield Johns, the designer of the 'plane, is standing in the centre of the second row from the back.

In the Basset Road photograph of 1928 all are remembered as are the school rugby team and those who made it to the Chiefs.

At the age of eight infancy suddenly ceased, and most Beacon children were shepherded off to Basset Road, although a few preferred to go to Troon. In Basset Road life took on a much more sombre aspect, although the teachers in the boys' school were men and discipline was harsher. More attention was paid to learning. It became a serious business with the teachers aiming to pass as many pupils as possible on to the Redruth County Grammar School, Truro Technical School or to pass the entrance examination to begin an engineering apprenticeship with Holman Brothers.

Nothing was ever the same again.

Some were shepherded off to Basset Road School, now a youth centre, 1983.

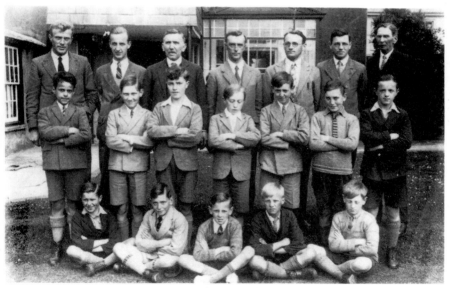

Basset Road Boys School, 1928
A. Richards, E. Rutter, T. C. Quintrell, H. S. Bond (Head), Magor,
O. Eddy, J. Gilbert
T. Treglown, T. Jones, S. Mayne, Bohay, R. Truran, J. Lawrence,
A. Stevens.
Trenowden, D. Parker, P. Pearce, C. Fidock, N. Truscott.

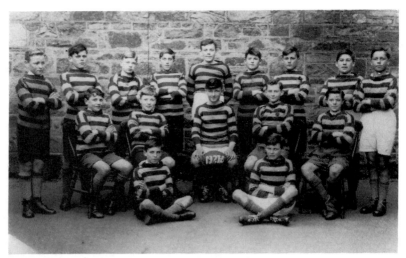

Basset Road School rugby team, 1927/8. Nursery for Camborne Chiefs.
C. Chenoweth, S. Harris, Tregonning, V. Knight, P. Shears, J. Trimm, House, C. Simcock, J. Roskilly.
Seated: J. Edwards, G. Blackwell, L. Tregenza, S. May, R. Oates,
Front: H. Thomas, P. Lawrence.

But not all made it by 1936.
Back row: F. Caldon, C. Selwood, R. Lobb, T. Kelly, C. Charleston, Liddicote, W. Carter, J. Boase, G. Blackwell, A. Pill, G. Thomas, -, -.
Seated: H. Thomas, Evans, L. May, B. Caddy, Treloar.
Front: Faull, Peno Knowles.

248

Ordinary People - Everyday Life

In August 1660, a proclamation was issued by Charles II ordering "that Smitike, alias Pennycomequick, should forever after that day, be called, named and known, by the name of Falmouth".

By the end of the eighteenth century there were three or four inns in the town and "a great number of very respectable lodging houses - where families and individuals may enjoy every comfort and accomodation".

Falmouth, in the seventeenth century was a small town, but one with great advantages. A fine harbour, protected by the castles of St. Mawes and Pendennis, with entry and exit rarely affected by the weather. As the colonial empire grew, communications with it were vital, and the Post Office, as it existed then, operated a fleet of Packet ships to carry mail to and from Britain. Other parts of the world were also served and the service grew, to become a valued part of the economy of Falmouth. In 1850, the Post Office Station was closed and the town suffered the loss of substantial trade and income. This placed the future of the town at risk. Fortunately, some business men who had prospered in the good years saw other prospects for Falmouth with its splendid harbour. With commendable foresight, they saw the advantage of building a dockyard.

Steamships were now passing regularly up and down the channel. Falmouth was the first port they could call at after a long voyage to Britain, and if docking and repair facilities were available, they would be used.

A company was formed and in 1860 the foundation stone of the dockyard was laid. The company, together with other influential people, had already created the Cornwall Railway Company and were building a line which would eventually link up with the Great Western Railway at Plymouth and thus to the growing national rail system. As the railway project was nearing completion and the town, the directors turned their attention to the passengers who, they hoped, would soon be flooding into Cornwall and Falmouth in particular, to enjoy the magnificent harbour and surrounding countryside. Accommodation would be required, and to supply the demand, another company was formed to build and appoint a large luxurious hotel, "The Falmouth". This was completed and opened with great ceremony on May 9th, 1865.

The directors of the companies involved in these ventures were always alert to exploit a situation and turn it to their advantage. The hotel was a short distance from the dockyard, which was now employing greater numbers of men, not only from the town but outlying districts as well. Some of these wished to bring their families with them and therefore required lodging. The company hit upon the idea of supplying this and so, on the ample grounds of the hotel, but a few yards from it, they built the "tap", a public house with twelve beds, where small families or single men could live. Here then was the ideal; rented accommodation, giving some of the valued engineers secure living quarters, food, and a public bar where they could enjoy a drink. All profits to the company!

Henry Blackwell junior had left Zelah day school in 1884 and was sent to Falmouth dockyard to serve an engineering apprenticeship. In the early 1890's he was living in the hotel tap; and there, too, lived the Collict family.

In April, 1892, the Royal Cornwall Gazette announced the marriage of Henry to Edith Mary, the daughter of Henry and the late Christian Collict.

Born in the Falmouth Hotel Tap, September 5, 1895. A Canadian Cornish lady visits her mother's birthplace.

Their first child, Lilian, was born in rooms over the public house "Hotel Tap", on September 5, 1895. When a request was made for a copy of the birth certificate, in 1983, there was some understandable concern at the Registrar Office. How could anyone be born in a "Tap"? The circumstances were explained, sanity had returned!

The Diary

I, Lily Blackwell, was born on 5 September 1895, at Falmouth, Cornwall. My parents were Cornish people, also my grandparents. We lived in rooms over a public house "Hotel Tap". My father was an engineer fitter working at the foundry in the docks. When I was about two years of age we moved into a house at 6 Vernon Place and just after this my sister Violet was born.

When I was about three years old my father was taken ill with typhoid fever, then my sister and I. My mother had quite a time looking after us and I can remember sitting up in bed with a big doll which a Mr Kelway gave me. Then my mother was taken ill and went to the hospital. My grandmother came to look after us, my father's mother Eliza

[Printed by authority of the Registrar General.]

CH 615030

B. Cert.
S.R.

CERTIFIED COPY of an ENTRY OF BIRTH
Pursuant to the Births and Deaths Registration Act 1953

Registration District   Falmouth

1895. :   Birth in the Sub-district of   Falmouth   in the   County of Cornwall.

Columns:—	1	2	3	4	5	6	7	8	9	10*
No.	When and where born	Name, if any	Sex	Name, and surname of father	Name, surname and maiden surname of mother	Occupation of father	Signature, description, and residence of informant	When registered	Signature of registrar	Name entered after registration
223	Fifth September 1895. Falmouth Hotel Tap, Falmouth. U.S.D.	Lilian	Girl	Henry Blackwell.	Edith Mary Blackwell, formerly Collict.	Fitter, Iron Foundry.	E.M.Blackwell. Mother. Falmouth Hotel Tap, Falmouth.	Twenty-eighth September 1895.	H.J.R. Corlyon. Deputy Registrar.	

Certified to be a true copy of an entry in a register in my custody.

.... Superintendent Registrar

.....20th July 1983.....Date

*See note overleaf.

Blackwell, but on 24th July 1899, my mother died and our home was broken up.

My grandmother took me back to live with her at Zelah and I can remember sitting up to the table when she was cooking, and I had a toy donkey with two baskets over its back which I would fill with currants and raisins. I can remember when playing outside I would see a flock of sheep coming and I would run inside the gate and stand up on the bar until they had passed. They would be going to the market. Another time I can remember standing outside and seeing the horse-drawn bus and then my dad would be there. Once my dad took me to where they were threshing corn and the men began to fight. Their faces were bleeding and my dad had to bring me home because I was crying so much.

I was nearly five years old when my grandmother Blackwell died on 30th July 1900, and I was taken back to Falmouth to live with my mother's father Henry Collict (1839-1906). My grandmother, Christian Collict, was dead. Grandfather had a garden and I can see the big Arum lilies growing in big pails. We would go to the cemetery at Swanpool when he could tend to my mother's grave.

Sometimes my dad would call for me and take me for a walk and we would meet Miss Laurence and she would give me tomatoes.

When I was six years old Miss Laurence became my stepmother and for the fourth time I had a new home. One Sunday before my dad married again, he came for me and we met Miss Laurence and took the train to Grampound Road to visit my dad's sister Aunt Annie Warne. We had our pictures taken that day. My grandfather Henry Blackwell and uncle Alfred were there as well. They were living there at 4, Railway Terrace.

My stepmother was kind of strict and she would tell my dad everything that we did and she would have a cane which was kept in the brass rod under the mantle shelf, but we were looked after very well as regards food and clothes, stepmother was a very good housekeeper.

I don't remember starting school again but I attended Clare Terrace Girl's School in Falmouth and paid three pence a week in the infants class and then two pence a week in the next class and I think three pence a week in standard six and seven.

My sister and I always had to set the table and wash the dishes. I did the washing and my sister wiped them and before we went to school in the morning we had to help with the housework. On Saturdays I had a lot of work to do, clean all the knives and peel potatoes for Saturday dinner and Sunday. We were six in the family, Henry, my father, his wife, Jane, grandfather, Henry Blackwell, uncle Alfred Blackwell, my sister Violet and myself.

Each Saturday there were extra to lunch because mother's people were farmers and they would come in to the market with their butter and eggs, cream and poultry. After the market they would come home to dinner. After the dishes were put away we would get ready and go to pay the butcher and grocer bills. With mother in the grocery store we had a few candies given us and in the butcher store, a penny each and then we would do some other shopping buying kippers or something like that for our tea.

Henry Blackwell, snr., Nell Sharp, Henry Blackwell, jnr., Miss
Laurence, Alfred Ernest Blackwell.
Annie Warne (Blackwell), Lillian Blackwell, Henry Warne.
Baby Warne, Minnie Warne.

Miss Laurence was brought to meet the family at Grampound
Road in 1901. Cousin Ellen Maria (Nell) Sharp came down from
Hartlepool. Her Mother was Anna Maria Scott (Keast). Her
husband, John Edmund Sharp was appointed General Manager
of Queenstown Dry Dock Shipbuilding and Engineering Co.,
County Cork in 1926.

When I had my school holidays I always went to stay on the farm.
There were four farm places and grandmothers home all within walking
distance of each other. My stepmother was always busy just before my
summer holidays making new underwear. I was always glad to go away
for my holidays. Once I remember staying with stepmother's brother and
he would have to go about three miles to get feed for the cattle and I
would always want to go with him for the ride and one night there was
another girl staying there as well so we went with uncle but he said we
would have to walk home, so we went and had to run at the back of the
trap and he would make the pony run. My feet were scarcely touching the
ground sometimes. When I stayed with one of my aunts I would have home
made plum jam and cream every morning for breakfast. When I was
twelve years old I would help to milk the cows. I could go out in the fields

and bring them in and chain them in their stalls. They would each know their own place and then I would throw the grain out for the chicken and fowls. I would get a basket and bring in the eggs. When I stayed with my grandmother I would have some crochet to do in my room which had a big bed with a top that came out over the bed and I would stand up on something to see what was on top. Sometimes there were lovely apples there and I was often tempted to take one.

On the first of each month grandmother would go out to the store for her groceries. It was a country store and when the door was opened the bell would ring. They sold everything in that store except meat but we could buy that from the butcher who came around once or twice a week with a horse and waggon.

Now I would have to come back home again and back to school. After school hours I could not go out to play. I would have to sit and mend my clothes or knit my own stockings. Each Monday evening I had to help fold the clothes and put some through the mangle. I would know each day what was for dinner. Sunday roast with potatoes followed by a milk pudding, Monday, stew, Tuesday pasties, Wednesday a little piece of meat roasted with potatoes, Thursday beef steak pie, Friday hearts roasted and Saturday, beef and kidney pudding. Stepmother did all her own business. I have heard her say that she only bought one loaf of bread

Clare Terrace Girls School, Falmouth, 1907.

Lily Blackwell born in the Falmouth Hotel 'Tap', 1895, back row centre.

254

in a ten-year period of time.

Sometimes when we came home from school we would see a man with lots of windmills so we would run home and get a jam jar, a stone one, then come back and he would give us one.

At Easter time I would stay with a Mrs. Berryman at Oak Cottage and Good Friday in the afternoon I would go with her to the chapel and help to set the tables for tea. I would like to do that. There would be saffron cake, cherry cake and bread and butter splits. We always saved some of the cherry cake for our tea as there never was very much of it, and then in the evening we would attend the service in the chapel. Mrs. Berryman had a girl named Minnie who lived with her to help with the work and I would have to share her bedroom. She was about ten or twelve years older than me. She was engaged to a young man and her brother would bring me home from the tea treats and one I remember I had a green linen dress and he bought me some black cherries. I stained my dress and after my holiday when I came home I got into trouble about it. My stepmother was very particular. Once I had a white felt hat with a green ribbon made of velvet on it. It blew off into the mud and I went into a store where step-mother's cousin tried to clean it and there was trouble again.

My school days were just ordinary. We had a new school building at Clare Terrace which I thought was fine. We could have our playtime if the weather was wet because our playground was under the school. I did not like school very much. When I lived at 10, New Street I could watch the soldiers going through their drill across the way from our parlour window. They came there every Sunday and then marched back to Pendennis Castle.

My grandfather Collict used to come and visit us every other Tuesday evening and bring us some fruit and every year he went to Penzance Fair bringing us ginger bread biscuits, comforts and pink and white almond candies.

One Sunday morning 29th April 1906, I remember my stepmother telling me that grandfather Collict had died that morning. He was buried in Swanpool Cemetery with my mother on Tuesday, 1 May. After the funeral my aunts and uncles came to see us but I did not remember seeing them before. I am now eleven years old. I think about this time my uncle Alfred Blackwell who was living with us went to Camborne to work and my grandfather Henry Blackwell left us as well and went to live with his daughter Annie and son-in-law Henry Warne at Railway Terrace, Grampound Road.

I took a place as house parlour maid. My father was not very pleased because I went into service but I got along very well, stayed there about a year and then my dad was taken sick so I stayed home for a while to help but then my father was taken very ill. He had been driving a gas engine which they had to run the other machines in the foundry and the fumes had got into his system. He died on Wednesday, 24th July 1912, at the age of forty two.

The road outside number ten, New Street, Falmouth was strangely quiet. Heavy layers of straw had been placed upon it to deaden the noise of the traffic of horses and the occasional motor vehicle. Church bells

*New Street, Falmouth where there were heavy layers of straw,
and the church bells hung silent.*

17th century church dedicated to King Charles the martyr.

remained silent at the request of doctors treating Henry Blackwell for an illness caused by the inhalation of poisonous fumes from the gas engines he had been installing and working in the dockyard. The doctors considered that any noise would have a dangerous affect on their patient but in spite of their precautions he passed away. For reasons that have never been explained his body was packed in the coffin with sawdust and as the funeral procession was making its way to Swanpool Cemetery the mourners were startled when a loud explosion was heard from inside the box.

After this I remember my aunt Emily Collict who had married Thomas Ingram writing me a letter saying she would be pleased to see me.

I took another situation as a house maid and stayed there until the next March when I left. I got one evening a week off and every other Sunday. We did not get much to eat there. Our dinners were served from the dining room and the cook made one small cake for a week. The old gentleman there was one hundred years old and some mornings I had to take him a cup of tea and he would be sitting up in bed with a long pole to point out the different ornaments for me to move around. I was always glad to get out of his room. He had a valet to look after him. (This was the Stephens family of Climax Rock Drill Co.)

Before my dad died I was writing to a young man in Africa. He was a brother to the young woman, Elizabeth Williams, who my uncle Alfred Blackwell married in Camborne. His name was Alfred and he sent me an engagement ring when I was seventeen. The next spring, just before I left the service of the old gentleman, he sent me a gold watch and chain.

I next went to Camborne to live with my aunt Elizabeth on 22nd March 1913. Her husband was in Africa working in the Johannesburg gold mines. (Alfred Blackwell)

One Sunday I went to see if I could find where my mother's sister Emily lived. She was the one who wrote to me when my dad died but when I got there she was out so I wrote her a postcard and said I would come one day in the week. My cousin Maude came to meet me but I was late and when I got near her house I saw some gypsies camping and after I passed them I ran so fast as I could. When I knocked at the door my cousin opened it and I received a very hearty welcome. My aunt Emily Ingram had not seen me since my grandfather Collict had died in 1906 and she began to cry. She said I looked like my mother. I had a good time there, they kept a small farm. I had three girl cousins there, Maud, Annie and Chrissie.

Then in May my boyfriend came home from Africa and then we went to visit my stepmother for a few days and then I took another situation as a house parlour maid but did not stay very long. When I left there I went to stay with my aunt Emily and my cousins.

During this time I was not going with the young man. We did not quarrel but I don't think his mother liked me very much. After this my cousin James Henry Collict started writing to me from Toronto.

End

Lily Blackwell later went to Canada and married James Collict. She died in Toronto in 1984.

The Norman Font in Crowan church is carved with strange animals resembling elephants. Henry Blackwell, a tinner turned publican was baptised here in 1747.

And buried in the churchyard.

XXVIII

GREAT EXPECTATIONS

In the preface to this book the question was asked. What do we expect or hope to find when we embark on the quest into the past? The answer is given in the foregoing pages and indicates to any would-be genealogist that a great deal can be accomplished in unearthing family roots.

In tracing one's family back along the main stream to its source, it is inevitable that what can be termed tributaries, will be seen entering at each new generation. There will be the temptation to follow these each to its own source, but this is time consuming and eventually the searcher will be engulfed in a sea of names of little meaning or consequence. Nevertheless, the urge to seek might reveal something of great interest or importance and must not be discouraged.

The author has researched several families which have made up his own particular tree, but it would be idle to speculate which traits, peculiar or otherwise, have been handed down and from which members of those families. The main line is Blackwell, but how much from the Williams, Keasts, Mitchells, Odgers make up the whole? They, too, had ancestors and many branches to their own trees. The immensity of the whole thing raises the question, just who are we? It is comparable to contemplating the origins of the universe and life itself. Better not to think about it!

In researching, snippets of information are sometimes revealed concerning some of these people, the importance of which can be measured only by the satisfaction it brings to the discoverer.

Henry, a brother of great-great-great-great-grandfather Thomas kept an inn at Crowan before he died in 1785; Thomas, a Crowan miner at the age of 21 volunteered to engage himself to be armed, arrayed, trained and exercised for the Defence of the Realm following an order from the Lord Warden of the Stannaries in 1798.

Francis, the author's great-great-grandfather, mentioned in Dr. Cecil Todd's book "The Search For Silver", sailed in 1842 from Liverpool for the Mexican silver mines. His brother Matthew, a Crowan blacksmith, who after marrying Anne Rogers in 1843 moved to Union Street Camborne, then in 1844 with four children to County Wicklow in Ireland before sailing from London to South Australia on the barque "Rachel", 383 tons, under the command of Captain R.H.Brown, arriving in Adelaide in September 1847 with an addition to the family in Isabella, born in Ireland. In 1872 at Kapunda, a town established in 1845 after the discovery of copper in the area in 1842, Isabella married John Polglase from St. Hilary in Cornwall. They lived for fifty years in the copper mining fields of Moonta (Australia's Little Cornwall) made famous by the Australian-born Cornish miner and author Oswald Pryor.

Matthew Blackwell set up a prosperous blacksmith's business in Kapunda. The Kapunda Herald in August 1865 advertised as follows "Matthew Blackwell, Stove and Oven Maker begs to inform his friends and the Public of Kapunda that he manufactures every description of the above at the shortest notice and most moderate terms. Iron fencing for cemeteries, palisading etc. manufactured to order on his premises, South Terrace." Much of the splendid iron lace work still adorns verandahs of houses in Kapunda.

According to Kapunda papers Matthew played a large part in local civic and political affairs. There is a street named after him in the town.

A great-grandson of Matthew is the Reverend A.E.E.Bottrell, an Australian Army Chaplain during World War II in the Middle East and the first Padre to serve with the Australian Commandos in the tough New Guinea campaigns.

In 1828 Elizabeth, a sister to Matthew, married copper miner William Trevarthen in Crowan. In 1839 they emigrated to New Zealand where William worked on Kawan and Great Barrier Islands until he was accidentally killed by a fall from his horse in Auckland in 1860.

Jenifer Blackwell, an aunt of Francis, Matthew and Elizabeth married John Trythall, a tinner from Camborne, at Crowan in 1776. Their direct descendant is Rear Admiral John Trythall C.B., O.B.E., K.St.J., an officer with a most distinguished career in the Royal Navy covering the years 1931 to his retirement in 1972.

James, a nephew of Francis, deserved a mention in the "West Briton" of 18 July 1872, his wife giving birth to a son at the Morro Velho Mine, Brazil. And there was Thomas Henry, a grandson of Francis. His story of great hardship in America in the 1870's is told in Dr.Todd's book, "The Cornish Miner in America"

Not much to make a song and dance about perhaps, but maybe sufficient to inspire you, the reader, to search. Who knows-you might find a famous ancestor, a peer of the realm or even royalty hanging about in the branches of your family tree. Don't let it go to your head!

According to the Bible we all have a common ancestor in Noah but to trace an individual line back to him is impossible. There is a huge gap in time between Biblical records and those that began with the parish registers about 1550. Registers of the established Church of England were first kept under a mandate devised by Thomas Cromwell in 1538. Since 1 July 1837 there has been a General Registry to record all births, marriages and deaths in England and Wales.

When I was young I failed to appreciate the narratives my parents and grandmother sometimes told me about their lives many long years ago. Now they are gone, as are all their generation who were part of our family. There is no one to question but the questions are many.

Some memories of the stories remained with me, sufficient to stir a curiosity and a very small inquisitiveness to discover something more about the forebears I had never known.

There is still much to learn.

Families can trace their histories back for many generations, discovering where their ancestors lived, who they were, how they earned a living and what effect they and history had on one another.
Genealogical work is absorbing, rewarding, frustrating and time-consuming. It can easily last a lifetime.

How does one put into practice the desire to trace the family tree.

An immaculate conception happened only once, therefore it is an inescapable fact that a person had parents, and also that the fact remained constant back through the ages.

Many families have withered and died, leaving no heirs. Some had attained prominence and were well known in their day but "some there be which have no memorial - who are perished as though they had never been and are become as though they had never been born and their children after them." Eccles.44.9.

First of all, one must bear in mind that the absolute essentials for a successful search are names and dates. These must be gathered and recorded from every conceivable source. Second, one must learn to play the part of Sherlock Holmes to unravel the mysteries of life. They are not all elementary.

Question relatives, never dismiss as irrelevant the smallest piece of information, even though it appears of no value. Somewhere in the puzzle it will fit into place as a vital clue. Write everything down while it is still fresh in one's memory with the date of the questioning. Tape conversations if possible. Many families still possess an old family Bible where births and deaths were recorded. Read the entries and then the Bible. It will do no harm and maybe a power of good.

Study old photograph albums, Names are sometimes written on the backs of the photos, many of which, even if more than a century old, are excellent.

Pore over church records. These can be found in the church in question, or increasingly likely, in the county record office. Armed with a name and a date certificates of births, marriages and deaths back to 1837 can be obtained from local registrars or the General Register Office, St. Catherine's House, Kingsway, London.

There are other documents available such as school registers, leases, apprenticeship indentures, travel documents, forces call-up or discharge papers and wills.

Newspapers going back for more than a hundred and eighty years are kept in some libraries. They will transport one to another age, in addition sometimes announcing marriages, births and deaths which might be of relevance.

Churchyards and cemeteries are to be solemnly explored and imagine the joy, properly subdued of course, of suddenly discovering the memorial stone of a long lost ancestor. At this time it would not be out of place to hold a pleasant conversation with the deceased. After all, is it absolutely certain that they cannot hear us? One precaution; make sure no-one else is within earshot; word soon gets around.

All the foregoing methods were included in producing the family trees shown on the following pages.

Blackwell

Line of descent

William, baptised 1596, St. Erth. Married Jane   St. Erth, 1633.
Thomas, baptised 1645, St. Erth. Married Sidwell   St. Erth, 1672.
Thomas, baptised 1676, St. Erth. Married Priscilla Williams.   St. Erth, 1698.
Thomas, baptised 1702, St. Erth. Married Jane Webster   Crowan, 1730.
Thomas, baptised 1732, Crowan. Married Jenefer Boterel.   Crowan, 1757.
Thomas, baptised 1764, Crowan. Married Elizabeth Rodda.   Crowan, 1797.
Francis, baptised 1802, Crowan. Married Jenefer Champion.   Crowan, 1822.
Henry, baptised 1825, Crowan. Married Eliza Whitford.   Kenwyn, 1844.
Henry, born 1846, Whitehall. Married Eliza Keast.   Kenwyn, 1867.
Alfred, born 1885, Bowling Green, St. Allen. Married Elizabeth Mary Williams.
          Camborne, 1908.

Children: Marion, 1909; Charles Alfred Irving, 1910; Richard Garston, 1914; Elizabeth Constance, 1916; Henry Cecil, 1918; Helen Renee, 1928.
All born at Beacon, Camborne.

Death: Charles Alfred Irving, 1985, Plymouth.
Richard Garston, 1970, at sea, buried in Darwin, Australia.
Elizabeth Constance, 1962, Camborne.

See also Williams line of descent.

Keast

Line of descent

Origins: From Kest, a straw basket, hence perhaps a basket maker from mid and north Cornwall.

John, baptised ? Married Grace Keast.	Ladock,1770.
John, baptised 1776. Married Elizabeth Batten.	St. Allen, 1795.
James, baptised 1806, St. Allen. Married Maria Batten.	St. Allen, 1832.
Eliza, born 1844, St. Allen. Married Henry Blackwell.	Kenwyn,1867.

Children: Annie, 1868; Henry, 1870; Charles, 1872; William John, 1875.
All born at Cost-Is-Lost, Perranzabuloe.
Alfred Ernest, 1885, born at Bowling Green, St. Allen.

Death: Annie Warne, 1925, Grampound Road.
Henry, 1912, Falmouth.
Charles, 1941, Germiston, South Africa.
William John, 1875, Cost-Is-Lost.
Alfred Ernest, 1968, Beacon, Camborne.

See also Blackwell line of descent.

Whitford

Line of descent

Origins: Probably from a fairskinned dweller by a river crossing.

John, baptised 1669, Kenwyn. Married Cathren Lawrens.   Kenwyn, 1695.

Mark, baptised 1710, Kenwyn. Married Catherine Eastlick.   Kenwyn, 1736.
John, baptised 1747, Kenwyn. Married Elizabeth Parnell. Perranzabuloe, 1769.
Mark, baptised 1770, Kenwyn. Married Mary Hale.   Perranzabuloe, 1797.
John, baptised 1798, St. Agnes. Married Ann Harris.   St. Agnes, 1822.
Eliza, baptised 1822, St. Agnes. Married Henry Blackwell.   Kenwyn, 1844.

Children: Eliza Jane, 1844; Henry, 1846. Born at Whitehall (Scorrier).
Mary, 1858. Born at Liskeard.

Death: Eliza Jane, not known.
Mary, not known.
Henry, 1911, Grampound Road.

See also Blackwell line of descent.

Williams

Line of descent

Origins: A name popular after the Norman Conquest.

John, baptised 1624, St. Keverne. Married Loveday.   St. Keverne.
Richard, baptised 1660, St. Keverne. Married Anne Gilbart. St. Keverne, 1686.
William, baptised 1697, St. Keverne. Married Mrs. Dorothy Richards.
      St. Keverne, 1726.
Richard, baptised 1729, St. Keverne. Married Ann James.   Grade, 1750.
Thomas, baptised 1751, St. Keverne. Married Mary Beel.   St. Keverne, 1778.
Thomas, baptised 1778, St. Keverne. Married Mary Huckin. St. Keverne, 1800.
Walter, baptised 1803, St. Keverne. Married Louisa Pearce.   Lamorran, 1833.
Richard, born 1854, Tolcarne. Married Ellen Annie Mitchell.
      Franklin Township, Michigan, U.S.A., 1874.

Children: William John, 1874; Florence, 1877; Walter, 1879; Richard, 1880.
All born at Franklin, Michigan.
Joseph Henry, 1884; Elizabeth Mary, 1886; Alfred, 1889; Lillian Ann, 1894.
All born at Beacon, Camborne.

Deaths: William John, 1955, South Africa.
Florence Mayne, 1960, Beacon, Camborne.
Walter, 1901, Mining accident, U.S.A.
Richard, 1939, Detroit, U.S.A.
Elizabeth Mary Blackwell, 1962, Beacon, Camborne.
Joseph Henry, 1963, South Africa.
Alfred, 1943, Beacon, Camborne.
Lillian Ann Timmins, 1977, Beacon, Camborne.

See also Mitchell line of descent.

Mitchell

Line of descent

Origins: A British name, the survival of which, as a surname, is due to the personal name Michel.

Thomas, baptised ? Married Honour Andrewartha.	Phillack, 1631.
Thomas, baptised 1644, Phillack. Married Margery Noall.	Phillack, 1678.
John, baptised 1682, St. Ives. Married Mary Upton.	Phillack, 1709.
James, baptised 1731, Phillack. Married Catherine Veal.	Phillack, 1755.
William, born 1764, Phillack. Married Sarah Jenkin.	Phillack, 1788.
William, baptised 1803, Phillack. Married Ann Negus.	Camborne, 1827.
William, baptised 1828, Knave-Go-By. Married Elizabeth Odgers.	
	Tuckingmill, 1855.

Children: Ellen Annie, 1856; Prudence Ann, 1860; Elizabeth Mary, 1864. All born at Beacon, Camborne.

Death: Ellen Annie Williams, 1929, Beacon, Camborne.
Prudence Ann Davey, 1938, Houghton, Michigan.
Elizabeth Mary, 1882, on board s.s. 'Republic', in Liverpool returning from America.

See also Williams line of descent.

Odgers

Line of descent

Origins: From personal name, Roger.

John, baptised 1772, Stithians. Married Elizabeth Williams.　　　Sithney, 1794.
William, born 1805, Sithney. Married Prudence Trevillion.　　Camborne, 1828.

Children: Elizabeth, 1828; Prudence Ann, 1830; William Henry, 1840; John, 1843.
All born at Condurrow, Camborne.

Elizabeth married William Mitchell at Tuckingmill, 1855. (See Mitchell line).

Prudence Ann married James Bennetts at Tuckingmill, 1849.

Children: William John, 1850; Eliza Ann, 1854; James Henry, 1858; Ellen, 1860.

William John lived in Calumet, Michigan in the late 1860's and early 1970's before returning to Beacon, Camborne, where he established his photographers business. He was a first cousin to Ellen Annie Mitchell who married Richard Pearce Williams in Franklin Township, Michigan, in 1874.

Trevillion

Line of descent

Origins: Place name near Trevelyan. Found in far west Cornwall.

Thomas, baptised 1755, Camborne. Married Honour Provis.   Camborne, 1783.
Prudence, baptised 1801, Camborne. Married William Odgers.   Camborne, 1828.

See Odgers line of descent.

Pearce

Line of descent

Origins: From Pierre - Peter, a common name latinised as Petrus.

John, baptised ? Married Eliza Jago.   Mevagissey, 1789.
Louisa, baptised 1809, Mevagissey. Married Walter Williams. Lamorran, 1833.

Children: Walter, 1842; Louisa, 1849.
Both born at Coswinsawsin, Gwinear.

Richard Pearce, 1854.
Born at Tolcarne, Beacon.

Death: Walter, 1892, Brazil.
Louisa ? Beacon, Camborne.
Richard Pearce, 1908, Beacon, Camborne.

See also Williams line of descent.

Negus

Line of descent

Origins: From Know - Gos. Nut Grove. The name appears as as Negatus in 1327.

John, baptised ? Married Jenifer Whennan.   Camborne, 1791.
Anne, baptised 1797, Camborne. Married William Mitchell.   Camborne, 1827.
William, baptised 1828, Knave-Go-By. Married Elizabeth Odgers.
                                                        Tuckingmill, 1855.

Children: See Mitchell line of descent.

Epilogue

And now, I stand on the hill of Camborne Beacon looking down across Cornwall to St. Erth, Crowan and the farmlands around Coswinsawsin, and in my mind's eye imagine the ancients passing from place to place, living, striving, dying in their time. I turn towards the great mining areas of Camborne, Redruth, Gwennap and St. Agnes, knowing that there, my forebears struggled to live. Away across the North Cliffs, the great oceans, over which so many sailed in their quest for better things. I see it all so clearly because I have reached back in time to touch the people who are my own.

The whole mystery of time past is waiting to be solved, and you too might discover that when you get so near the dead, they seem more real than the living, and being near them there is the sense of coming home after a long time away.

H. C. Blackwell

The author was born in Beacon, Camborne in 1918, and was educated at Beacon Infants, Basset Road School and Camborne Technical College.

He served his engineering apprenticeship at Holman Brothers, Camborne, and joined the Royal Navy on the outbreak of the second world war, seeing service afloat and in Egypt.

In 1946 he was employed by the West African Gold Corporation at the Marlu Gold Mine as the Mill Engineer, in what was known as 'the white man's grave'.

In 1951 he moved to Kirkuk in Iraq as an engineer employed by the Iraq Petroleum Company Ltd., and, working under the direction of Lloyd's Register of Shipping, was engaged in the survey of mechanical plant and equipment. In 1960 he was transferred to Umm Said in Qatar, as Senior Engineer Inspector responsible for the inspection of the Associated Oil Companies installations throughout the areas covered by Lebanon, Syria, Jordan, Bahrain, the Trucial Sheikdoms and Qatar.

He retired in 1974 but in 1975 was asked to return to Qatar as the Construction Supervisor for the Qatar General Petroleum Corporation, a post he held until relinquishing it in 1982.

The author has travelled extensively, including an intensive tour in 1983 of the Michigan Copper Country where his grandparents lived in the 1870's.

A Fellow of the Institute of Petroleum, Henry Blackwell lives in his native village of Beacon.

Glossary of Mining Terms

Adit - A horizontal drift or tunnel through which the water pumped or drawn thereto by the engine from the bottom of the mine and also the water descending from above by percolation, passes off by gravitation.

Adventurer - Shareholders in a mining company.

Air Shaft - A shaft sunk into existing tunnels for ventilation purposes.

Alluvial - Deposit of earth left by flood.

Amalgam - Mixture of metal with mercury as gold amalgam.

Attal or Attle - Refuse, dumps or waste from a mine.

Bal - An old Cornish word meaning mine.

Balance Bob - A counterpoise of the rods in the engine shaft.

Beu or Beuheyl - A 'Living Stream', the productive part of a tin stream.

Bob - The lever or beam transmitting power from engine to pit.

Bob Pit - The pit in which the balance bob works.

Breast - A man-made cliff used in washing tin ores.

Buddle - An appliance round or square, concave or convex, used in the separation of ores from the waste by means of water.

Bunch - Rich patch in a lode.

Burrow - Pile of rubbish from the mine working.

Cage - For lowering or raising men in the shaft.

Calciner - Apparatus for roasting ore.

Coffin or Koffen - Old workings open to the surface made by the ancient miners.

Collar of a shaft - Timber or masonry built around the inside of a shaft to prevent it from caving in.

Core - The miners working shift.

Crib or Crouse Time - Miners' meal time.

Cross Cut - A level at right angles to drives on the lode.

Dead Ground - A portion of the lode in which there is no ore.

Dish - That portion of the produce of a mine which is paid to the mineral owner, also called a royalty or dues. On the mines of the Gold Coast of West Africa a similar word, dash, is used when giving something.

Drive - A level generally on the course of the lode.

Dry - Where miners dry their clothes.

Engine Pool - A pond for supplying the engine with condensing water.

Engine Shaft - Through which the water is drawn by the engine from the depths of the mine to the adit or surface.

Fathom - Six feet, the Cornish miner's unit of measure.

Flopjack - Water raising contraption.

Fork - Water in fork - water all drained out to the bottom of the engine shaft.

Frame and Rack - A table made of boards and inclined to allow a stream of water to wash off waste from slime tin.

Gad - Steel wedge.

Gard - Sand with tin.

Gounce - Oblong pit with inclined floor for separating materials.

Grain Tin - Oxide of tin in the form of grains or pebbles in alluvial tin.

Grass - Surface of mine. In uncomplimentary terms to dismiss a person, he or she would be told to "Go to grass"!

Griddle or Riddle - A sieve.

Grizzly - A flat screen for sizeing ore.

Halvans - Waste from dressing of ores.

Horse Whim - Machine as described in the book and worked by a horse for drawing up materials from the mine.

Huel - Alternative Cornish spelling for Wheal, a mine.

Jigging - Jigging the griddle or sieve to separate the ores.

Keenly or Kindly - Ground that gives the appearance of being favourable for ore.

Kibble - Buckets for bringing up materials from the shaft.

Kieve or Keeve - Large iron-bound vat or tub for washing ore.

Killas - Clay slate.

Koffens - Surface excavations resembling coffin shape.

Lander - Man who stands at the top of the shaft to receive the Kibble.

Launder - Wooden water carrier or race.

Leat - Water course.

Levels - Mine workings driven along the course of the lode.

Lode Stuff - The undressed mineral from the lodes.

Looby - To toss.

Mundic - Iron pyrites.

Open Cut - Working or excavation open from the surface.

Outcrop - Where the lode appears at the surface.

Packing - The final dressing of ores in a kieve or vat with water after stirring and striking the sides of the container.

Pass - The slide by which ore for crushing is carried down to the stamps. Openings left for lowering stuff to levels.

Pitch - Limits to the piece of ground set to tributor.

Pitwork - The pumps and apparatus of the engine shaft.

Plunger Pole - The piston or forcer of a forcing pump.

Plunger Lift - The pipes attached to a forcing pump.

Pyrites - Either of two sulphides of iron.

Rack - An inclined automatically worked frame on which slimes are washed.

Rise - The connection between a higher and lower level for mining the ores or ventilation.

Ruddle - Sloping frame of iron bars.

Set - A frame of timber ready made for putting into a drive or shaft.

Sett - A mining area or mine.

Shode - Tin ore found in stones.

Skimpings - Skimmings of the light ores in the dressing.

Skip - An iron or steel box-like carriage for raising materials from underground to surface.

Slimes - Mud containing metallic ores.

Smelting House - Where the ore is reduced to metal by means of fire.

Spalling - The breaking of ore at the surface into small pieces before being cobbed. The Cornish used the word to threaten..."If you are not careful I'll spall to 'ee."

Spitzkasten - V-shaped boxes for classification of sand and slime. *Stope* - Ground in the mine containing a lode ready for excavating.

Stoping - Breaking ore from the lode. When upward, termed overhand, when downwards underhand stoping.

274

Stannary - Tin Mine, Tin Mining District. Court for regulation of mines.
Stent (1) - The extent within which the miners work during one 'taking'.
Stent (2) - Waste material.
Strake - A launder or chute used for washing ore stuff.
Strike of the Lode - Bearing of the lode.
Stiling - Walls on each side of the Tye.
Sump - The bottom of the mine shaft.
Tacknote - A licence to search for minerals before a lease is granted.
Tail of Adit - The place where the adit water leaves the adit.
Tappets - Projecting timbers on axle of a crushing mill.
Tailings - Refuse from the last dressing operation.
Tin Bounds - The limits of a given area for mining anciently set out by order of
    the Vice Wardens of the Stannaries when the landowners of waste land
    declined to grant license for mining therein.
Tin Ore - Black tin ready for smelting.
Tin Pyrites - Sulphide of copper - tin.
Tossing or Tozing - A process consisting of suspending ores by violent agitation
    in water, their subsidence being accelerated by packing, the lighter and
    worthless matter remaining at the top.
Tongues - Timber attached to the vertical lifters of a crushing mill.
Tribute - Proportion of the value of the ore which the miner gets for his work.
Trommel - A barrel-shaped sieve for sizing ore stuff.
Tutwork - Piece work or contract work.
Tye - The under level where lighter parts of ground were carried away.
Tying - Sluicing.
Underlie - Angle of lode.
Van - Tin ore washed on a shovel.
Vugh, Vugg or Vogle - Natural cavity in the rock.
Whim - A machine for raising ore and men worked by horses or steam.
Winze - A sink on the lode communicating one level with another.

Index

Chinese, 130, 131, 154
Chin-wang-tao, Treaty Port, 130
Chippewa Indians, 60
Chiverton Mine, 25, 226, 227
Christian Fellowship, 31
Christianity in Cornwall, 196
Church of England, 199, 260
Church, Central Mine Methodist, 66
Churchtown, Mevagissey, 55
City Deep Mine, 158
City Engineer, Bulawayo, 172
Civil War, American, 147
Clare Terrace Girls' School,
    Falmouth, 252, 254, 255
Clarence, Duke of, 26
Cleave, 118
Cleveland, 46
Cliff Mine, Michigan, 41
"Climax" Rock Drill, 229
Clowance, 208
Cock, Mr. Ben, 164, 168
Cole, Rev. Thomas, 116
Collict, 249
    Christian, 252
    Edith Mary, 249
    Emily, 257
    Henry, 252
    James Henry, 257
Collins, 16
Colorado, U.S.A., 97
Columb, St., 186
Columbus, 45
Comanche Indians, 79
Commando, Boer, 127
Commission, Miners' Phthisis, 125
Communist Party, South Africa, 157
Condurrow, 32, 34, 36, 58, 71, 114,
    122, 210
Confederate States, 147
Congress, Library of, 68
Consolidated Mines, Gwennap, 21
Constantine, St., 194
Construction Engineer, Rhodesia,
    158
Consultant, Mining, 184
Copper, **passim**
Copper Country, 45, 49, 62, 67, 213,
    218,
Copper House Company, Hayle, 164,
    193

Corbett, Gentleman James, 217
Cornish, **passim**
"Cornish Miner in America, The",
    95
"Cornish Rock Drill", 164
"Cornubia", Steam Tug, 147
Cornwall, passim
Cornwall, Earl of, 8
Cornwall, Easter Sessions, 120
Cornwall, Folklore of, 194
Cornwayle, 71
Cornwall Technical College,
    172, 182
Cornwallia, 1
Cortes, 45
Commons, M.J., 217
Coster, 16
Cost-Is-Lost, 25, 147, 158, 223, 227
Coswinsawsin, 57, 96
Couch of Philadelphia, 124, 164
County Courthouse, Houghton, 61,
    78
County Wicklow, 259
Cousin Jack, 41, 137
Coward, Noel, 49
Cowes, 27
Cox & Co., Falmouth, 143, 147, 229
Crassus, a Roman, 4
Cromwell, Oliver, 194, 199
Cromwell, Thomas, 260
Cross, Military, 154
Cross Street, Camborne, 49, 246
Crousa Downs, 52
Crowan, 15, 21, 22, 25, 95, 97, 201,
    202, 206, 208, 258, 259, 260
Crown Reef Rugby Team, 212
"Crystal Sapphire", m.v., 182
Cuba, 36, 37, 38
Curtiss, Rev David, 66
Curnow, Andrew, 245
Currie, 159
Curry, Mary Jane, 68, 87
Curry, Nicholas, 168
Custer, General, 76
Customs and Excise, 36

"Daily Mail", Rand, South Africa,
    158
Dame School, 36, 37

280

World War II, 50, 260
Wrestling, 210

Yale University, 219
Yellow Jacket, Calumet, 43
Yeoman, 201
Younger Brothers, The, 76
Yucatan, Mexico, 45
Yugoslavia, 50

Zelah, 130, 147, 222, 223, 226, 227,
    228, 229, 236, 240, 249, 252
Zennor, 122
Zoar, 52
Zoutpansberg, 127, 128
Zulu Chief, 126